Men's Rights, Gender,
and Social Media

Men's Rights, Gender, and Social Media

Christa Hodapp

LEXINGTON BOOKS
Lanham • Boulder • New York • London

Published by Lexington Books
An imprint of The Rowman & Littlefield Publishing Group, Inc.
4501 Forbes Boulevard, Suite 200, Lanham, Maryland 20706
www.rowman.com

Unit A, Whitacre Mews, 26-34 Stannary Street, London SE11 4AB

Copyright © 2017 by Lexington Books

All rights reserved. No part of this book may be reproduced in any form or by any electronic or mechanical means, including information storage and retrieval systems, without written permission from the publisher, except by a reviewer who may quote passages in a review.

British Library Cataloguing in Publication Information Available

Library of Congress Cataloging-in-Publication Data

Names: Hodapp, Christa, 1980- author.
Title: Men's rights, gender, and social media / Christa Hodapp.
Description: Lanham : Lexington Books, 2017. | Includes bibliographical references and index.
Identifiers: LCCN 2017033836 (print) | LCCN 2017030851 (ebook) | ISBN 9781498526173 (Electronic) | ISBN 9781498526166 (cloth : alk. paper)
Subjects: LCSH: Men's movement. | Social media. | Men--Social conditions.
Classification: LCC HQ1090 (print) | LCC HQ1090 .H623 2017 (ebook) | DDC 305.31--dc23
LC record available at https://lccn.loc.gov/2017033836

∞™ The paper used in this publication meets the minimum requirements of American National Standard for Information Sciences Permanence of Paper for Printed Library Materials, ANSI/NISO Z39.48-1992.

Printed in the United States of America

Contents

Introduction vii

1 How the Men's Rights Movement Works 1
2 Identity, the Internet, and Masculine Discourse 27
3 The Men's Rights Movement and Political Revolution 53
4 Oppression, Harm, and Masculinity 83
5 Fathers' Rights, Parenting, and Power 105
6 Men, Violence, and Oppression 137

Conclusion 169
Bibliography 171
Index 177
About the Author 187

Introduction

It is not uncommon for men to perceive feminism as accusatory and insulting, frequently feeling that feminism creates more divisions than bridges by blaming men for social problems. Claiming that they are not individually responsible for the harms and oppression that feminists describe, some men feel unjustly persecuted by feminist politics. Combining this with feelings of disenfranchisement in contemporary economic and social contexts, feminism has become the enemy in the eyes of many men who reject its arguments, reinscribing hegemonic masculine identity to cement this dismissal. In light of this backlash, feminists have at times seen certain men as enemies as well, resulting in a fully politicized battle of the sexes.

The phenomenon of feminist backlash is far from new, and feminist authors such as Susan Faludi,[1] Anita Superson,[2] and Ann Cudd[3] have worked to document and analyze these actions in both academia and the wider culture. However, in recent times, the backlash these authors describe has taken on new forms. The anger and frustration of men has been escalating, and this escalation is both encouraged and given voice to by online platforms. Because the Internet allows individuals from all over the globe and from all walks of life to connect, men came to realize through these connections that other men were just as angry as they were. Online blogs, message boards, and social media (just to name a few), allow men to communicate the pain they experience in contemporary culture, as well as the deep feelings of resentment stemming from the fact that society seems to have no platform for addressing such pain. In general, the world is changing, and certain men feel as though they have been left behind, marginalized and victimized for simply being men.

A combination of factors have escalated this resentment and backlash into what is referred to as the "men's rights movement" (MRM). This movement arises from the intersection of several sociopolitical forces. First, in terms of western culture, there has been notable backlash to progressive politics on the whole, marked by outcries against "political correctness" and a nostalgia for traditional social structures previously criticized as racist, sexist, and so forth. Second, failing economies and shifts in capitalist market structures have increased dissatisfaction levels in this society, creating a pervasive sense of disenfranchisement and loss of identity as jobs are lost, poverty is on the rise, and the gap between classes increasingly widens. Third, feminist critiques have interrupted masculine value systems, demanding change and an abandonment of various power structures. Some men feel as though this is a personal attack on their innate identity, and the lack of constructive interrogation and reformulation of masculine identity creates a scarcity of resources for a critical reconstruction of gender identity on the whole. Finally, these factors occur in the age of the Internet, which is often portrayed as a sort of last bastion of truly free speech, providing a platform for individuals to eschew political correctness and speak one's true mind.

Out of this context, backlash becomes politicized and organized, at least to some degree, into a movement. As with other social movements, the MRM is not uniform, but there are certain principles or beliefs uniting its various factions. One of the central claims of the MRM is that society, both contemporarily and historically, revolves around women, and that arguments claiming female oppression are a farce. Although feminism allegedly demonizes men, the MRM argues that men have consistently been required to sacrifice for women to unjust degrees. Pointing to examples such as economic providing, chivalry, military service, and so forth, the MRM claims that men's income and lives are regularly put on the line in order to serve women.[4] Consequently, this movement argues that women systematically oppress men, an oppression that is reinforced and falsely legitimized through feminism. Additionally, the MRM generally puts forth highly dichotomous and essentialist concepts of gender, relying heavily on hegemonic masculinity to explain male struggle and experience. This essentialism is then used to support the argument that maleness is the primary source of oppression for men, superseding other aspects of identity such as race, ethnicity, class, or sexual orientation. Furthermore, while they admit that women can realize the error of their oppressive ways, they also argue that women are generally vengeful, power-driven, selfish, and irrational.

Notably, this movement has an unusual political strategy. The MRM is almost exclusively an online movement, and its discussions and literature are generally posted in various online platforms. In terms of political action, many MRMs reject the possibility of engaging constructively with the current "gynocentric" culture, and thus refuse to work within mainstream society. Rather, the generalized goal is not to engage with the culture at large, but to disrupt or destroy it all together. This goal manifests itself online as trolling, spamming, doxxing, and an overall policy of harassment directed at suspected sources of male oppression. Occasionally these behaviors manifest themselves in the real world as MRM led protests or conferences, but generally speaking group action is limited to the Internet, a supposed safe haven for unpopular opinions and social outsiders. The MRM strategy for intervention is mainly one of disruption.

The MRM self-perception varies somewhat, but there are distinct traits regularly exhibited by its adherents. One is the reliance upon aggressive and even violent language. Many MRM posts read as extraordinarily angry, if not enraged, which is explained as a proportional reaction to longtime marginalization.[5] There is a belief that now is the time to express this rage as a form of self-preservation, and that one is merely speaking a truth that had been obscured for far too long. Coupled with this emotive sensibility is the belief that the MRM is a source of logic and rationality, a somewhat curious pairing with rage. Nonetheless, MRMs often present themselves as legitimately angry "truth tellers," who, under the surface of anger and resentment, are committed to pure logic and argumentation.[6] Using this logic propelled by righteous anger, these men seek to reclaim masculinity, and reassign the lost value to traditional male values.

As a feminist scholar, I find the MRM simultaneously tragic and deeply disturbing. The tragedy of the MRM comes from the legitimacy contained in some of their complaints—masculinity is indeed toxic, men do experience harm and suffer under current gender systems, and men are certainly feeling increasingly exploited in contemporary society. However, the real problem is the MRM's inability to accurately assess this damage, rejecting progressive strategies and politics, while embracing the problematic norms at the source of masculine pain. I do believe these men are angry, and I do believe these men are suffering, however, feminists and other progressives cannot accept the expression of such pain through virulent misogyny and regressive nostalgia. Furthermore, there appears to be an increase of regressive misogyny on the whole within our culture, and the MRM is a symptom of this larger problem. While some individuals consider the MRM outliers or a fringe group, I argue that the MRM is merely a visible manifestation of the deep misogyny that has resurrected itself in recent years. The MRM has managed to morph itself into feminism's doppelganger, co-opting its language, issues, and arguments for the purpose of defending a masculinity that has been increasingly criticized and rightfully challenged.

The purpose of this work is to examine this movement from a variety of angles, assessing its strategies, identification as a political movement/revolution, and its general claims and arguments. In doing so, I hope not only to provide a philosophical understanding and analysis of the MRM itself, but also to shed light on the current masculinity crisis occurring in various sociopolitical contexts. The MRM can be viewed as an exemplar of contemporary masculine backlash and angry men in general, giving insight to the sources and problems revolving around and informing current regressive social conditions.

HISTORY OF THE MRM

In order to clarify the focus of the arguments and critiques contained in this work, it is necessary to provide a brief history of the MRM, including its origins, influences, and various manifestations. While some MRM members argue that the history of the movement stretches back into the 1800s,[7] the most relevant influences on contemporary men's rights issues begin in the 1970s with the advent of the men's liberation movement. Thus, this section will provide an overview of the history and development of the current MRM starting with the men's liberation movement, as well as a discussion of current branches and embodiment of the movement in various online platforms. Finally, I will provide an argument for this project's focus on Paul Elam and his website, A Voice for Men (AVFM) as exemplars of the contemporary MRM, based upon the overall evolution and focus of the movement.

According to the AVFM website, the men's rights movement has two waves, with the second wave beginning in 2009 with the start of AVFM. In the first wave, the movement was not cohesive or well organized, but can rather be identified with a variety of initiatives concerning the status of masculinity and the rights of men. Oftentimes, these initiatives and proposed interventions concerned issues directly impacting men, including but not limited to, alimony, custody, and workplace protections. Furthermore, these concerns also addressed broader sources of alleged male oppression, such as feminism, male gender roles, issues in sexuality, and misandry, the hatred of men (parallel to the concept of misogyny). AVFM argues that these issues propelled a wide variety of individuals toward action to protect the rights of men, and that the movement gained significant momentum with the publication of Warren Farrell's work, *The Myth of Male Power*, in 1993. The second wave later distinguishes itself from the first wave by claiming to be more inclusive, organized, and less insular than the previous wave.

Men's Liberation

Although there is evidence that the promotion of men's rights was a political and social concern more than one hundred years ago, the contemporary movement in the United States has close ties to the men's liberation movement of the 1970s, particularly through the work of leading men's rights activist Warren Farrell. This discussion of the men's liberation movement will focus heavily on Farrell and his evolution from a male feminist working within feminism for men's liberation to a men's rights activist (MRA) committed to rejecting feminism and bringing an end to what he sees as male oppression. My reason for focusing on Farrell is that he is often named as a "father" of the contemporary MRM, and is still considered a major author and influence on MRM arguments, issues, and discourse. His shift from a feminist sympathizer to an MRA mirrors the changing attitude of certain men toward the political implications of masculinity as both a personal and political identity.

The men's liberation movement of the 1970s was heavily invested in second wave feminism, focusing on the implications of feminism for men and masculinity following critiques such as Betty Friedan's in *The Feminine Mystique*. Feminist critiques of femininity and feminine gender roles resonated with certain male activists, inspiring parallel critiques concerning masculinity. Many men involved in the men's liberation movement noted that men suffered from both the economic and emotional divisions of labor as well, and that masculine gender expectations often resulted in emotional impoverishment, being overworked, and feelings of exploitation in both public and private realms. Consequently, men's liberation supported the notion that systems of gender roles and expectations harmed both men and women in analogous ways, and the feminist project of emancipation from such roles was thus in men's interest.

While this approach to male liberation worked to attract men toward feminism, certain problematic tendencies began to arise within the context of these groups. The main objection to male liberation was the presentation of gender issues for men and women as parallel, and hence symmetrical in terms of harm and oppression. Michael Messner argues, "The language of sex role theory allowed men's liberationists to sidestep a politicized language of gender relations, in favor of a falsely symmetrical call for women's and men's liberation from oppressive sex roles."[8] In other words, some men's liberationists failed to note the impact of patriarchal structures, institutions, and power relations on gender, and thus denied the import of male privilege and power in various contexts. Furthermore, this movement also restricted its account of masculinity to mainly the experiences of white, middle class, heterosexual men.

Messner argues that these tendencies in the men's liberation movement caused a fissure within the group, resulting in one set of men focusing on what they referred to as "men's rights" and the other set remaining sympathetic to feminism. According to Messner, the advent of the MRM is based upon an over-reliance on what was referred to as "sex-role theory," namely the idea that "sex" (more accurately gender) roles for both masculine and feminine identity are harmful. As mentioned previously, what this analysis lacks is a discussion of gender relations in the context of such roles, which requires a significantly more complex analysis of power, standpoint, and intersectionality than a simplistic analysis of masculine vs. feminine expectations. Messner points out, "In this usage, the concept of *oppression* was depoliticized and seemed to only refer to a general condition faced by everyone living in a sexist society."[9] This analysis avoids responsibility for the harms inflicted on women by men in a society as a result of gender, such as sexual violence, spousal abuse, harassment, and the like. Some men working within feminism recognized these failings, aligning themselves with feminism by recognizing men's power in patriarchal contexts in spite of the various harms inflicted upon men through gender roles. However, men insisting upon the primacy of gender roles in discrimination and oppression created a sense of symmetry in the experience of oppression for both men and women, creating a new movement that was not only separate from feminism, but also critical and even hostile to its aims.

Warren Farrell follows this trajectory, and was a well-known male feminist in the 1970s. As a prominent member of the National Organization for Women (NOW), Farrell was an early supporter of the Equal Rights Amendment (ERA), and organized a variety of workshops and consciousness raising events focusing on men's issues and relationship to feminism. Farrell argued for the symmetry of oppression and harm between men and women in terms of gender roles, and famously highlighted this concern in role reversal workshops, most notably utilizing a male beauty pageant to raise awareness of the impact of beauty standards and objectification.[10] Farrell's work, *The Liberated Man*, illustrated the ways in which male and female oppression was comparable and symmetrical, arguing for a variety of phenomena concerning male experiences that functioned as an analogy for female experiences, such as the "masculine mystique," and being objectified as "success objects." While some feminists were open to Farrell and men's liberationists, other feminists expressed concern, citing, as noted previously, the neglect institutional power issues in the gender role symmetry argument, as well as the issue of blaming women for men's issues in stereotypical ways—such as nagging, and so forth.[11]

Although feminist criticism and rejection of gender role symmetry arguments played a role in the rising tensions between feminism and the men's liberation movement, an additional factor contributing to the increasing fractures was the problem of custody and divorce. While men's liberationists were often supportive of feminist agendas and goals, second wave feminism's support of women as a priority in custody disputes and reproductive decision making alienated and angered many men in the men's liberation movement. One such individual was Warren Farrell, who explained, "Everything went well until the mid-seventies when NOW came out against the presumption of joint custody. I couldn't believe the people I thought were pioneers in equality were saying that women should have the first option to have children or not have children—that children should not have equal rights to their dad."[12] Increasing clashes between fathers' rights advocates and feminism served to increase frustration within the men's liberation movement, deepening the fissures already present.

With tensions on the increase, various authors contributing to issues of men's liberation began to increasingly focus on men's overall disadvantages and the distinct costs of being a man. Such focus began to lead some men to conclude that not only were men harmed by gender roles, but men were also being actively harmed and oppressed by both women and feminism. Writers such as Herb Goldberg began to argue that male privilege and power does not exist—it is a myth.[13] These writings and theories starting in the late 1970s can be identified as early manifestations of the contemporary men's rights movement.

The Men's Rights Movement—History of the First Wave

According to Messner, the men's rights movement took shape in the 1970s through various organizations, such as Men's Rights Inc. and the Coalition of Free Men. These organizations, combined with a growing fathers' rights movement, provided further momentum for the growing sense of anger, disillusionment, and paranoia experienced by disenfranchised men's liberationists. Much of this backlash was directed at feminism, and men's rights advocates such as Goldberg argued that feminism was a plot to cover up the reality of women's power and privilege over men. Men's rights discourse shifted to conversations concerning the reality of a matriarchal gynocentric (woman oriented) culture, and the fact that men in such a culture were the true victims of a variety of gender issues, such as domestic violence, sexual assault, harassment, parenting, and divorce. Messner points out that while the issues addressed by the men's rights movement do serve as important rallying points, the most prominent and central issue to the men's rights movement has been fathers' rights.[14] The centrality of fathers' rights will be a thread running throughout this history, and will be addressed more directly in later chapters.

In order to fully understand the emergence of the MRM, Messner argues that it is useful to examine the "slippage" from a discourse concerning equal oppression to one arguing that men are overwhelmingly oppressed by women and feminism. According to Messner, this repositioning is the result of assumptions built into men's liberation rhetoric from early on. Men associated with men's liberation often expressed feelings of frustration and even anger over the fact that women and feminists did not seem to take their complaints concerning male oppression seriously. Messner argues that there are three themes that arise in many MRA autobiographies:

First is the claim of having been an early and ardent supporter of (liberal) feminism in hopes that it would free women and men from the shackles of sexism. Second is the use of the language of sex role theory that equates sexist thoughts and attitudes with oppression without discussing gendered institutional arrangements and intergroup relations. And last is the sense of hurt and outrage when women do not agree that men's issues are symmetrical with those faced by women, coupled with an enthusiastic embrace of an angry and aggressive anti-feminist men's rights discourse and practice.[15]

This trajectory represents both the evolution of individuals and the movement at large. In order to address this more clearly, I will return to the example of Warren Farrell and his turn from male liberation to men's rights activism.

In line with the themes above, Farrell was clearly aligned with feminism in the early to mid-1970s, with his frustration growing in the later 1970s due to what he saw as a failure on feminism's part to take seriously the issues concerning men as fathers. Maintaining his reliance on symmetrical experiences of gender exploitation, Farrell continued writing and working on various consciousness raising projects, with the stated goal of understanding women's anger toward men and the feelings of misrepresentation that many men experience. In 1986, Farrell released another book on these issues, entitled, *Why Men Are the Way They Are*. This work represents Farrell's attempt to discuss men's nature and behavior in a way that he felt truly represented men's thoughts and feelings, and Oprah Winfrey's support of the work furthered its success. However, in the work, Farrell maintains that women continue to wield a large amount of (sexual) power over men, and that men are exploited by women and others in economic/work contexts.

At this point, the shift in Farrell's worldview is apparent. Susan Faludi points out that Farrell was coming to portray men as the "new downtrodden," arguing that women were directing far too much criticism and anger toward men. Faludi explains, "Soon he [Farrell] was running workshops that emphasized *female* re-education, sensitivity training sessions to teach women to hear, and heed, men's grievances against them."[16] In an interview with Farrell, Faludi describes Farrell as committed to his new views on gender and male oppression, but regretful and sad over his abandonment by prominent feminists such as Gloria Steinem. Continuing his work, Farrell released *The Myth of Male Power* in 1993, which represents Farrell's full shift into men's rights theories, and it is still considered a classic and centerpiece text within the MRM. In this work, Farrell argues that feminist arguments concerning men's social and economic power are actually based on myths, and men are systematically disadvantaged and even oppressed. These shifts and changes in Farrell's thought reflect the themes that Messner describes, and work as an individual example of the evolution of the MRM and MRM thought throughout the 1980s and 1990s.

At this point in time, the MRM had established itself as a persistent worldview concerning gender and gender relations. According to Michael Kimmel, a professor of sociology specializing in masculinity studies, this movement at this point had further morphed into a movement that not only brought to light the oppressive nature of masculinity, but also promoted traditional masculinity as a role and identity to be celebrated. Consequently, traditional masculinity was not viewed as necessarily toxic or damaging as the men's liberation movement of the 1970s had argued; rather, the problem was women and women's reactions to this masculinity.[17] This view came into prominence during the 1990s and 2000s, but was not universally adopted. Some MRAs supported a return to traditional gender roles, while others rejected much of masculinity outright. Fractured approaches and thought processes at this time, combined with an overall lack of cohesion and agreement on specific issues, caused the MRM to remain a loosely associated network of individual men and groups that maintained that men are oppressed and damaged by society as well as feminism. However, the advent of the Internet supplied the MRM with a new platform for promoting their views, communication with other MRAs, and an avenue for recruiting other concerned men to the cause.

The Men's Rights Movement and the Internet

The Internet had a significant impact on the MRM, and various discussion boards and websites contributed to the creation of what is currently described as the "manosphere." The manosphere is a group of loosely associated websites, blogs, and forums all concerned with masculinity and men's issues, and includes input from the MRM, pick-up artists, anti-feminists, and fathers' rights activists. Caitlin Dewey points out that the manosphere contains its own jargon, and argues that the manosphere philosophy can be reduced to several core tenets: "(1) feminism has overrun/corrupted modern culture, in violation of nature/biology/inherent gender differences, and (2) men can best seduce women (slash save society in general) by embracing a super dominant, uber masculine gender role, forcing ladies to fall into step behind them."[18] Because the manosphere is so large, I will attempt to characterize it by focusing on several sites, blogs, and forums that have become central to and defining of MRM principles and beliefs. Due to their popularity and influence, I will be discussing the Red Pill forum on Reddit, the pick-up artist site "Return of Kings" (ROK), MGTOW.com (Men Going Their Own Way), and Paul Elam's AVFM.

Reddit is a site that is a compilation of postings from users, functioning as a sort of online bulletin board for users. Users, called redditors, can sign up and log on for free, and are able to post on various subreddits, which are divided by topic and theme, as well as to vote on various posts from other users. Posts on Reddit can be up or down voted by other users, and upvoting causes a post or comment to increase in visibility on the site. Generally, Reddit prides itself on its openness in terms of content and speech, and users post on an astoundingly wide variety of topics and interests. The "Red Pill" subreddit arose as a forum for men and sympathetic individuals to discuss the belief that men are actually the oppressed and disenfranchised gender in society. The "red pill" is a reference to the film, *The Matrix*, in which a character is offered the choice between a red pill and a blue pill. The blue pill will allow the individual to go back to a normal life, forgetting the nature behind reality, while the red will allow the individual freedom from a simulated world, consequently allowing the individual to know the truth behind the world and reality. Thus, the "red pill" of Reddit implies that its users have woken up to the nature of gendered reality, and no longer accept feminist myths concerning women's oppression and male privilege and power.

The Red Pill subreddit does not function as a space for political organization or mobilization; rather, it tends to function as a platform for individuals to post various "rants," discuss gender problems, reflect on strategies for picking up women, and to share information on various modes of "masculine" self-improvement. Since the Red Pill is a public thread, individual participants lie along a fairly wide spectrum, with some individuals exhibiting what appears to be a virulent hatred of women to others who merely demonstrate frustration with certain aspects of contemporary male experiences. Nonetheless, there are certain things that are fairly consistent within the Red Pill. Dylan Love explains:

> For Red Pillers, genuine reality goes something like this: Female oppression is a myth and men are the ones holding the short end of the stick. That said, men and women are inherently different due to evolution, so each gender should carry out its designated role in society. For example, women should raise children at home and men should work and have sex with women.[19]

Love then points out that a large amount of the focus within the group concerns sexual relationships with women and how to pick up mates, which is somewhat ironic given the Red Pill tendency to be highly critical of women in general. Nonetheless, useres on the site often discuss various "pick-up" strategies, as well as marking their progress in terms of diet in fitness, related to general quests to achieve idealized forms of masculinity.

The Red Pill has its own jargon and rhetoric, which are highly reflective of its ideals. Most notably is the distinction between alpha and beta males, with members actively striving for alpha male status. According to the post, "Alpha vs. Beta traits," no one is completely alpha or beta, but individuals will lean toward one or the other based on background and other personal factors.[20] However, the post also argues that individuals must be self-determining, stop blaming others, and work to be the type of man they want to be. Generally, alpha males are confident, collected, controlled, hard to impress, and are not controlled by desires for approval from women or others. Other posts further these arguments, pointing out that alpha male status not only frees men from dependence upon female approval and attention, but that women's supposed tendency to be attracted to non-needy men contributes to alpha males' successes with women.[21] Overall, these themes and tendencies in the Red Pill reflect several wider MRM tendencies to value traditional masculinity, challenge what is perceived as feminine dominance and control over men, and a sense of disempowerment due to women's control over sexuality and sexual relationships.

While the Red Pill does tend to focus on "picking up" women as sexual partners, other sites explicitly function as resources for men to manipulate women in the interest of gaining sexual access. One particularly notorious "pick-up artist" (PUA) site is "Return of Kings" (ROK), established and maintained by Roosh V following a falling out between Roosh and the Red Pill when Roosh accused the Red Pill of publishing his content without permission. This site promotes a worldview referred to as "neomasculinity," which is a more extreme version of the beliefs frequently promoted on the Red Pill. ROK has a significant amount of PUA literature, but also covers a wide variety of other topics. In the "About" section, ROK states that the site is explicitly for heterosexual men, and that "women and homosexuals are strongly discouraged from commenting here."[22] Central beliefs focus on men having "game" with women, how to become and stay an alpha male, and the current degeneracy of progressive, feminist, "liberal" culture. Roosh encourages men on the site to stop taking no as an answer from women, to devalue women in order to increase pick-up game, and the positives in being aloof when interacting with women. In addition to misogyny, the site regularly utilizes racist, homophobic, and transphobic language, framing these prejudices as normal aspects of an appropriately masculine psyche. More disturbingly, Roosh has been accused of sexual assault, and has described various experiences that fit general definitions of rape.[23] Nonetheless, ROK and other Roosh-associated sites repeatedly deny the reality of rape, claiming that coercion by males is a normal aspect of heterosexual experiences.[24]

In stark contrast to PUA sites and the Red Pill, another group of MRAs has taken an alternate approach to combatting the perceived damage and oppression caused by women and feminism, namely, to avoid women and relationships altogether. This group, Men Going Their Own Way (MGTOW), claim to be acting in the name of self-preservation, which can only be achieved by cutting women out of their lives completely. In general, MGTOW argues that feminism has made women so toxic and dangerous for men that it is no longer safe for women to engage with them. The MGTOW wiki claims that men involved with this movement place their self-interest first, and do not look to others for approval nor for definitions of what masculinity means. In line with these tenets, there are four levels of being a MGTOW, namely: 0) Situational awareness, that is, the Red Pill type of awareness; 1) Rejecting long-term sexual relationships; 2) Rejection of short-term sexual relationships; 3) Economic disengagement; 4) Social disengagement.[25] Many MGTOWs are quick to point out that they are not MRAs, since they are not a political movement nor do they seek to alter society—rather they seek to distance themselves from society as much as possible. Nonetheless, the MGTOW community is a well-known part of the manosphere and holds many of the same concerns about women, gender, and identity as many MRAs and MRM sites.

Clearly, these websites indicate the broad spectrum of beliefs and approaches to masculinity contained within the manosphere. While often identified with the MRM, these sites serve more as discussion, lifestyle guides, and support networks as opposed to resources for organized political action or input. As seen in the description of some groups and members, many of these outlets are explicitly suspicious of political engagement or reject it outright. According to Paul Elam, the MRM did not gain significant coherence until the advent of his site, AVFM, in 2009, bringing about what he refers to as the second wave of the MRM. This second wave was allegedly brought about by increased communication, networking, inclusivity, and a focus on men's rights as human rights. The next section will provide a more detailed overview of Elam and AVFM, discussing its function and impact on the contemporary MRM.

The Second Wave of the MRM and AVFM

Paul Elam claims that a turning point in his life was reading Farrell's *The Myth of Male Power*, and that this was the source of his own "red pill" moment in the 1990s. Mariah Blake, a reporter for *Mother Jones* magazine, states that Elam was working as a drug and alcohol counselor during this time, and his increasing concern for men's rights caused him to begin to regularly question and react to what he perceived as bias against men in this context.[26] Eventually, Elam found his way onto the manosphere. According to Blake, Elam claims to have been put off some of the bigoted language and theories; he nonetheless saw great potential for the MRM via online platforms. As a result, Elam launched AVFM in 2009, hoping to attract people of all races, genders, and so forth, who shared concerns over masculinity and men's issues.

Although Warren Farrell was wary of AVFM at first, due to its reputation for anger fueled rhetoric, he later came to see the site as a valuable resource, and Elam became a sort of protégé. Many individuals see Elam as the unofficial leader of the MRM, in spite of his conflicts with other MRAs such as

Roosh V. Elam regularly endorses and utilizes aggressive language and tactics in his approach to men's rights, for instance, calling for "Bash a Violent Bitch" month and running a site, register-her.com, which was a site that released the personal information of women who allegedly played a role in false rape reporting or other actions against men. Elam justifies his approach, arguing, "I don't know any social movement that has made progress without anger. We all saw what happened with Warren Farrell. He spent 40 years engaging in very reasoned, polite, discourse about men and boys, and society basically said, 'So what?'"[27] Consequently, while Elam has been widely criticized for his aggressive language and tactics, he sees this as a necessary aspect of raising awareness and forcing intervention. If no one will listen to the concerns of men and men are suffering in increasingly damaging and dangerous ways, then such action is often justified as self-preserving as opposed to merely violent.

According to Elam, what makes AVFM particularly compelling and important is its inclusiveness and diversity. In fact, one of the points included on the description of the second wave on AVFM states, "[The second wave of the MRM is] inclusive to all: women, men, straight and gay, trans, white, black are actively involved (as opposed to predominant hetero white of the 1st wave)."[28] Posts on the site repeatedly emphasize the lack of tolerance for any form of racism on AVFM, and regularly highlight female MRAs as invaluable allies. MRM books directly addressing gay males are regularly promoted and discussed on the site. Such promotion of "inclusivity" is reflected in the reference to the MRM as the MHRM (men's human rights movement), with the concept of human rights serving to create connections over and above individualized experiences of certain groups of men. The commitment to such human rights and diverse membership stands in stark contrast to sites such as ROK, and some parts of the Red Pill.

Overall, AVFM is explicitly political, even if the site does not often (if ever) promote direct political action and/or engagement with current political structures and institutions. It contains a detailed mission statement, regular editorial and writing staff, well organized lists of issues and ideologies, detailed histories, and regularly updated videos and posts on various issues and events. Furthermore, Elam and AVFM have been involved in organizing MRM conferences and events. The site is very issue oriented, denying any sort of affiliation with specific political parties or religious sects. Generally speaking, the site is dedicated to narrowly focusing on masculinity and male oppression as universal sources of moral wrong and sufferings, arguing that such concern transcends individual identity and partisan politics or religion.

Thus, while the manosphere is scattered and diverse in many ways, AVFM serves as a central organizing point for the MRM. It has served to create consistent points of concern and discussion, and provides clear direction and leadership that varies from the scattered nature of the MRM in earlier times. Because of these factors, this work uses AVFM as a central reference point for several reasons. First, it is the most consistent and coherent source of MRA issues, theories, and concerns. Second, it is the most consistently political, containing its own mapped out logic and approach to gender. Third, its politics are allegedly mainly motivated by some form of desire for gender justice, and the site repeatedly denounces any form of sexism, racism, homophobia, and so forth. This approach is of interest because it demonstrates an attempt on the part of AVFM to legitimize itself as a social, political, and personal resource, because it avoids the appearance of a mere outlet for the airing of random frustrations and dislikes by men who may or may not be adequately informed or appropriately motivated. Overall, in order to adequately analyze the MRM, I believe that one must take the movement seriously, and AVFM is arguably the most reliable and organized branch of the MRM to date. Merely focusing on the vicious sexism, racism, homophobia, and so forth, found on sites like ROK and certain Red Pill threads might be informative, but it does not address the MRM as a sociopolitical movement with coherent assumptions and reasoning mechanisms.[29]

PARAMETERS AND METHODS

As the previous section demonstrates, attempting to assess the MRM is overwhelming, due to the extraordinary number of websites, blogs, discussion boards, and individuals claiming to identify as part of this movement. Due to the sheer volume of sites and discussions, the scope of this project reflects the scope of MRM arguments most commonly made on sites like AVFM. However, this focus creates several consequences that impact the nature and context of my discussion. First, although the MRM movement claims to be global, most of this discussion will refer to issues in western culture and the United States, and western culture is the predominant context given on sites such as AVFM. Consequently, references to "society" and "culture" in this work reflect the western/U.S. context. Furthermore, the MRM's use of terms such as "men" and "women" reflect biologically based concepts of essentialist gender that often, if not always, neglect the concept of gender as fluid and socially constructed. As a result, these gendered terms erase the identities of individuals who identify as transgender and gender queer. While I am committed to the belief that such erasure is morally unacceptable, these identities are notably absent in this discussion due to the MRM's failure to engage such issues on the whole. Thus, my usage of gendered terms and pronouns in this work reflect common MRM usage, which should be read as indicative of my subject and sources, and not as an endorsement of such usage and constructs.

This work is divided into six chapters of content. Chapter 1 provides an in-depth overview of the MRM, analyzing its central tenets and arguments, and contextualizing these arguments in relation to feminism. Chapters 2, 3, and 4 attempt to provide a philosophical analysis of the politics, methods, and foundational claims of the MRM. Specifically, chapter 2 is an analysis of the MRM as an online phenomenon, interrogating the impact of the Internet on identity, communication, and politics. Once the conditions and identities contributing to the MRM are established, chapter 3 engages the MRM as a political movement, interrogating its claims of revolutionary and liberatory politics. This analysis suggests that the MRM, while highlighting certain important issues and concerns, ultimately fails as a social movement due to its inability and, at times, outright refusal to recognize or engage with larger social structures contributing to and maintaining domination. Chapter 4 creates a transition between the assessment of the MRM as a movement and the specific areas of concern engaged by the MRM. Because the MRM's foundational claim is male oppression, this chapter describes the nature of oppression, and under what conditions oppression can legitimately be claimed to occur. This model of oppression is then combined with the more general assessments of the MRM to critically examine two prominent themes in MRM forums, namely, male oppression in the family and male experiences of violence.

My analysis should be read as a feminist and progressive philosophical engagement with gender, masculinity, and politics. It relies on feminist philosophy and theory, as well as reflecting an overall criticism of contemporary capitalism. Generally, this work suggests that while the MRM gets many things wrong, they do get one thing right—our culture is overwhelmingly oppressive and damaging, full of contradictions and irrationality. However, instead of retreating into archaic or traditional forms of identity as resistance, we must imagine a new political future that transcends and overcomes current systems of domination and exploitation.

NOTES

1. Susan Faludi, *Backlash: The Undeclared War against American Women* (New York: Three Rivers Press, 1991).

2. Anita Superson, "Sexism in the Classroom: The Role of Gender Stereotypes in the Evaluation of Female Faculty," in *Theorizing Backlash: Philosophical Reflections on the Resistance to Feminism* (Lanham, MD: Rowman and Littlefield, 2002).

3. Ann Cudd, "Analyzing Backlash to Progressive Social Movements," in *Theorizing Backlash: Philosophical Reflections on Resistance to Feminism* (Lanham, MD: Rowman and Littlefield, 2002).

4. This is commonly referred to as "gynocentrism" in MRM circles. The website, Gynocentrism and Its Cultural Origins, is frequently referenced as the primary site for information on this phenomenon.

5. Paul Elam, a central MRM figure and founder of AVFM, commonly uses this approach. For example, he justifies his anger and revolution in the piece, "A Little Blood in the Mix Never Hurt a Revolution," last updated March 26, 2015, http://www.avoiceformen.com/mens-rights/a-little-blood-in-the-mix-never-hurt-a-revolution/.

6. Adam Kostakis regularly makes this point in his Gynocentrism Theory Lecture Series, posted at: https://gynocentrism.com/2014/05/25/gynocentrism-theory-2/.

7. Peter Wright, "The First and Second Wave of the Men's Rights Movement," last modified August 6, 2014, https://www.avoiceformen.com/mens-rights/first-and-second-wave-of-the-mens-rights-movement/.

8. Michael Messner, "The Limits of 'The Male Sex Role': An Analysis of the Men's Liberation and Men's Rights Movements' Discourse," *Gender and Society*, vol. 12 (1998): 255–276.

9. Messner, 261.

10. A detailed discussion of Farrell's life and events can be found in: Mariah Blake, "Mad Men: Inside the Men's Rights Movement—and the Army of Misogynists and Trolls it Spawned," *Mother Jones*, January/February 2015, http://www.motherjones.com/politics/2015/01/warren-farrell-mens-rights-movement-feminism-misogyny-trolls.

11. Messner provides several quotes from feminists on these issues, including Nancy Henley and Carol Hanisch, in his article.

12. J. Steven Svoboda, "Interview with Warren Farrell," MenWeb.com, last accessed May 3, 2017.

13. See, *The Hazards of Being Male: Surviving the Myth of Masculine Privilege* (Berkshire: Nash Publishing, 1976).

14. Messner, 267.

15. Messner, 269.

16. Susan Faludi, *Backlash*, 317.

17. Kimmel, *Angry White Men*, 107.

18. Caitlin Dewey, "Inside the 'Manosphere' That Inspired Santa Barbara Shooter Elliot Rodger," May 27, 2014, last accessed May 3, 2017, https://www.washingtonpost.com/news/the-intersect/wp/2014/05/27/inside-the-manosphere-that-inspired-santa-barbara-shooter-elliot-rodger/?utm_term=.34b0f4a9079f.

19. Dylan Love, "Inside the Red Pill, the Weird New Cult for Men Who Don't Understand Women," *Business Insider*, September 15, 2013, last accessed May 4, 2017, http://www.businessinsider.com/the-red-pill-reddit-2013-8.

20. "Alpha vs. Beta Traits," last updated May 2016, last accessed May 2017, https://www.reddit.com/r/TheRedPill/comments/3j7b3q/alpha_vs_beta_traits/.

21. "Signifiers of the Alpha Male, Signifiers of the Beta Male," last accessed May 4, 2017, https://www.reddit.com/r/TheRedPill/comments/3j3pbl/red_pill_101_signifiers_of_the_alpha_male/.

22. Last accessed May 4, 2017, http://www.returnofkings.com/about.

23. Dave Futrell, "Are Roosh V's 'Bang' Books How-To Guides for Rape?" last accessed May 4, 2017, http://www.wehuntedthemammoth.com/2015/08/14/are-roosh-vs-bang-books-how-to-guides-for-date-rape/comment-page-2/; http://www.wehuntedthemammoth.com/2016/02/14/an-icelandic-woman-has-come-forward-to-accuse-roosh-v-of-rape-blogger-reports/.

24. "When No Means Yes," last accessed May 4, 2017, http://www.rooshv.com/when-no-means-yes.

25. MGTOW Wiki, last accessed May 4, 2017, http://mgtow.wikia.com/wiki/MGTOW.

26. http://www.motherjones.com/politics/2015/01/warren-farrell-mens-rights-movement-feminism-misogyny-trolls.

27. http://www.motherjones.com/politics/2015/01/warren-farrell-mens-rights-movement-feminism-misogyny-trolls.

28. Peter Wright, "Welcome to the Second Wave," January 25, 2013, last accessed May 5, 2017, https://www.avoiceformen.com/mens-rights/welcome-to-the-second-wave/.

29. This should not be read as an endorsement of AVFM or its tenets, but rather an identification of AVFM as one of the most reliable resources concerning the MRM in the manosphere at present.

Chapter One

How the Men's Rights Movement Works

As the introduction to this work makes clear, characterizing the men's rights movement (MRM) is challenging. However, in order to focus this discussion, the current chapter will examine the rhetoric, ideals, and methods of core MRM groups and sites such as AVFM in order to provide a more detailed description of the movement and its engagement with politics and feminism. This chapter will attempt to discern patterns of discourse, narratives, and representation across the MRM and "manosphere" in order to create a more coherent working definition of the movement that adequately reflects its central claims. Throughout this chapter, I will be discussing the vocabulary and terminology as well as the ideals and issues that commonly appear within MRM discussions and writings. By establishing this base of understanding, the following chapters will be able to elaborate on specific issues in MRM identity, methods, and politics more specifically.

CORE PRINCIPLES AND IDEOLOGIES OF THE MEN'S RIGHTS MOVEMENT

In order to represent MRM arguments concerning male oppression, it is important to focus on the following centers of such alleged oppression: gynocentrism, misandry, and feminist rhetoric. MRAs argue that these principles function to both motivate and sustain male oppression. The following sections will attempt to provide a clear overview of each principle and how it functions in MRM rhetoric, creating a clearer definition of the purpose, mission and functioning of the movement overall.

Gynocentrism

Generally speaking, gynocentrism is the claim that society has historically revolved around women and femininity, at a great cost to males. More specifically, this is the notion that there are deeply entrenched historical norms that put women first and demand the repeated sacrifice of males to uphold the feminine center. Contemporary feminism, then, is the further entrenching of women's power, as opposed to a political movement working for the liberation of women. Adam Kostakis explains, "The traditional idea under discussion is male sacrifice for the benefit of women, which we term Gynocentrism. This is the historical norm, and it was the way of the world long before anything called 'feminism' made itself known. There is an enormous amount of continuity between the chivalric class code which arose in the Middle Ages and modern feminism, for instance."[1] If this is true, then, MRAs argue, feminism is not liberatory it is oppressive—the myth of female oppression exists in the interest of furthering the oppression of men. Furthermore, the centrality of femininity culturally makes it the case that men are repeatedly disempowered, and the services men are called on to perform for women's benefit are presented as sources of honor while actually creating further weakening of men's position. More importantly, the existence of gynocentrism is claimed to completely undermine the feminist belief that society has a patriarchal structure. Patriarchy is then argued to be the ultimate feminist myth, an argumentative straw man or red herring.

One of the most common examples used to support arguments for the existence of gynocentrism is the notion of male sacrifice for women—both physically and economically. Farrell argues, "What is consistent among men is not violence but men's willingness to protect. When they can protect by killing enemies, they kill enemies; when men can protect by 'making a killing' on Wall Street, they do that. Men's underlying motivator is neither swords nor plowshares . . . it's adapting to love and adapting to approval."[2] Therefore, while feminists and others have read such behaviors as demonstrating the power to rule or control political and economic forces, men like Farrell read these actions as fulfilling social requirements for male sacrifice and the placement of women on a pedestal. Women wait around to be served and rescued, while men labor to provide for and protect them on this model. As Farrell puts it, being a hero is actually being a slave.[3]

A common MRM argument, then, is that women have significantly more power than men overall, in spite of feminism's insistence to the contrary:

> The perception of women as powerless makes us fear limiting the expansion of women's power. Fear of limiting the power of the sex with the greater spending power, the greater beauty power, the greater sexual power, the greater net worth among wealthier heads of households, and the greater options in mar-

riage, children, work and life creates the corruptness of absolute power which will ultimately lead to a much bloodier battle of the sexes.[4]

In other words, men make money and women spend it; men ask for sex and women grant occasional permission; men contribute to children economically but women control parenting. Everything men do is in the service of women's needs and demands, and the consequences are degrading and deadly. For writers like Farrell, being a man is a thankless and often humiliating job.

As mentioned previously, MRAs argue that the myth keeping this system in play is patriarchy. For men to continue to allow themselves to be degraded and taken advantage of, they must believe that the system is correct or just. Feminists further this so-called propaganda by denying gynocentrism/gynarchy and focusing on patriarchy. Kostakis argues:

> As such, The Patriarchy™ is not a real thing. It is only an imagined thing—a fetishized object of imagination that exists in the minds of feminists and other morons. It exists to perpetuate a shallow and one-dimensional narrative that presents women as objects-of-victimization. It is the sort of thing that feminists love to hate. It is loved because it can be blamed for everything. It is hated because it is the villain. Without The Patriarchy™, there would be no feminist narratives. Without Snidely Whiplash, there would be no Dudley Do Right.[5]

For the MRA, the patriarchy is the feminist-created boogey man, a shadow figure looming over everything serving only to affirm and further feminist claims. More simply put, the concept of patriarchy helps feminists to rig the system by begging the question—they have already assumed in the patriarchy everything they want to demonstrate, argue for, and resist. Finally, and most importantly, the alleged myth of patriarchy distracts us from the real issue—gynocentrism and the degradation of males.

If the world is gynocentric, MRAs argue, then it is critical that men refocus their efforts. Roger Devlin points out that it is far past time for men to abandon the protector role by refusing to economically support women, take care of all their needs, and refuse to die in wars for them. Furthermore, he argues, it is this protector tendency that has led many men to endorse feminism—they feel obligated to protect women from the shadowy oppression of patriarchy and all of the other "evil" types of males in the world.[6] Consequently, the need to protect and provide has caused men to repeatedly endorse the movement directly responsible for their own oppression. In this way, men are frequently characterized as well-meaning dupes of a vicious and destructive feminist movement driven by female narcissism and self-service. The only way out for men is to realign personal and political priorities—take women out of the center and place men and their well-being there.

Misandry

The next step in demonstrating male oppression is to show not just that women are at the center of society and law, but that men are degraded and hated as a result of this structure. Much as gynocentrism acts as the foil to feminism's concept of patriarchy, the concept of misandry is used to counter feminist accusations of misogyny. Kimmel describes the MRM definition of misandry as one focusing on the alleged fear, loathing, degradation, and hatred of men as a complete inversion of feminism's misogyny.[7] For the MRM, contemporary western society exhibits a pervasive dehumanization and brutalization of men through violence, devaluation, and economic and physical objectification. Evidence for such misandry is commonly cited as being present in feminism's descriptions of men and the hostility of feminism toward individual men as well as masculinity on the whole.

The concept of misandry is central for Elam. On his website, he claims:

> It [the MRM philosophy] is the radical notion that men are human beings, and should see themselves as human beings first, and should be afforded the same rights and considerations as anyone else. It is the radical notion that men, collectively and as individuals, owe women nothing whatsoever. We do not owe women our protection. We do not owe women provision. When it comes to protecting anyone else, our first question is, "Why should we?" And when it comes to things like intimate relationships, marriage, children, we ask, boldly and without apology, "what's in it for us?"[8]

Notice the language Elam uses closely reflects famous feminist quotes and rhetoric.[9] This strategically presents the MRM as the truth about society and gender, asking us to go through the proverbial looking glass in order to see the truth. The problem is not patriarchy or the general gender system; the problem is the persistent and unrelenting targeting of males as scapegoats and resources, which is upheld by dehumanizing narratives about men.

For Elam, women and feminists refuse to take any responsibility for the problems that men face. Furthermore, feminism has a particularly humiliating strategy—picking out individual males as feminist whipping boys and pariahs to scare other men into submission. Kostakis further argues that men are picked out as fetishized villains to be relentlessly disciplined and punished within feminist circles and rhetoric. The general force or motivation behind these actions, according to men's rights authors such as Kostakis and Elam, is a general hatred and disdain for men. Kostakis explains:

> Feminism provides more than the opportunity for catharsis. The feminist soon realizes that she need not restrict herself to echo chambers, but might try her hand at real change. A thrill rushes through her at the thought of not just disparaging, but actually hurting men. Backed up by an extensively organized, generously funded and institutionally-connected movement—one that enjoys a rosy reputation as defender of that greatest virtue of our time, equality—she sets to work. Feminism is a misandrist's dream.[10]

According to Kostakis, feminism does not create misandry but provides an outlet for enraged, male hating women to focus and organize their persecutory disdain. This, then, is not portrayed as a political action, but as merely spiteful, hateful abuse hiding beneath the banner of a social/political movement.

The charge of misandry is included in most criticisms and theories offered up by men's rights activists, giving an edge of persecution to general complaints. It is not just that men are neglected, marginalized, or made invisible; women hate men with such virulence and commitment that there appears no end in sight to the alleged persecution. Such arguments are then used to justify some of the seemingly and obviously drastic conclusions and methods recommended by various men's rights activists.

Feminism as an Oppressive Force

Because feminism is argued to be a driving force behind misandry and the alleged oppression of males, it is imperative to further explore the MRM conceptualization of feminists and feminist work, especially since the MRM regularly targets individual feminists and their work. As was previously discussed, feminism is seen as the predominant contributor to male oppression, and is framed as a sham political movement that gives women a platform to vent their dislike or hatred of men in general. Thus, feminism is a threat to men but it's framed as a threat motivated and furthered by emotionally charged hatred and a desire for power, as opposed to an organized movement that strategically oppresses men through a variety of deliberate and powerful interventions.

When perusing the various takes on feminism, a common theme that arises concerning feminism is the notion of a movement out of control. In fact, many contributors and authors in the MRM claim that feminism started out with some reasonable requests, but quickly degenerated. Feminist women, according to these men, will never be content with what they have—each victory creates a greater desire for power and further confirmation of women's alleged misandry. Furthermore, this misandry causes feminists to completely ignore any wrongdoing on the part of women, causing women to continue to avoid responsibility for certain social and/or gendered realities. Dean Esmay argues:

> Feminists claim to be rebelling . . . but in their talk of "oppression" they are never looking at women's role in creating and maintaining the status quo, never acknowledging the special privileges women have always enjoyed, and never acknowledging that when they ask for "rights" they almost never want the responsibilities that go with them, laying the responsibility for whatever goes wrong on men (or "The Patriarchy").[11]

Consequently, Esmay concludes that feminism asks for rights for women without wanting to give up the advantageous gendered norms of previous eras. For example, women are asking for "equal rights" as long as it's not inconvenient—thus, there is little interest in equality in terms of military drafts or expecting polite deference on the pars of men (opening doors, giving up seats, etc.). On this view, it seems like women want it all and they want it for free.

However, these complaints seem to grant women a lot of power in terms of oppression while simultaneously maintaining a misogynistic representation of women/feminists as emotional, irrational, and lacking organization. Thus, there appears to be a contradiction concerning how supposedly irrational and unintelligent women are creating and maintaining this seemingly intricately created social structure of male oppression. Nonetheless, MRAs such as Elam and Kostakis emphasize the fact that feminists are mostly emotional, and their driving emotion is an irrational rage. Feminism is described as a movement appealing to vindictive, irrational, selfish, immature and unintelligent women. Kostakis elaborates:

> The power of suggestion is particularly pronounced in the feminist crowd because it is mostly composed of women, and women are more impressionable than men. This is not an inherent difference between the sexes, but a socialized defect. A lifetime of privilege, of parasitic exploitation and entitlement, of juicing the fruits of another's labor, has left many women devoid of character, with unrealistic views of the world which leave them open to certain kinds of manipulation that men are not so easily taken in by. Feminism is ideological snake oil, and impressionable women are its customers.[12]

These portrayals present feminism as a sort of unhinged bratty sister, making irrational demands and throwing tantrums at every turn.

In order to maintain the coherence of this portrait of feminism, MRAs supply an answer for feminist effectiveness in spite of their unintelligent irrational nature—feminists are dupes. Elam explains:

> The answer to that is as simple as it is forbidding. Feminism is not for feminists. Feminists are idiots, but they are the useful idiots in the description previously reserved for Soviet sycophants in cold war America. Feminism, in reality, is for governments and corporations. And it is the most effective tool for control of the masses since the riot baton and water cannons. Feminists are

not a bunch of nut cases that have taken over the world. They are just a bunch of nut cases that have assisted some really smart and devious people in erasing any impediments they might have ever had at putting a leash on all of us.[13]

To be clear, Elam does not elaborate here on the forces of oppression behind all of this. It's not a thoroughly explained position, however, it is an effective tactic for engaging with feminism as an MRA. This explanation/view allows the MRM to portray women in degraded, misogynistic terms while making the notion of feminism's oppressive nature as highly effective consistent with the former claim. In other words, feminists are "idiots" but they are able to do damage because they are puppets of the powers that be—we can blame feminism for many things while not giving feminism any credit (good or bad).

The MRM presents the problem with feminism as an issue of equality, based upon arguments that feminism creates an unequal distribution of goods, opportunities, and responsibilities. The notion of equality as central to a larger concept of social justice is not new, however, an appropriate definition of equality has been a persistent and plaguing philosophical issue. The MRM helps itself to a simplistic notion of equality in terms of certain issues—for example if men must register for the draft then so must women, or if women can make choices about pregnancy then so can men. At the same time, many MRAs present models of gender that are deeply traditional and essentialist. Thus, it is often unclear how the MRM thinks equality can be achieved between two sexes that are fundamentally different, because a sense of equity in this context requires a significantly more complex understanding than the definition presenting itself on MRM sites.

It can be argued that what really drives MRM conversations and arguments is a sort of competition in terms of resources and victimhood. Eva Cox summarizes this phenomenon as follows:

> It strikes me this whole debate is getting into what I call the "competing victim syndrome." This is basically about trying to claim that "I'm worse off than you are, because there are limited resources and if I can prove I'm worse off than you are and look at my scars, look at my pain, look at my misery—I can have more of the existing resources than you can."[14]

As a result of this, she argues that social justice has begun to devolve into a competition based on showing who is really the worst off, creating a reactionary position contributing to deep and antagonistic social divisions. When people have victim based political conversations, the inability of individuals to identify with the problems of another person, that individual will develop "compassion fatigue"—you are no longer relatable, but merely an "other" whom you cannot fully recognize.[15] This encapsulates what happens on many MRM platforms. There is no coherent exchange with feminists, no conversation, no coming to terms, but rather a squabbling over an unquantifiable sense of pain, suffering, and the resulting oppression. Consequently, discussions easily spiral into ad hominem attacks or straw man responses until one side disengages, leaving the conversation to be had among individuals who all agree and reassure one another of given positions and perceptions.

Thus, the MRM has a very specific strategy in furthering its agenda through criticisms and engagements with feminism. First, throughout the literature on feminism and women and general, traditional and misogynistic notions concerning femininity and women are upheld, and these constructs are presented as innate and essential female identities. If this is the case, then the MRM can argue that women are out of control, it is their nature to be this way, and hence avoid any requirement to constructively engage or interact with feminists, especially feminist women. Furthermore, if women are naturally irrational and out of control, then giving them any power and/or voice inevitably leads to disaster. Thus, the MRM can suggest an ultimate return to traditional gender roles as an answer to this alleged male oppression in a society out of control. Second, a focus on resources creates the ability to construct a competing victimhood to discredit feminism's claims of oppression, and so forth. If the MRM can eventually achieve a return to traditional male gender roles, and in turn reinforced masculine power, then furthered access to resources under the banner of distributive justice can only work to reinforce the foundation for male privilege and power. Overall, the MRM presents itself as a sort of feminist doppelganger, inverting feminist claims and strategies under the rubric of liberation, working toward the goal of social power.

WHO ARE THE MRAs?

Membership and Mission

As pointed out previously, the MRM is related to the manosphere, a loose association of websites and organizations promoting certain forms of masculinity and generally expressing a disdain for feminism. Because of the nature of the manosphere, it is not possible to accurately assess the precise make-up of MRM populations or the demographics of all individuals that identify as MRAs. Nonetheless, there are very clear patterns in terms of MRA identification: white, heterosexual middle class males of varying ages. Notably, MRA sites often claim to only be concerned with issues impacting men qua men: they do not specifically address issues arising from race, class, sexual identity, and so forth. Interestingly, this seems to suggest that there is such a thing as an essential masculine or male experience, feeding into the alleged "humanism" of the men's rights movement that purports to work toward equality.

Elam's website recently began identifying itself as a platform for the MHRM—the men's human rights movement. This shift is a strategic move for the organization to present itself as operating in line with humanist values, presumably in order to counteract accusations of misogyny and woman-hating. According to the website, the goal of the movement is to secure freedom and rights for all persons, regardless of gender. The site has a detailed mission statement, listing a variety of concerns and demands, with the following serving as an introduction:

> It is time for equity-minded men and women to engage in the final push for freedom for both sexes, and indeed for all human beings. It is time for the interests of humanity to take precedence over the interests of men and women as political factions and social adversaries. It is time for a movement that truly favors humanity, not a particular sex. It is time for feminism to fulfill its promise of equality, and to quit making a mockery of it.[16]

This presentation creates a potential rallying cry for all persons—the problem is not the respect for difference but the overemphasis of difference, suggesting a slippery slope concerning social activism. It's not a new complaint—if we keep talking about how different we are, how can we all ever truly work together? If we keep giving certain people special rights based on these differences, how can we ever be equal? It rings of simple lessons about color-blindness and gendered worth, urging us to whitewash our differences in the name of an uninterrogated and hyper-literal sense of "equality."

The use of the term "human rights" is also a strategic move in the MRM arguments for male oppression and in denying the use of misogynistic interventions and language. Generally speaking, human rights are norms used to protect all people everywhere from severe forms of abuse. In other words, simply by being human, you should have the right to be protected from certain kinds of harm and intervention, and this right creates a duty for all persons to respect these rights in others. When the term "human rights" is invoked in social and political contexts, it usually evokes a sense of rights protecting deeply important goods and freedoms, not simple or mundane issues. In other words, the term often creates a feeling of profound importance or a deeply important call to action for the protection of other humans. This sense of priority and universalism makes the term very useful for a movement/organization that has repeatedly been accused of misogyny, harassment, hate speech, and violence. The MRM identification with "human rights" simultaneously emphasizes the perceived severity of men's oppression and suffering while allowing the group to present itself as non-partisan, peaceful, and communitarian.

By presenting itself as "humanist," groups like "A Voice for Men" also explains away their lack of concern with diversity among men, often glossing over differences in race, class, and sexual preference. The egalitarian model being used in these contexts suggests that men deserve equal dignity and respect (an uncontroversial demand), but that men share a common bond in being men in terms of identity, experience, and deprivation of these basic rights. There is no clear denial in most instances on the part of the MRM that certain men experience other oppressions such as racism, classism, or homophobia, but the point is that these forms of oppression are often secondary to the overwhelming gender oppression men are claimed to experience. This position is very similar to problematic assertions made by feminists in the second wave, carrying over in some degree to certain forms of current feminism. Many white middle class straight women assumed their position as a starting point or given, creating the baseline for all discussions concerning "women" and "femininity." The problem with this is erasing other standpoints, failing to recognize interlocking oppression, and an overstating of women's shared experience. Such moves alienated many women from feminism, and it seems to have the same effect on the MRM, given its generally white, straight, middle class make-up. The old mistakes repeat themselves over and over—privileged positions become the "human position." In other words, the "human rights" the MRM seeks come from the standpoint of a certain kind of man, not all men qua men. It's counterproductive and alienating to distill men's concerns down to a sort of "men qua men" analysis, yet it seems to be the cornerstone of many MRM discussions and commitments.

Nonetheless, as a movement seeking certain "rights" it is imperative to analyze and discuss the nature of the rights the MRM seeks. The specifics are very broad in range, but generally focus on the following areas of concern: custody/parental rights, rape law, education, violence, and incarceration. These areas have been the topic of many social theoretical analyses and political movements/interventions. What makes the MRM unique as an analytical lens is the claim that the problem at the root of these issues is misandry and the oppression of men. While the MRM notes and rallies around these alleged abuses against men, there is no clear political organization to move forward with legislative demands, and so forth. Rather, MRAs like Elam claim that there is no recourse for action given current cultural and sociopolitical structures at play. Thus, Elam and other individuals aligned with the MRM see the movement as a counterculture as opposed to one focused on creating political change. Elam states, "We don't want to break in to the mainstream. We just want to break it. And even that is somewhat of a misstatement. The mainstream is already broken. It is the mainstream that is the problem. We are not dumb enough to think it holds the solutions."[17] This position portrays the MRM as a rogue movement set on disruption and resistance as opposed to the creation or potential improving of existing rights.

Consequently, it can be argued that the MRM seeks a broad negative right of noninterference concerning the maintenance of hegemonic masculinity. The refusal to cooperatively engage with current politics and other movements accomplishes several things. To begin, it reinforces the MRM's desire to dismiss feminism completely and to continue to dismiss any and all points coming out of this referential framework. Additionally, the unnamed search for a negative right to noninterference in the experience of hegemonic masculinity allows for the creation of a world view that is deeply narcissistic, reverting to notions of humanism that ignore the location of a claimed "objective" standpoint. Finally, this rejection of the mainstream creates a sense of permission in terms of method; namely it lends itself to "breaking" social structures or general strategies that are destructive. This overall opens the door for certain types of violent exchange based upon anger and resentment, pushing gender progress further back as meaningful linguistic exchanges all but vanish.

Methods of Intervention

The drive to "break the mainstream" provides insight to the methods used by the MRM. Overall, the MRM strategy is mainly linguistic, promoting its views online in articles and blogs, and disrupting dissenting individuals through a variety of online interactions. Because the general content and ideals informing the blogs and writings of the MRM were previously discussed, the focus here will be on the methods of intervention used by the MRM concerning individuals and organizations, often feminist, who advocate views and agendas they see as promoting misandry, male oppression, and disseminating bad and/or ignorant information. Elam advocates the use of provocation, stating. "We set out to provoke an obtuse, downright stupid media apparatus into sending people our way. They graciously and obliviously complied. They could not help themselves. Pissing on their sacred cows is just too much for their propaganda addled minds to handle. Their outrage and indignation, just like ours, had to be vented."[18] The point is to get attention, evoke outrage, and disrupt conversation, with the overall goal being to garner members and support while derailing feminists and feminist allies with rage and frustration through the illumination of their so-called idiocy. The movement both creates and feeds upon rage, making it deeply toxic and dangerous, to the point of becoming self-defeating as opposed to liberating.

The MRM commitment to rage and disruption are most obvious in the online surveillance of others combined with various disciplinary and silencing techniques. One of the most common types of disruption is referred to as "trolling." This term is used in a variety of ways in online communities, but it commonly refers to people who anonymously post comments, and so forth, online with the sole purpose of disruption. It's often thought of as a sort of aimless activity with arbitrary targets, thus, the use of the term here may not fall in line with more specific definitions. Nonetheless, it is helpful for thinking through the more low-level disruptive behaviors we see by MRAs in online forums. It has been commonplace for these individuals to insert insulting and degrading comments on anything containing any sort of perceived feminist content in order to derail the post or writings. Oftentimes, it contains no arguments, just insults, creating a refusal to actually engage, coupled with destructive intentions. In addition to trolling, many MRAs have escalated online interference to various forms of harassment, often with sexual or other types of violent threats, directed at feminists, women who speak in certain threads, or women who simply engage in typically "boys only" activities, like gaming. In general, the goal is to silence, shame, degrade, and remove women and feminist speech from contexts the MRA values, which could be anything from a subreddit thread to (apparently) the entirety of the Internet.

While the above interventions can create stress and exclusion, there are significantly more forceful and damaging sorts of behaviors the MRM uses in its search to destroy the "mainstream." Individual MRAs might "infiltrate" certain feminist organizations or blogs, and have been known to crash websites with fake reports and spamming as a form of "protest." For example, an individual referred to as "Agent Orange" infiltrated the interactions of a group named "radfem," effectively shutting down the website and disabling future group organizing.[19] In terms of spamming, one particularly severe example involves the 2013 posting of fake rape reports on an online form for Occidental College that allows students to anonymously report sexual assaults. Coverage for this story reports, "The spamming of Occidental's complaint form follows a comment posted Tuesday on 'Men's Rights' pages on the websites Reddit and 4chan . . . that blamed 'feminists' at Occidental for creating the online form. 'You just fill out a form and the person is called into the office on a rape charge,' the post says, falsely. 'The "victim" never has to prove anything or reveal their identity.'"[20] In response to this perceived injustice, MRAs and so-called off-campus Internet trolls posted more than 400 obviously false reports in a 36-hour period, using names like "Fatty McFatFat" for these fictional accusers. While this is often perceived as one of the more egregious interventions spurred by sites like Reddit, the strategy is not unusual for the MRM. A call for similar action on Dartmouth's anonymous reporting forum emerged in February 2014.[21] Another well-known MRA intervention involves a poster campaign in Edmonton at the University of Alberta created in answer to an anti-sexual assault ad campaign with the tag "Don't Be That Guy." MRAs responded with a counter campaign with the slogan "Don't Be That Girl," warning against false rape reporting. The MRM campaign gained momentum when it created new posters featuring a photo of Lise Gotell, chair of women's studies and gender studies at the

University of Alberta, featuring the tag, "Theft isn't black. Bank fraud isn't Jewish. And rape isn't male."[22] While this is not Internet behavior, the intense covering of the town and campus with these posters and the targeting of a specific individual mirrors many online "trolling" actions and bullying tactics. Overall, it seems that instead of creating sound arguments and political debates, the movement rallies to crash, destroy, and disrupt the offending target under the "the mainstream is too broken to engage" defense.

Perhaps the most distressing method of silencing and surveillance utilized by the MRM is the use of registries and personal information to intimidate the targets of MRM criticism. Because this "doxxing"[23] behavior is quite common, Elam's use of this method will be discussed as paradigmatic in order to establish the methods and purpose of this intervention. Elam's most notable disciplinary apparatus utilizing doxxing is the site "Register-Her.com," established in 2011 and was shut down in 2014. The purpose of this site is to publish the personal information of individuals who "have caused significant harm to innocent individuals either by direct action of crimes like rape, assault, child molestation and murder, or by the false accusation of crimes against others."[24] Much of the site targets women who claim to be victims of male on female rape who are labeled as false accusers.[25] Other individuals listed on the site are women labeled as "anti-male bigots," usually due to feminist activities. While the information on the site usually just contains names and affiliations, Elam has pointed out that the site could potentially list the addresses, phone numbers, and so forth, of the targeted individuals, creating anxiety on the part of those listed concerning harassment, stalking, and so on. In the past, Elam has put out "bounties" or cash rewards to get the name of an anonymous feminist blogger.[26] These sorts of lists and exposures work as indirect threats by pointing out that these women are known, they have been located and they can be found at any time. The assumed strategy here is the creation of silence through fear.[27]

These strategies, while mainly verbal, are often perceived as violent actions and threats. The harassment and exposure, coupled with the directly and indirectly violent threats make the MRM an intimidating force to reckon with. As Raewyn Connell points out, "Violence is part of a system of domination, but is at the same time a measure of its imperfection. A thoroughly legitimate hierarchy would have less need to intimidate. The scale of contemporary violence points to crisis tendencies . . . in the modern gender order."[28] Thus, the violent reactions of the MRM relate directly to a contemporary crisis in masculinity. Feelings of loss concerning masculine power and a perceived degradation of male identity result in a deep sense of shame for some men. According to James Gilligan, shame is central to an understanding of violence, especially for male perpetrators. Gilligan argues that men are subject to a sort of honor code, and any shame experienced within this honor code can be undone by violent action, because violence connotes power and power counteracts shame. For men, women often act as a potent source of shameful feelings, particularly through sexual behaviors and interactions.[29] Thus, it is unsurprising that the shame men feel as a result of feminism and perceived disempowerment is answered with rage, anger, and violence on the part of the MRM. Furthermore, it is notable that the subject that appears to elicit the most violent responses on the part of men and the MRM is rape and heterosexual interactions with women.

While there is a great deal of anger, shame, and violence involved with the strategies of the MRM, it would be a mistake to assume that their methods are disorganized and ineffective. The actions of the MRM against targeted women and feminist create an effective system of discipline and surveillance similar to the workings of power Michel Foucault describes in *Discipline and Punish*. According to Foucault, disciplinary power is absolute and indiscreet, because the gaze of power is both everywhere and constantly alert.[30] The Internet makes this form of discipline highly effective for the MRM due to its public nature. Thus, the gaze of the MRM is everywhere, watching language, action, and response; it intervenes, interrogates, and infiltrates at any given moment. Its constancy as a threat works to silence, dissuade, and discourage. However, Foucault reminds us that power is not negative but productive; "truth" is a mode of power that produces, regulates, and distributes information.[31] Thus, while the MRM silences and represses on the surface, what they are actually seeking is to establish a different narrative concerning oppression through these disciplinary actions. It seeks to create a regime of truth not by ignoring feminism but constantly engaging the topic in order to produce a narrative in line with the power structure of hegemonic masculinity. Discipline, according to Foucault, reduces multiplicity by arresting movement.[32] Hence, the MRM seeks to create or in some ways resuscitate a regime of truth concerning men and masculinity through the production of truth coupled with a homogenizing of feminist views and masculine standpoints. This creates greater control and enhances the ability to secure truth through controlled narrative.

In conclusion, the MRM has developed effective strategies of intervention for silencing and dismissing feminism. It takes up issues that feminists and other social theorists have long acknowledged as legitimate sources of concern and purports to provide a narrative concerning the "truth" about these issues. These contextualized truths are then presented within a wider context of truth concerning the nature of male experiences and oppression. This is then coupled with the notion that the situation for men is dire and intolerable, and that feminism is not only misguided but also immoral or even evil. To prove and reinforce these notions, feminism is frequently compared to hate groups such as the KKK or Nazis, lending legitimacy to the use of extreme forms of intervention and violence through harassment by the MRM as a response. In other words, the narrative presented is that feminism and society have left these men no other choice but to create a counter-disciplinary regime through surveillance and harassment in the name of exposing the "truth" about society and power. It is through the control of "truth" that power is to be obtained, maintained, and distributed. Thus, the MRM claims that it is time to take back control of this narrative.

HOW THE MRM HAPPENS: CULTURE, GENDER AND POLITICS

The emergence of the men's rights movement should not be dismissed as a simple uprising in feminist backlash or an excuse to express misogyny in an increasingly politically correct world. Rather, this movement should be understood within the context of what has been called a "masculinity crisis" in contemporary culture. The notion of masculinity and crisis has been a theme throughout this chapter, and this section will provide a deeper development of the relevant issues in order to provide a thorough backdrop for understanding the emergence of the MRM as a notable cultural force. Specifically, this section will discuss the nature of the masculinity crisis, how it deeply informs the MRM, and contemporary issues in feminist theory/politics as it relates to the masculinity crisis and backlash politics.

Masculinity and the MRM

Michael Kimmel persuasively argues that the MRM is a movement that comes out of a general sense of anger in contemporary males. As Kimmel explains, men are experiencing a very real and potent sense of anger in current society, and this anger comes out of feelings of being cheated out of the rewards society told them they would be entitled to as "good" men.[33] Cultural shifts result in a sense of emasculation, uselessness, and humiliation for many of these men. "Economic and social changes that are bewilderingly fast and dramatic are experienced as the general 'wimpification' of American men—castrated by taxation, crowded out by newcomers who have the rules bent for them, white men in America feel as if they are presiding over the destruction of their species."[34] Consequently, men feel as if they have been cheated, lied to, and mislead, creating backlash directed toward the perceived sources of this loss—women, feminism, and minorities. The MRM provides a platform for these men in which they can regain hope for a restoration of the previous order and communicate with like-minded men for sympathy, validation, and the creation of responses. As Kimmel points out, anger creates a commitment and makes one feel as a stakeholder. Thus, anger seeks an outlet as well as connections with others.[35] It would then seem like the MRM is such an outlet, creating bonds based on anger, resentment, and perceived shared oppression/persecution.

The question, then, is how men in our society reached this point, which requires a further examination into what type of "masculinity" is actually in crisis. As previously indicated, white, heterosexual males constitute the MRM majority. Consequently, it is unsurprising that the baseline of masculinity for the MRM is based upon properties they directly identify with, erasing the complex social interactions that create the standpoints of men in highly varied contexts. Connell claims that masculinity is not an ideal or a removed archetype, but rather a complex social identification forged out of and organized by social relationships. In other words, gender emerges through interactions with others and the world,[36] and masculinity and femininity are mutually dependent identifications that engage each other dialectically. This mutual dependence, however, also suggests an inherent vulnerability on the part of both sides. The vulnerability of women/femininity is often expressed in feminist rhetoric that identifies men as having power, exhibiting high levels of aggression, and acting out violently. These perceptions coupled with patriarchal norms and expectations result in the hegemonic masculinity referred to above. Connell is careful to point out that there is no monolithic absolute sense of masculinity, but hegemonic masculinity serves a very important function. She explains, "Hegemonic masculinity can be defined as the configuration of gender practice which embodies the currently accepted answer to the problem of the legitimacy of patriarchy, which guarantees (or is taken to guarantee) the dominant position of men and the subordination of women."[37] In other words, this is the culturally exalted form of masculinity that is often presented as an ideal. The problem emerges when this hegemonic view of masculinity clashes with men's own experiences and perceptions of reality.

While feminist discussions and hegemonic masculinity present a male identity based on power, many men who are alleged to enjoy such power (white heterosexual males) actually feel disempowered in current cultural contexts. Thus, many men come to deeply resent the "myth" of power that they do not feel they have. For instance, one arena in which this is evident is economics, particularly for middle class and working males. The ability to provide for one's self and family is a central value for masculine identity. However, with economic changes and recessions coupled with increased earning power on the part of women, the role of the male of power comes increasingly under threat. Bell hooks points out that men struggle with the contradiction between what is expected of them and the inability to fulfill these expectations, leading to emotional responses to the lack of privilege and power society seemed to promise men.[38] It can begin to feel like women are taking over and taking advantage of men when they can have the same jobs as men but still have the privilege of male care and protection. Susan Faludi argues, "The economic victims of the era are men who know someone has made off with their future—and they suspect that thief is a woman.... If there has been a 'price to pay' for women's equality, then it seems to these men that they are paying it."[39] Furthermore, once male identity in terms of economic provider was compromised, western culture failed to provide an adequate or desirable alternative for men's identity.

Without a viable or appealing alternative, many men rejected contemporary changes in gender norms and expectations and became nostalgic for a romanticized past of male identity. As Kimmel puts it, "Their entitlement is not aspirational; it's nostalgic."[40] Susan Faludi points out older forms of masculinity showed men how to function within the greater context of society and sold this as a sort of price for admission into male adulthood.[41] However, Fauldi also points out that male power and control has been increasingly limited. The problem is that men seem unable or unwilling to recognize that the source of their economic and social exploitation is a larger systemic issue, leading to the scapegoating tactics previously discussed in terms of women, minorities, and feminism. The rhetoric turns to a nostalgic longing for a time when "men were men," and this loss is projected onto these scapegoats as opposed to social systems at large.

These frustrations also arise in the context of sexuality, particularly in terms of heterosexual interactions with women. The feminist movement brought about an awareness of the fact that women were not merely sexual objects and had a right to say no. However, the ability to say no and refuse sexual advances for women increases male anxiety concerning sexuality, particularly in terms of losses of power and role coupled with constant fear of rejection and reprimand. As Kimmel points out, white males express a high level anger at the perception that women are often beautiful, sexy, and available yet turn them down with a perceived sneering disdain.[42] It can start to feel like a game, where men are led on by women's sexuality and contemporary sexual liberation but then are rejected and discarded without a thought. It contributes to shame and humiliation, which is then counteracted with anger and even violence.

These perceptions and frustrations create a significant crisis in masculinity for traditionally privileged men. They are told they have power, but they don't feel like they have any. The loss of identity and power create feelings of shame, anger, and embarrassment. Connell points out that violence and attempts to restore a traditional masculinity are signs of crisis tendencies in identity.[43] Thus, the more angry and nostalgic the responses, the more likely it may be that the identity in question is deeply threatened and unstable. Furthermore, as Connell also points out, the alteration of fundamental power structures, as in the collapsing legitimacy of patriarchal power, create the most significant evidence for an identity in crisis. The fact that masculinity is in crisis is not doubtful. Hence, the issue of real concern is how this crisis is being managed.

What is troubling is the crisis is being managed through a refusal to engage in wider sociopolitical conversations in order to establish a new and healthy form of identity for these men, coupled with a reactive and defensive hypermasculine performance enacted with the intention of deflecting any feminist encroachment on traditional male identity. Susan Faludi explains this problem in-depth:

> Men don't see how they are influenced by the culture either; in fact they prefer not to. If they did they would have to let go of the illusion of control. Today it is men who cling more tightly to their illusions. They would rather see themselves as battered by feminism than shaped by the larger culture. Feminism can be demonized as just an "unnatural" force, trying to wrest men's natural power and control from their grasp. Culture, by contrast, is the whole environment we live in; to acknowledge its sway is to admit men never had the power they imagined. To say that men are embedded in the culture is to say, by the current standards of masculinity, that men are not men. By casting feminism as the villain that must be defeated to validate the central conceit of modern manhood, men avoid confronting powerful cultural and social expectations that have a lot more to do with their unhappiness than the latest sexual harassment ruling.[44]

Unleashing anger and frustration on women is significantly easier than facing the large socially structured institutions shaping male experience and identity. For instance, it is easier to scapegoat feminism than to admit that the American Dream is just that—a dreamlike myth in many instances that contains no guarantees. Facing such realities may create an overwhelming sense of powerlessness and can amplify the feeling that one has no control. Faludi further points out that the male paradigm itself offers no answer to any alterations in identity or an adequately politicized response to these issues. This situation can be explained in light of the fact that if men are already labeled the oppressors they cannot be oppressed. Consequently, men will often create "paper tigers" to chase, resulting in unlikely explanations and hollow victories at best.[45] Given these conditions, it seems that men are stuck on a wheel that never moves forward, thus repeating over and over the same issues that are at the heart of many problems.

The conditions do not seem to be any better for young men, either, demonstrating the fact that these young men did not learn some critically important lessons from the experiences of older men. Faludi argues that one major contributor to the problems the men in question experience is the creation of a culture of ornament, and this ornamental tendency appears to deeply impact young men. According to Faludi, male purpose and community connection has been replaced by a superficial and materialistic culture, where youth, attractiveness, and "swagger" are the ruling orders of the day. She describes the experience of contemporary manhood as a filling of personal void with consumption, gym-workouts, "hypermasculinity," and empty compensations of a masculine mystique.[46] This type of masculine existence can arguably lead to what Michael Kimmel describes as "Guyland"—a space for young men aged 16–26 that is a suspension between being a boy and being a man, marked by homosocial male bonding and acting out.[47] As Kimmel points out, these boys, like the men described above, are highly defensive, and their desire to "prove themselves" as men has an air of desperation to it.[48] The distinctly homosocial nature of Guyland is a sort of defensive measure, in which young men create bonds and social orders to exclude external threats to the power and affirmation they desire. This sort of order then perilously sets the stage for the masculinity crisis older males are already experiencing—the anger will likely grow alongside an increasing sense of purposelessness or lack of direction as one drifts toward adulthood.

Taking into account the above descriptions of masculinity and the mounting masculinity crisis, the MRM is an unsurprising consequence of such tension. As men become increasingly frustrated and their "paper tiger" battles increasingly empty, the desire to politicize feelings of victimization and oppression greatly increase. An organized movement or minimally the appearance of one has great appeal. The creation of written work, in books, blogs, and other platforms, under the umbrella of the MRM creates a sense of community where men can create a new form of "Guyland"—a largely homosocial bonding platform where other men express shared feelings and resentment. The creation of such community can start to fill the voids Faludi describes, substituting bonds with the wider community for in-group bonding with an alleged purpose. The MRM allows angry and frustrated men to bond and receive a purpose—addressing and ending the oppression of males in society through the actions of feminism. Furthermore, this movement reinforces the desire for power and control in men's life, and makes the option not to engage in wider social criticism and analysis not only unnecessary but also pointless and perhaps even dangerous.

The masculinity crisis looks for resolution in the assertion of power and control, as well as a return to hegemonic masculinity, and the MRM offers the promise of such resolution through a staunch resistance to feminism and the resolute assertion of men's rights. Some of the demands stated by MRM sites seem reasonable—a reassessment of custody law, an examination of education issues applying specifically to boys, and fair treatment in resource allocation, responsibilities, and care. However, underlying all of this is a potent level of anger and resentment, coupled with a refusal to engage with feminism or collaborate with other movements in the interest of social change and justice. In line with the masculinity models discussed in this section, the MRM presents itself as a safe haven for all men, young and old, caught in the throes of an identity crisis that refuses to fulfill their desire for power and control. It claims to offer solutions without sacrifice: retention of

Contemporary Feminism, Masculinity and the MRM

The rage directed at feminism can partly be understood as a reaction to a crisis in gender and masculinity, with the MRM blindly directing anger and intervention to a perceived source of harm. However, the issue with feminism is arguably not so simple. In many ways, certain versions of feminism have contributed to this widening chasm between genders, amplifying issues and concerns that are easily exploited by the MRM. This section will address certain problems in feminism that have contributed to backlash culture through the creation of sociocultural divisions that create both a sense of political harm and potential for targeting.

Definitions of feminism can vary widely, but at the root of all these definitions is a commitment to end sexist oppression.[49] Liberal feminism, radical feminism, difference feminism and a wide variety of other forms within the third wave of feminism attempt to work toward this goal by utilizing different strategies and emphasizing different problems. However, the MRM focuses on two specific types of feminism, namely liberal/egalitarian feminism and contemporary radical feminism. Generally speaking, these are the two ends of the feminist spectrum that are most visible in popular culture and discourse. However, within more popular contexts, these forms of feminism tend to create similar tendencies of victim and resource competition as previously attributed to the MRM.

Because liberal/egalitarian feminism is perceived as the most mainstream, the analysis will start with this version. The principles motivating this form of feminism center on the importance of equal rights for women. One persistent criticism of this approach to feminism is its tendency to have an inappropriately narrow scope. Bell hooks points out that feminism is generally perceived to be a movement focused on making women the equals of men, but the problem is that not all men are equal. Thus, it seems as though this understanding of feminism strives to make women equal to certain types of men, namely privileged, white, heterosexual men of middle or higher class. However, as hooks points out, this does very little to deconstruct general systems of domination that limit and oppress people in multiple and complex ways. In some ways, this kind of feminism works to insert women into an oppressive system without radically altering the system itself. Hooks argues:

> Consequently, it is now necessary for advocates of feminism to collectively acknowledge that our struggle cannot be defined as a movement to gain social equality with men, that terms like "liberal feminist" and "bourgeois feminist" represent contradictions that must be resolved so that feminism will not be

continually co-opted to serve the opportunistic ends of special interest groups.[50]

The framing of feminism as a struggle on the part of women to have a part of or access to the resources of privileged men entails failure due to the fact that it does not challenge the structural issues at hand. Furthermore, it shows that simplistic notions of equality will not suffice to create significant changes contributing to the creation of a progressive society, whether these notions arise in the context of feminism or the MRM.

This concept of feminism and its related failings make it particularly vulnerable to attack from groups like the MRM. First, it sets the stage for the victim competition Cox describes by essentializing two groups of people and framing social justice struggles as a competition for resources. Once this happens, the two groups become antagonistic toward one another—feminists might start viewing their work as a war of the sexes and men see themselves as the unrecognized victims of this war. Hooks summarizes this situation, stating:

> Unfortunately, this has made it appear that feminism was more a declaration of war between the sexes than a political struggle to end sexist oppression, a struggle that would imply change on the part of women and men. Underlying much white women's liberationist rhetoric was the implication that men had nothing to gain by feminist movement, that its success would make them losers.[51]

Additionally, the equality that this version of liberal feminism strives for targets privileges held by the types of men that prototypically make up the men's rights movement. Thus, it becomes a tug of war for social privilege, with the MRM emerging as the male driven inversion of generalized second wave feminism. The problem is that neither group adequately recognizes that the problem is not the distribution of privilege but the nature of such privilege itself. Women want to take part in privilege and men don't want to surrender it, if these men admit to having it at all.

The other form of feminism consistently targeted by the MRM is so-called radical feminism. The radical feminism that many MRMs refer to appears to be a more contemporary formulation of seventies radical feminism that focused on issues concerning the primacy of the woman, female separatism, political lesbianism and essentialist concepts of gender. The most notable current manifestation of this type of feminism within general culture is the blog radfemhub, a website advocating female only spaces, separatism, and the resistance of what they see as the toxic influence of men and masculinity on women. As mentioned previously, radfem is currently inactive and exists only as archives following an intervention from an individual referred to by the MRM as "Agent Orange." This individual gained access to private messages, blogs, and interactions occurring within the radfem site in order to expose the group's alleged misandry. To be fair, the interactions were often degrading to men, making jokes at men's expense or degrading typical male attributes, and so forth. Given the information presented by the "Agent Orange Investigation," it is not obvious that these radical feminists are committed to misandry. Nonetheless, their venting of frustrations toward men appears shortsighted, ignoring the importance of men and all people of all genders as potential comrades in the struggle to end sexist oppression.[52] However, the MRM (specifically Elam's organization) focused in on these findings and decried the group vehemently, leading to a shut-down of the site and ensuing problems for the group to hold meetings and conferences due to protests. The MRM reveled in these findings as undeniable evidence that feminism is rife with man-hating and oppressive gender norms.

It is not unreasonable to argue that the forms of feminism targeted by the MRM are at the very least ineffective or shortsighted. However, it is not clear that these versions of feminism are representative of the current movement as a whole. First, both the liberal and radical feminism described by the MRM seem to better represent second wave feminism as opposed to more contemporary versions presented in the third wave. This is not to say that the issues with these types of feminism do not persist—they do, especially in more popular and less academic feminist thought and input. However, the characterization of feminism presented by the MRM comes of more as a straw man argument than an accurate characterization of a complex movement. Feminism is pared down to a couple of very basic and outmoded versions that can easily be made vulnerable to MRM criticism. The problem is that the portrayal is also not completely inaccurate. Such feminism obviously exists and is advocated for in certain contemporary formats. Second, these understandings of feminism make it easier to treat feminism as a kind of scapegoat for the current issues and anger that white heterosexual males are facing in western culture. Kimmel argues that men, in this case MRAs, often scapegoat their perceived problems onto other people, stating:

> Scapegoating . . . directs the blame for your predicament away from the actual institutional forces of our problem and onto other groups who are far less powerful. It grants them far more power—the power to take away from you that to which you are entitled—than they actually have; the "other" always looms large in the analysis of your own plight.[53]

If frustrated and angry men want to scapegoat women, the most obvious target is feminism. In its work for equality, feminism contributes directly to the perceived problems of these men, and its simplified forms make adequate scapegoats and villains of feminist activists. Thus, the MRM capitalizes on this scapegoating and organizes itself in many ways as a resistance to this representation of feminism.

In conclusion, the MRM presents a deeply problematic representation of feminism, although it may not be entirely false. The spirit of the MRM criticism is that feminists are misguided at best, "idiots" at worst. In order to explain how a group of "idiots" or an intellectually unfounded movement has had such an impact, the MRM claims that feminists are puppets of the powers that be, and point to the infusion of misandry and gynocentrism within our culture as further explanation. While I previously point out that the MRM capitalizes on some feminist errors in terms of concepts of equality and progress, the question remains as to how feminists should respond. Many feminists and feminist sympathetic authors have suggested that it may be appropriate to ignore unsympathetic and unfair backlash to the movement. Keith Burgess Jackson argues in his piece on backlash to feminism in philosophical communities that feminists have a right to ignore backlash, especially if it is bullying.[54] He further claims that the strategy of ignoring backlash must be held until bullying ceases and the bully recognizes and supports feminist values. This certainly sounds ideal—wait until the bully comes around and if not, just don't engage. However, it is not obvious that this is a feasible option when engaging with the MRM. The movement continues to grow, and its tactics are disruptive. In other words, it seems like these words can often hurt. The issue is, then, how feminists should engage.

The engagement should involve the following two aspects: using the criticism as fuel for self-reflection and a reassessment of men as comrades. In terms of self-reflection, feminism should note the issue of victim competition and take it seriously. Recognizing injuries against men in a variety of forms does not weaken feminism. In fact, it further focuses feminism on the fact that the issue in sexist oppression is not individual men but a system of sexist domination and exploitation. The rhetoric of the MRM serves as a reminder to avoid engaging on this level and to maintain focus. This leads directly to the second aspect—engaging men as critical members of the feminist movement who are dedicated, worthy, and admirable. Hooks argues, "Men are not exploited or oppressed by sexism, but there are ways in which they suffer as a result of it. This suffering should not be ignored. While it in no way diminishes the seriousness of male abuse and oppression of women, or negates male responsibility for exploitative actions, the pain men experience can serve as a catalyst calling attention to the need for change."[55] Working this way can work to help men see that, not only is feminism important, but feminism is in their interest, not their enemy. Overall, it is clear that feminists are not obligated to engage directly in hopeless, abusive, or pointless conversations with MRAs, or to respond to every accusation or criticism. The response should occur when it is constructive and works to build community. If this does not occur, the MRM serves as a potent reminder to feminism to maintain appropriate focus, build connections and communities and to work at all times for the liberations of all people as the ultimate end goal of feminist theorizing.

CONCLUSION

Researching and discussing the MRM can serve several important political functions. To begin, it requires us to take the masculinity crisis quite seriously. While feminist progress is critical to the creation of a just society, many of these changes resulted in a void for men, leading many males to feel aimless, disempowered, and disrespected. The MRM provides an extreme yet clear crystallization of these feelings and perceptions. Thus, it gives great insight into masculinity, backlash, and the problems involved in theories of equality. Second, its extreme criticisms suggest a renewed effort on the part of feminists to engage men as comrades and to work for recognition of the complexity of standpoint and oppression as it impacts all peoples. This is not to say that feminists are obligated to "save" or interact with MRAs; rather, feminists should build communities with men to create new, healthy versions of masculinity that work to deconstruct sexist oppression. Such work can provide new outlets for men, giving them greater options than the promises of the MRM. Thus, the remainder of this book will focus on the specific issues concerning the MRM. The goal will be to focus on the political functions stated above in order to address complex social issues and the underlying gender politics involved.

NOTES

1. Kostakis runs a website dedicated to mostly issues in what he terms "gynocentrism." Elam recommends the site and links it on his "Voice for Men" site: http://gynocentrism.com/2013/08/02/feminism-the-same-old-gynocentric-story/.
2. Farrell, *Myth of Male Power*, 1551.
3. Farrell, *Myth of Male Power*, 1551.
4. Farrell, *Myth of Male Power*, 6520.
5. Adam Kostakis, "Gynocentrism, Humanism and the Patriarchy," last updated May 24, 2014, http://gynocentrism.com/2013/08/15/gynocentrism-humanism-and-the-patriarchy/.
6. Devlin, Roger. "Sexual Utopia in Power," last accessed March, 2015, https://dontmarry.files.wordpress.com/2009/03/sexualutopia.pdf.
7. Kimmel, *Angry White Men*, 131.
8. Dean Esmay, "Breaking the Pendulum: Tradcons vs. Feminists," last updated March 26, 2014, http://www.avoiceformen.com/gynocentrism/breaking-the-pendulum-tradcons-vs-feminists/.
9. The quote in question is "Feminism is the radical notion that women are people," which has become a common feminist slogan/rallying cry.
10. Adam Kostakis, "The Eventual Outcome of Feminism: Part I," last updated May 24, 2014, http://gynocentrism.com/2014/05/25/the-eventual-outcome-of-feminism-part-i/.
11. Esmay, "Tradcons," http://www.avoiceformen.com/gynocentrism/breaking-the-pendulum-tradcons-vs-feminists/.

12. Adam Kostakis, "The Eventual Outcome of Feminism: Part II," last updated May 24, 2014, http://gynocentrism.com/2014/05/25/the-eventual-outcome-of-feminism-part-ii/.

13. Paul Elam, "The X%: What Feminism Is Really About and Why Anyone Who Values Freedom Should Fight against It," last updated November 19, 2013, http://www.avoiceformen.com/feminism/the-x-what-feminism-is-really-about-and-why-anyone-who-values-freedom-should-fight-against-it/.

14. Eva Cox, "Boys and Girls and the Costs of Gendered Behavior," Keynote Address (Promoting Gender Equity Conference, Canberra, February 22–24, 1995), 74.

15. Cox, "Boys and Girls," p. 75.

16. "Mission Statement," last accessed November 16, 2016, http://www.avoiceformen.com/policies/mission-statement/.

17. Paul Elam, "Counterculture," last modified October 22, 2013, http://www.avoiceformen.com/mens-rights/counterculture/.

18. Elam, "Counterculture," http://www.avoiceformen.com/mens-rights/counterculture/.

19. This incident is explained by Elam on the following link: http://www.avoiceformen.com/?s=radfem.

20. Tyler Kinkade, "'Men's Rights' Trolls Spam Occidental College Online Rape Report Form," *The Huffington Post*, December 18, 2013, http://www.huffingtonpost.com/2013/12/18/mens-rights-occidental-rape-reports_n_4468236.html.

21. Emily Matchar, "'Men's Rights' Activists are Trying to Redefine the Meaning of Rape," *New Republic*, February 26, 2014, http://www.newrepublic.com/article/116768/latest-target-mens-rights-movement-definition-rape.

22. "Don't Be That Girl Sex Assault Posters in Edmonton Spark Anger, Debate," *HuffPost Alberta*, July 10, 2013, http://www.huffingtonpost.ca/2013/07/10/dont-be-that-girl-posters-edmonton_n_3575338.html.

23. For an overview of doxxing (or doxing) please refer to: "What Doxxing Is, and Why It Matters," *The Economist*, March 10, 2014, http://www.economist.com/blogs/economist-explains/2014/03/economist-explains-9.

24. Links to register-her.com have been removed as of April 14, 2014, with plans in place to replace the site.

25. General standards for labeling a woman a "false accuser" is, at minimum, someone whose accused rapist is not fully convicted in a trial. Anything less than a full conviction result puts a woman at risk for being named.

26. http://rationalwiki.org/wiki/Paul_Elam.

27. The use of violent threat is not subtle in these cases. The slogan FTSU (Fuck Their Shit Up) is part of Elam's Register-Her site/movement.

28. Raewyn Connell, *Masculinities*, 2nd ed. (Berkeley: University of California Press, 2005), 84.

29. James Gilligan, *Violence: Reflections on a National Epidemic* (New York: Vintage Books, 1996).

30. Michel Foucault, "Disciplines and Sciences of the Individual," in *The Foucault Reader*, ed. Paul Rabinow (New York: Pantheon Books, 1984), 192.

31. Foucault, "Disciplines," 74.

32. Foucault, "Disciplines," 193.

33. Kimmel, *Angry White Men*, 9.

34. Kimmel, *Angry White Men*, 14.

35. Kimmel, *Angry White Men*, 34.

36. Connell, *Masculinities*, 35.

37. Connell, *Masculinities*, 77.

38. bell hooks, *Feminism: From Margin to Center*, 2nd ed. (Cambridge: South End Press, 2000), 75.

39. Susan Faludi, *Backlash: The Undeclared War Against American Women* (New York: Three Rivers Press, 1991), 81.

40. Kimmel, *Angry White Men*, 63.

41. Susan Faludi, *Stiffed: The Betrayal of the American Man* (Harper Collins, 2011), Kindle edition, 731.

42. Kimmel, *Angry White Men*, 17.
43. Connell, *Masculinities*, 84.
44. Faludi, *Backlash*, 284.
45. Faludi, *Stiffed*, 12983.
46. Faludi, *Stiffed*, 845.
47. Michael Kimmel, *Guyland: The Perilous World Where Boys Become Men* (New York: Harper Perennial, 2009), 7.
48. Kimmel, *Guyland*, 18.
49. Hooks, *Feminism*, 32.
50. Hooks, *Feminism*, 34.
51. Hooks, *Feminism*, 34.
52. This phrasing is borrowed from hooks in *Feminism*.
53. Kimmel, *Angry White Men*, 24.
54. Keith Burgess Jackson, "The Backlash against Feminist Philosophy," in *Theorizing Backlash: Philosophical Reflections on the Resistance to Feminism*, ed. Anita Superson and Ann Cudd (Lanham, MD: Rowman and Littlefield Publishers, 2002), 33.
55. Hooks, *Feminism*, 73.

Chapter Two

Identity, the Internet, and Masculine Discourse

This philosophical analysis of the MRM will begin with a discussion of the context in which the MRM takes hold, namely the Internet. In order to assess the MRM as a sociopolitical phenomenon, it is necessary to examine the underlying assumptions and methods contributing to the rise of the phenomenon of "angry white men" generally and the MRM specifically. In this chapter, I will argue that there are certain social forces interacting in the creation of gendered selves, and that these identities can be altered in specific ways in online platforms. Such alterations allow for specific hegemonic codes of gender to arise as idealized selves, and that the values of cyberlibertarianism and the phenomenon of group polarization interact in the creation of extremist backlash movements such as the MRM.

NARRATIVE IDENTITY AND THE IDEALIZED GENDERED SELF

In order to address the issue of online identity, I will be utilizing the concept of narrative identity, relating to the establishment of character and self for individual persons. While experiences, character traits, and relationships all generally contribute to the narrative of self, structural norms such as gender also deeply impact our sense of who we are and how we relate to the world around us. In order to create a full account of selves, care must be given to both the personal and political, as well as the contexts of our self-expression. I will argue that online interactions and online identity engage issues of narrative self, character, and gender in unique ways due to the possibilities contained in anonymity and lack of embodiment in online platforms. These issues are important in discussing the content and nature of MRM rhetoric as a mainly online phenomenon that directly engages and reflects issues of gender, identity, and politics.

The establishment of "identity" is a lifelong project for most human persons. Historically, the philosophical problem of identity over time has taken on a variety of forms, with a plethora of different criteria used to determine "sameness." However, as Marya Schechtman points out, there is a distinct and important difference between questions of characterization and questions of reidentification. Philosophy has often focused almost exclusively on the problem of reidentification, creating debates concerning how to establish a relation of strict numeric identity for human beings over time. While this is certainly an important endeavor in some respects, authors such as Schechtman and Derek Parfit point out that the aspects of identity we seem to care most about are not adequately captured in these theories. Specifically, Schechtman claims the four features of identity that we, as humans tend to focus on or care most about, are: survival, moral responsibility, prudential concern, and compensation. According to her argument, an examination of these four features leads to the conclusion that they relate significantly more to the problem of characterization as opposed to reidentification.

The characterization question for human identity can be summarized as follows: "Most simply put, this questions asks which actions, experiences, beliefs, values, desires, character traits, and so on . . . are to be attributed to a given person."[1] In other words, these types of questions ask what it means for a certain characteristic to belong authentically to a given person, thus establishing some form of explanation concerning the nature of one's true character and personality. One of the most obvious ways that the characterization account varies from the reidentification problem is the fact that characterization admits to degrees, as opposed to the "all or nothing" nature of strict identity. The reason for this is that different behaviors and characteristics of an individual contribute to personality and the self in different ways, with some having a more central role than others.[2] It is clear that all characteristics in a person's history contribute to her character to some degree, but some characteristics are more important than others in the creation of an individual self.

According to the characterization view of persons, there is a sense of "true" identity for individuals based upon traits playing a central role in the establishment of a person's character. However, when a person engages in online relationships and communication, the establishment of character-based identity is not externally constrained by personal history or relationships with others. Instead of adhering to the reality of our characters based upon these external restraints, the Internet allows us to "start over" in some sense, based on the lack of embodiment and the possibility for anonymity present in online interactions. Thus, the establishment of online identity provides us with an opportunity to create an idealized version of the self, filtering out the characteristics about ourselves we find undesirable or troublesome, and focus on the traits that we admire or desire but lack full realization in our current "real life" state.

The use of an idealized self in online interactions is arguably an outgrowth of self-interested concern, which Schechtman identifies as one of the four features of character identity. Generally, self-interested concern is the desire to fulfill one's own personal desires and goals. According to Schechtman, such goals and desires can be characterized simplistically as pleasure and pain, but are often more complex, reflecting a desire for personal development or doing something significant with one's life.[3] Thus, if one's character identity is based upon certain central characteristics, then these characteristics will influence the goals and second order desires possessed by a given individual.[4] Consequently, the goals that are important enough for an individual to make sacrifices for reflect the most central internal values of that individual.[5] For example, I may have the desire to have a toned and muscular body because I think that is an ideal body shape and I want to be attractive. However, this body will require some work—I must go to the gym regularly, adhere to strict nutritional guidelines, and give up certain behaviors I might enjoy, such as drinking alcohol or eating dessert every night. It may be the case that I have no interest in working that hard, and such a body is a dream that I do not realistically consider. Thus, it appears that this goal is not something reflecting an important internal characteristic for me, and may in fact say very little about my character or self.

However, suppose that while I am not willing, or perhaps am unable, to meet this goal, my inability does bother me and I develop a poor body image. I begin to feel somewhat helpless to improve myself, developing anxiety over the fear that no one will find me attractive as I am. It is precisely this anxiety that contributes to online behaviors such as "catfishing."[6] I can create an identity that lines up with my valued goals and desires that I am, for whatever reason, unable to achieve. My falsified online identity creates an outlet in which I am exactly who I want to be, temporarily relieving my anxiety and feelings of failure. Consequently, I may try to use this online identity to then fulfill other aspects of my self-interested or prudential concern, such as finding a romantic partner, friends, or merely being the object of admiration and desire.

This use of online identity for the creation of an idealized self suggests that the mere lack of sacrifice for a goal does not indicate that at least some part of that goal is not central to my character. Rather, it may be the case that I have a variety of fears preventing me from the development of proper second order desires contributing to my success. In the given example, my preoccupation with body image suggests that I deeply value physical attractiveness and the perceived acceptance, love, and attention that goes with it, indicating it as a central characteristic of my self. However, perhaps I also deeply fear failure, and perceive my current physical state as inevitable. The prospect of repeatedly failing to achieve something I value so highly creates an internal dissonance in myself, causing me to abandon this goal. However, this abandonment, while allowing me to avoid failure, may create a feeling of despair or lack. The creation of an online persona exhibiting my concept of an idealized body creates the opportunity for occasional relief from this paradoxical tension, and allows me to access some sense of what it would be like to embody an ideal, even though the experience is clearly false and somewhat delusional.

While online identity seems to offer a wide range of possibilities for personal presentation, role/identity adoption, and so on, research indicates that individuals online tend to be generally honest, especially in terms of one's gender. As Susan Herring describes, many individuals online report that behavior such as gender switching or false identities require too much effort to maintain, and thus it is simpler to interact as one's self online.[7] The reasoning behind this type of response reflects the general schemata of narrative identity in at least two ways. First, if the purpose of creating a narrative self that reflects one's values and central properties, then the gender one identifies with will be the most desirable persona. Outside of a sense of curiosity concerning the experience of a different gender, individuals placing gender as a core aspect of identity might find it difficult or simply uninteresting to alter that part of their identity in any context. Second, if individuals see gender as an innate and thus unalterable property of the self, then it may be very difficult to maintain the persona of another gender without detection online or otherwise. Because of the anonymity involved with online interactions, there was some initial hope that the Internet would provide users with a gender-neutral platform for communication. However, even in text-only forums individual communication styles are generally considered reliable indicators of a user's gender. Certain "tip-offs" are contained in user discourse, such as verbosity, use of profanity, politeness, length of messages, and tone used in disagreements.[8] Consequently, even if someone "poses" as another gender online, there is a belief that such individuals will quickly be detected due to linguistics, and so forth. If this is true, one might conclude that gender masquerading in online forums requires significant diligence and risk of detection with little personal satisfaction for the average user.

Nonetheless, even if users do not completely alter their gender when communicating online, it may be the case that idealized gender identity plays an important role in online contexts. Thus, while individuals may not want to be a different gender in online forums, they may want to express their gender in idealized sorts of ways in these contexts. For instance, if a male identified person feels emasculated in his daily life by any number of factors (loss of male privilege, feminism, lack of masculine-identified skill sets), the Internet allows this individual to express the masculine self in its fullest sense without real world situations impinging on such expression. Consequently, it is unsurprising that MRAs, who argue that they are oppressed as men and victimized by women, often rely upon aggressive, hypermasculine rhetoric and identities in online postings and interactions. While the real world seems to prevent them from expressing what they see as their authentic gendered selves, the Internet provides a format in which masculine identity can be established in a controlled way without the external constraints these men claim to experience in everyday interactions.

GENDER PERFORMANCE ONLINE

When discussing the nature of gendered selves online, the concepts of gender that regularly emerge are highly dichotomous, stereotypical, and based on persistently essentialist assumptions. The masculine-identified discourse online often reflects various aspects of hegemonic masculinity, such as aggression, adversarial approach, self-promotion, and directness.[9] On the other hand, feminine-identified behavior frequently involves supportive communication, apologetic, lessened entitlement, alignment strategies, and shorter messaging.[10] In order to conceptualize the predominance of these communication styles, it is crucial to compare and contrast the everyday realities of gender and the alleged sociopolitical progress being made in terms of gender norms, with the lapse into highly traditional, simplistic, and nonprogressive gender presentation in online text communication platforms. I argue that gender is performative, and that such performances are naturalized through the integration of such performative norms into narrative concepts of self. If online platforms provide freedom from certain restraints on identity due to the lack of embodiment, then the prevalence of hegemonic gender online suggests that such constructs of gender are deeply entrenched and that progressive politics has significant work remaining in the project of transforming gendered realities.

If gender is considered a critical part of self-narrative and concept, then the emergence of gender within the self and in relation to others is central to any discussion of social identity. Everyday concepts utilize gender not only as a theoretical or abstract aspect of identity, but also as an essential feature of an embodied self. Authors such as Susan Bordo, Judith Butler, and Michel Foucault argue that the body is not a mere physical object propelling us through the world. Rather, the body is a highly significant symbol of cultural relations, expectations, and power. Susan Bordo explains, "Not chiefly through ideology, but through the organization and regulation of the time, space, and movements of our daily lives, our bodies are trained, shaped, and impressed with the stamp of prevailing historical forms of self-hood, desire, masculinity, femininity."[11] Bodies are thus inherently social entities, molded and disciplined to reflect cultural norms and expectations. Bordo argues that dualistic tendencies within culture contribute to this disciplining of bodies, because the concept of self is often separated from the body. Thus, the self is in a constant struggle against an unruly body to get it to "behave" or work/look the way one wants it to.

A critical aspect of this struggle is the creation of a docile body—one that is amenable to disciplinary intervention. Foucault claims that discipline is a technique operating upon bodies. Thus, he argues, "A body is docile that may be subjected, used, transformed and improved."[12] Bodies enter a machinery of power that explores, breaks down, and rearranges with the goal of creating a body with maximal utility or usefulness and a decrease of individual force (no opposition or the achievement of obedience). Thus, "Discipline 'makes' individuals; it is the specific technique of power that regards individuals both as objects and instruments of its exercise."[13] Docile bodies are created through hierarchical observation, normalizing judgment and the examination. In hierarchical observation, individuals are placed under surveillance that is also internalized. Normalizing judgment then functions as an evaluation of docile bodies under surveillance, establishing dichotomous conceptions of good/bad with resulting corrections. Finally, the examination brings together power and knowledge, making individuals the subjects of investigation and scientific study.

Judith Butler discusses the construction of the self in Foucaultian terms in her work, *Giving an Account of Oneself*. According to Butler, Foucault's concept of "regimes of truth" creates a framework and terms making subject recognition possible. In other words, norms contained within a given regime of truth places restraints on what one can be as a subject in a given social or cultural context. The construction of the subject within this regime of truth is not simply deterministic but a project of negotiation. She explains, "We are not deterministically decided by norms, although they do provide a framework and the point of reference for any set of decisions we make."[14] Consequently, to question a social framework or truth regime is not merely to question an external structure, but to question the very basis and nature of one's self. In the context of disciplinary truth regimes, the creation of docile bodies through the mechanisms Foucault describes work to create a sense of determinism and circumvent the individual possibility of such questioning. Thus, in order to create maximally docile bodies and subjects, disciplinary truth regimes must create norms relating to the most central aspects of self-identity, the most critical of which is arguably gender. One's gender is portrayed as an inherent determining factor of the self, set within the limits of a socially marked and readable body.

From the moment one is born, the body is placed into one of two strict categories of sex: male and female. Sex is often portrayed as a biological given, while gender is described as a set of behaviors associated with or exemplifying a given sex. This central aspect of identity can be understood in terms of Foucault's matrix of power and discipline in relation to the body. According to Judith Butler, bodies are not passive instruments that take on cultural meaning, but rather that bodies come into existence through culture. Thus, she argues, "Gender ought not to be conceived merely as the cultural inscription of meaning on a pregiven sex (a juridical conception); gender must also designate the very apparatus of production whereby the sexes themselves are established."[15] For Butler, docile bodies are not merely contained in order to receive and reflect the inscription of normative power in a given society; rather, bodies emerge through and become intelligible by the workings of gendered norms and expectations. Identity is a normative ideal constituted by the regulatory practices of gender formation and division.[16] Consequently, she points out, "Inasmuch as 'identity' is assured through the stabilizing concepts of sex, gender and sexuality, the very notion of 'the person' is called into question by the cultural emergence of those 'incoherent' or 'discontinuous' gendered beings who appear to be persons but who fail to conform to the gendered norms of cultural intelligibility by which persons are defined."[17] While Butler's analysis deviates from Foucault's in some sense, the relationship between the two is clear. Building on Foucault's analysis of the body as a locus of normative cultural power, Butler focuses on the body as a primarily gendered entity that emerges within a field of normative prescriptions and expectations. Various means of surveillance and normalizing judgments are paramount in the enforcement of binary gendered codes, and individuals become subjects of interest and intervention through the ability to enact the "correct" gendered behaviors and bodies.

Gender is, therefore, a disciplinary production reflecting a cultural fantasy projected on the body through constructed presence and absence.[18] Butler argues that this disciplinary production creates a false sense of stable gender, and that the gendered nature of the body contributes to the illusion of an interior and organized gendered core.[19] Gendered behavior and desires create this sense of substance, and Butler characterizes this set of bodily acts as performative. She explains, "Such acts, gestures, enactments, generally construed, are *performative* in the sense that the essence or identity that they otherwise purport to express are *fabrications* manufactured and sustained through corporeal signs and other discursive means. That the gendered body is performative suggests that it has no real ontological status apart from the very acts which constitute its reality."[20] If this is the case, then gender is a fabrication and a fantasy as opposed to an ontological fact or truth. Consequently, Butler argues that gender can be understood as the effect of a cultural discourse concerning truth and identity.

The import of gender as a discursive practice or effect of discourse is critical in understanding the nature of gendered identity in online practice. Generally speaking, our bodies often limit our options in terms of gender identity and gendered relations. Within cultural confines, gendered bodies will be read in certain ways, resulting in certain responses, identifications, and categorizations. Bodies that do not conform are labeled as unintelligible, often receiving rejection and scorn, and at worst, violence and annihilation. The desire to enact alternate gendered possibilities safely often requires one to master the performance of an opposite gender, done within the boundaries of "passing" as another gender or choosing certain acts or behaviors that do not go too far or violate some established boundary of gender appropriate crossings. Consequently, the body often appears to be a limiting factor in terms of gender expression, but online interactions seem to neatly avoid this confinement or limitation.

Due to the lack of confinement enacted by embodiment or bodily norms, the Internet is often described as a space of free expression, a sort of libertarian idealized space in which one can express oneself in any sense one sees fit. The alleged lack of limitation on self-expression and self-presentation creates the sense that online communication provides a platform for postmodern play in identity, or that it frees people from concerns about bodily realities, whether these are issues of gender, disability, physical shape, and so forth. However, as discussed previously, such postmodern play and possibility do not seem to be regularly utilized by online communicants, due to the trouble of maintaining alternate identities and the high likelihood of detection. In other words, while bodies do seem to constrain gendered expression in important ways, the performance of gender involves significantly complex modes of expression that go far beyond bodily realities. Thus, physical realities are not the only modes of gender that are essentialized—behavior, thought processes, and so on. are also frequently considered innately gendered properties of an individual. In order to unravel the complex nature of gendered performance in online platforms, one must consider the commonalities and contrasts of gendered performance in embodied and non-embodied interactions.

GENDER AND RELATIONALITY ONLINE

Returning to the notion of character identity, Steve Matthews emphasizes the importance of character identity in terms of our sense of self and our relationships with others. While his analysis of character identity lines up in many ways with Schechtman's discussion of narrative identity, Matthews points out the importance of embodiment in the establishment of identity. According to Matthews, our identity is deeply tied up in our relationships with others, and our self-presentations are highly dependent upon our embodied selves. He explains, "Our identities are partly a function of the relations we bear to *embodied* others: to alter our self-preservations to exclude these bodily aspects will tend to eliminate a rich source for the development of identity."[21] Thus, his argument suggests that we cannot consider character or narrative identity in isolation from social relationships and exchanges with others. As beings in the world, we encounter one another as physical beings, and confront each other as bodies presenting or made possible by the normative and social demands described in the previous section.

Butler argues that our bodies are necessarily social and political due to the unavoidably public aspect of our physical beings. She argues, "This means that each of us is constituted politically in part by virtue of the social vulnerability of our bodies—as a site of desire and physical vulnerability, as a site of publicity at once assertive and exposed. Loss and vulnerability seem to follow from our being socially constituted bodies, attached to others."[22] Consequently, Butler claims that while we may strive to claim ownership or autonomy over our bodies, they are never fully our own, describing the body as a social phenomenon in a public sphere.[23] This is not to say that autonomy is not possible or something not to be valued, however, Butler claims that individuation of this type is an achievement not a given, since our bodies place us outside of ourselves and for others.[24] Relating this to Matthews' arguments concerning bodies and identity, Butler's claims reinforce the primacy of embodiment in the creation of identity, but she greatly emphasizes and expands the concept of identity as inherently social and externally constrained and determined through our relationships with others.

If our identity is inherently social, Matthews claims that this further implies that identity has a normative aspect contained in the ability for social communication as well as in self-reflection. These abilities imply not only an individualistic sense of self, but also a self-image that is mediated through the views of others. In other words, the way I see myself is often deeply impacted by the ways that others see me.[25] Consequently, one can argue that narrative identity is deeply mediated by a complex internal/external audience—the narrative must be coherent not just for the narrator but, in many ways, for the individuals one relates to in the world. Thus we can understand narrative/character identity as a dialectic between the individual and the world of persons the individual inhabits.

In normal everyday interactions, individuals possess certain qualities and traits that they lack control over as an embodied being. Matthews describes these traits as nonvoluntary bodily aspects to which the possessing individual has three attitudes: indifference, dislike (implying a desire to not disclose), and lack of awareness.[26] He describes eye color as something to which an individual may be indifferent, as opposed to a speech impediment, which one may wish not be disclosed. In any case, the body creates a sense of vulnerability to others that individuals cannot fully control. One cannot force someone to recognize them or perceive their body in precisely the way they themselves do, nor can they provide a clear and concise account of the self with complete control of the interpretation and assigned meanings provided by others.

This vulnerability arguably creates a moral claim on others. According to Butler, one cannot control the terms by which one is addressed, since an individual exists within certain sets of predetermined norms and social matrices.[27] However, the address and its corresponding effect of subject recognition is a critical aspect of identity and self-establishment. Butler presents the problem of "giving an account of oneself" in these terms, corresponding to the notion of narrative identity discussed previously. However, Butler claims that the creation of self-narratives is never a straightforward endeavor, since the identity is always opaque for the individual subject. This opacity, Butler argues, is due to the fact that from the start of our very existence we are dependent upon others, formed within the context of relations that are not recoverable. She then states, "Indeed, if it is precisely by virtue of one's relations to others that one is opaque to oneself, and if those relations to others are the venue for one's ethical responsibility, then it may follow that it is precisely by virtue of the subject's opacity to itself that one incurs and sustains some of its most important ethical bonds."[28] Thus, we come to know ourselves not merely through an internal narrative, but through our interactions with others, which are mediated through truth regimes and normative expectations. These norms set the conditions for ethical recognition by providing a framework for humanity that causes us to recognize others as human. Butler argues, "In a real sense, we do not survive without being addressed, which means that the scene of our address can and should provide a sustaining condition for ethical deliberation, judgment and conduct."[29] Consequently, moral interventions such as judgment, condemnation, and so forth, must operate along with a sustained recognition of the subject of such intervention.

It seems clear that the narrative account of self-identity suggests a variety of true and accurate concepts concerning individual self-establishment and elaboration. However, what this theory does not encompass is the centrality of relationships, recognition and embodiment in terms of selfhood. While the goal of human beings is often to provide a coherent narrative account of an internal self, this narrative account is limited and interrupted by inherent opacities and normative limits on recognition through and by other beings in the world. Although we may like to consider ourselves insular and autonomous, we are determined by external norms and other selves from the first seconds of our existence and continue to be vulnerable to these externalities throughout our lives. Our existence as embodied beings furthers this sense of vulnerability. Furthermore, our bodies work within social frameworks and relationships as readable sorts of texts, often functioning as disciplined or docile physical phenomena reflecting normative traits making us readable human subjects for the others we encounter. Overall, our narrative identity is deeply mediated through our embodied interactions with others, and this is an inescapable aspect of human existence.

Because embodiment, relationality, performativity and recognition are all central aspects of character/narrative identity, online text-based communication provides a direct challenge to our understanding of the self in terms of both narrative content and normative status. When communicating online, specifically in text-based formats, there are no other physical bodies to encounter nor must one be bound to the real and involuntary aspects of one's own physical self. By eliminating embodied interactions, online text-based communication alters the conditions of recognition in important ways, and undermines the very nature of vulnerability one might experience as an embodied being in everyday interactions.

Clearly, online communication takes a variety of forms, some of which do involve embodied presentation—video chatting, picture based communication, and so forth. However, outside of direct video communication, most presentations can be manipulated, as seen in the co-opting of others' pictures, and so on, in catfishing, or the simple picking and choosing of individual pictures in social media accounts to put the "best self" forward for public viewing and consumption. Nonetheless, of direct interest in the discussion at hand is text-only communication. This type of communication dominates the interactions and speech actions of the men's rights movement or MRA sympathetic individuals online. Specifically of interest are comments and discussions in online forums such as Reddit, blogs posted on sites such as AVFM, the actions of trolling or general disruption on comment threads and websites, and the use of anonymous social media accounts to express various views and opinions.

The use of text-only communication online presents a variety of possibilities but also a host of potential problems, moral, normative, and otherwise. Online communication does present some potential advantages for controlling self-presentation. Matthews explains, "It is precisely things like anonymity, the capacity to control how one presents, and the lack of pressure in time-delayed communication which confers the benefits of online text-based communication."[30] Thus, text-based online communication eliminates the nonvoluntary aspects inherent to embodied interactions, conferring significant control to the individual in terms of what is presented about the self and how. Furthermore, these types of conversations do not demand the immediate verbal responses expected in face-to-face verbal interactions, giving an individual time to consider and carefully construct responses that line up with self-concepts and desired presentations. Consequently, these text-based interactions eliminate much of the mutuality and vulnerability present in embodied exchanges, creating what Matthews refers to as an "egalitarian or flattening" effect.[31]

What is particularly problematic about the nature of online identity in terms of text-based communication is the ability to construct the self in terms of an idealized character—in other words I can easily become the self I most want to be almost instantly. Matthews points out that there exists a gap between real and ideal self-image, and a crucial aspect of this gap is its role in self-development.[32] The distance between my self and the ideal encourages me to strive to be different, work toward the ideal, and to develop myself consistently in the name of such goals. However, if one can immediately become an idealized self online, the gap is obliterated. There is certainly a sense in which the idealized ego online is not "real" but the ability to at least escape into this ideal lessens my need to strive toward it in real life.

At this point, the evidence and theoretical insight seem to create a somewhat conflicting picture. In some ways, individuals online appear to be generally honest about their identities and selves, particularly in terms of gender. However, it also seems to be the case that the lack of embodiment allows users of text-based communication to enact and achieve idealized self-identity online that may not in fact line up with the lived realities of a given gendered existence. It can then be argued that the issue at hand is not one concerning honesty about facts of the matter, but rather an issue of self-perceived authenticity. In other words, if my performance of gender online lines up with what I perceive as an appropriate expression of my gender identity, then online interactions may provide me with a forum for expressing my authentically gendered self. The facts of the matter constraining such performance in my everyday life do not make my online performance dishonest, rather such constraint merely reflects my inability to assert myself authentically in the real, embodied world.

"AUTHENTIC" MASCULINE SELVES

As argued in previous chapters, many men currently perceive masculine identity as being threatened, creating a sense of resentment and backlash to feminist and gender progress in personal, social, and political contexts. Michael Kimmel argues that men in contemporary culture are experiencing a sort of "masculinity crisis," resulting in very real feelings of anger and resentment due to the perception that they have been "cheated" out of societal rewards promised to them for being "good men." Cultural shifts result in a sense of emasculation, uselessness, and humiliation for many of these men. Consequently, men may feel as if they have been cheated, lied to, and mislead, creating backlash directed toward the perceived sources of this loss—women, feminism, and minorities. Many men report feeling a complete loss of identity, and in order to protect against such loss, these individuals often resort to a hyperbolic masculine performative identity as a sort of wall against the persistent forward motions of feminism and other progressive movements.

In the introduction to *Theorizing Backlash: Philosophical Reflections on the Resistance to Feminism* the authors claim, "The response to feminism is not argument but disdain, not rational disagreement but irrational resentment, not dispassionate debate but sexist attack."[33] The gains made by feminism politically, academically, representationally, and otherwise are frequently met with aggressive resistance, bullying, and even outright harassment. Ann Cudd provides a framework for understanding the nature of backlash, pointing out that social progress often requires a redesigning of social institutions in the interest of lessening oppression. Such redesign will often fail to be in the interest of other social groups, since they will be deprived of certain advantages and privileges held under previous conditions.[34] Cudd points out that there are cases in which progress can be unclear due to competing demands of justice, pointing to the example technical progress and capitalism (the problem of efficiency vs. equality). Thus, there may be instances in which progress for one cause or group of individuals comes into legitimate conflict with another cause or group of individuals. However, it must be emphasized that the gains and harms of progress are not simple utilitarian sums. In other words, the simple loss of privilege does not constitute an unjustified harm and thus a conflict of justice. Cudd explains, "For example, the abolition of slavery deprived the slave owners of property. . . . This was an entirely justified harm, because the ownership of slaves was unjustifiable."[35] This claim can easily be extended to the case of sexism, or male privilege. Feminism creates a certain loss for (white heterosexual middle class especially) males in terms of sociopolitical privilege, but this privilege, based solely on power-based social constructs, is not justifiable.

Although the loss of privilege appears to be politically and ethically justifiable, feminism's encroachment into areas of male privilege has created a wide array of frustrated and angry responses from men in recent times, resulting in the "angry white men" Kimmel describes. When faced with a loss of privilege and a threat to hegemonic masculinity, some men react by retreating into traditional masculine identity, valuing dichotomous gender constructs, and criticizing what they see as an overabundance of "political correctness" that infringes on their right to express themselves in traditional (often misogynist) ways. In other words, these so-called angry white men perceive the embodied world as a space in which they are prevented from expressing their authentic masculine identity due to over-reaching feminist interventions and demands for political correctness and sensitivity. They reside in a world that has recently failed to recognize them in a way they find adequate, instead condemning certain aspects of masculinity some men continue to value.

In addition to the problematics of feminist backlash, masculinity is a gendered construct that inspires certain high levels of anxiety due to its tenuous construction and maintenance. As Butler points out, gender is a performance that must be repeated over and over in order to appear natural and innate. Because masculinity is compulsory, one must strive to create a flawless performance, but such performance is impossible. Consequently, masculinity is fraught with potential and actual failures in performance, and such failures result in cultural punishment often through the use of shame. James Gilligan argues, "Men are honored for activity (ultimately violent activity) and they are dishonored for passivity (or pacifism), which renders them vulnerable to the charge of being a non-man ('a wimp, a punk, a pussy')."[36] Emasculation through feminizing males who fail to uphold hegemonic masculine performance creates a sense of shame often resulting in violent or aggressive behavior. Gilligan points out that male gender roles expose men to shame if they are not violent or aggressive and rewarding them with honor when they are.[37] However, many men cannot achieve this honor-inducing aggressive masculinity in everyday contexts due to a variety of factors, including but not limited to legal or workplace restraints, competition from women intellectually, athletically, or professionally, romantic rejection by women, or limited physical capabilities ranging from lack of athletic ability to lack of an idealized male body type.

In such situations, we can observe the conflict between lived reality, recognition, and the perceived authentic self discussed earlier in the chapter. Men may see themselves as innately masculine, that is, aggressive, powerful, intellectual, and rational. Furthermore, this sense of self will be a key aspect of one's self narrative, due to the centrality of such identification and the presumption that such qualities are innate and gender essential as opposed to performative or socially constructed. Because of this belief system, it is unsurprising that certain men come to feel unjustly limited or oppressed by certain social standards or progressions that prevent their assertion of a supposedly innate aspect of their identity. The staunch denial of gender's performative, socially constructed, and fluid nature, combined with a belief in an externally limited authentic self-expression, increases the number of "angry white men" in western contexts reacting against and rejecting progressive social movements and evolving social normativity.

One reaction to such perceived limitation and denial of masculine identity is the withdrawal of men into masculine social spaces. Such social spaces serve to shield men from female interaction/intervention, feminine value systems, and from the shaming involved in both masculine failure and/or progressive rejection of masculine value systems. Additionally, male homosocial bonding spaces serve to affirm, instruct, and reinforce hegemonic masculine expectations. Michael Kimmel argues that several strategies for the restoration of manhood can be traced historically, and that the strategy of escapism has been one dominant mechanism.[38] According to Kimmel, men throughout history have attempted to escape so-called feminizing forces through the creation of boys only clubs, fraternities, male lodges, men's weekend retreats and revivals, as well as within male targeted media outlets.[39] In each instance and over time, male participants in such escapist activities are often members of privileged racial and social classes who actively resist mechanisms of social change that threaten their sense of entitlement and social power. Such masculine safe havens provide relief from external progressive social threats while assuring individuals of the essential reality of their own masculine identities.

While men of all ages and contexts utilize this form of masculine escapism, Kimmel notes that it is particularly prominent for young men, specifically adolescent and post adolescent males. Kimmel dubs this social phenomenon/space "Guyland." This space is founded upon a base of middle-class and masculine entitlement, giving rise to purely homosocial bonding behaviors unrestrained by the responsibilities of adult life.[40] What makes this space particularly problematic is the effort to prove masculinity in the absence of any real guidance, leaving young men at the mercy of their peers in their attempts to prove and assert themselves as men.[41] This does not provide the context for a healthy development of identity, and the reliance upon problematic masculine values such as aggression, violence, and competition can often make "Guyland" a risky space to inhabit.

The absence of women in such spaces is notable and deliberate, which Kimmel encapsulates in the well-known adage, "bros before hos." Kimmel explains, "American men want to be a 'man among men,' an Arnold Schwartzenegger-like 'man's man,' not a Fabio-like 'ladies' man.' Masculinity is largely a homosocial experience: performed for, and judged by, other men."[42] Thus, Kimmel argues that women are for possessing not for emulating. The assertion, maintenance, and judgment of masculinity is left to men themselves, and this homosocial space of gendered performance and reinforcement is supplemented by "guy" groups, activities, and media. When women participate in these spaces, they are generally peripheral and only permitted access through an unstated agreement to support and participate in the masculine discourse present. Kimmel points out that girls can even become guys to some extent, as long as they don't pose too serious a threat to male dominance in "Guyland"—for instance know sports but not too much, and so forth. Consequently, girls must live with "Guyland" and can even become a part of it in some respects, but they do not define the space.[43] Even though women have some access, this sort of male space is for and about males and masculinity first.

The list of behaviors that can be identified as stereotypically masculine or constitutive of "Guyland" type spaces is lengthy. Activities involving competition, aggression or risk such as sports, binge drinking, and violent video games are common. Additionally, hypermasculine sexuality is reflected in pornographic media and media that objectifies women as sexual conquests or possessions for masculine characters. Media that is marketed for male audiences stereotypically includes action films, violent television series, and violent video games. Women can certainly watch and/or participate in these activities, but as Kimmel points out women do not make the rules in these contexts—women negotiate as opposed to determine. Furthermore, women viewing media such as action films will often be required to identify with male protagonists in the film, creating a significantly different form of spectatorship in some ways than male spectatorship. As Laura Mulvey points out, women spectators may identify with the narcissism, omnipotence, and freedom of male characters in films such as westerns (and by analogy, action films), but female characters enacting these values often end up annihilated by the end.[44] Male characters, on the other hand, have choices—they may opt for a heroic narcissism by walking off into the sunset alone, or they can gain social capital through adherence to the law and cultural order. In any case, such film and media representations reinforce the centrality of male only spaces, and the freedom/power masculinity offers to men that women can only reach through (often tragic) fantasy.

The perceived need to "save" masculinity through a retreat into traditional masculine values maintained via homosocial masculine spaces deeply informs gendered behavior in online contexts. In contemporary times, "Guyland" has extended far beyond sports and fraternities, and into a wide variety of gaming and message board systems online. The appeal of online masculine expression is multifaceted. First, as was previously established, masculinity online is not constrained by embodiment—masculinity is all about attitude and discourse, not about your body, muscles, or visible athletic ability. In this sense, the access to hegemonic masculinity becomes somewhat more equally available, since the requirements are merely the right mindset, rhetoric, and some appropriate skill set (which can be anything from hyperintellectualism in some area ranging from science to sports, all the way to skill in online gaming). Second, the Internet allows individuals a wide reach in terms of audience, combined with the ability to carefully consider and construct responses in text-based communication. Thus, masculine reinforcement can come from a remarkable number of individuals from a vast number of contexts, widening the boundaries of "Guyland" in incredible ways. Furthermore, men can observe one another online, learn proper masculine rhetoric, and take time to craft a desirable response when engaging in text-based communication. This allows for a perfection of masculine performance that is significantly less likely to create a sense of shame or failure, thus reinforcing masculine value systems and performance as rewarding, inherent, and valuable.

MASCULINE SPACE ONLINE

The creation of masculine space online is often the effect of men essentially taking over open forums and making certain spaces undesirable for women. Women report a lack of participation in forums for a variety of reasons, including aggressive language and argumentation, harassment, and silencing. According to Susan Herring, there is a significant difference in values used by men and women posting online, and these values impact individual posting behavior as well as interpretations and the related interpretations of other posts. She explains, "Women preferentially evoke an ethic of politeness and consideration for the wants of others, especially the desire to be ratified and liked, while men evoke an ethic of agonistic debate and freedom from rules or imposition. The male ethic predominates in official netiquette guidelines and in discourse about the Internet in general."[45] Consequently, the masculine values dictating Internet forum postings favor masculine rhetoric, which simultaneously devalues and alienates female users from certain online contexts.

Herring recognizes that characterizing posting styles as "masculine" and "feminine" runs certain risks, namely the potential implication of gender essentialism coupled with exposure to the accusation of making sweeping gender assumptions. However, the purpose of her discussion and other studies like hers is to detect certain trends in gendered behavior, and the cause of these trends is not directly named. Certainly, female users can adopt masculine rhetoric and vice versa, but empirical evidence suggests a high frequency of stereotypical rhetoric coupled with specifically gendered users. Furthermore, the source of the rhetoric need not be identified as innate qualities or properties of masculinity and femininity rooted in essential gendered differences. These variations could just as easily be explained in terms of gendered performance or other social constructionist views that identify gendered behavior as originating in socially imposed norms determining behavior throughout development in a person's lifetime.

Therefore, generally speaking, Herring claims that male users in online text-based communication forums rely heavily upon adversarial rhetorical style, involving language that is often loaded with challenges, a sense of superiority, and a higher frequency of length posts.[46] The adversarial rhetorical style runs along a continuum from the mainly innocuous to the extreme form often referred to as "flaming" or "trolling."[47] In general, male users typically promote themselves as clear and succinct thinkers, but evidence contradicts this self-conception. The contradiction lies in the tendency for such male users use of adversarial linguistics dominated by long posts based upon self-promotion that often dominates conversations and alienates other users.[48] Herring identifies three types of typical behavior exhibited by male users: self-promotion, rhetorical coercion, and adversality. Individuals engaged in self-promotion will frequently refer to their titles, name drop, mention other connections, and gratuitously mention publications.[49] Rhetorical coercion occurs when such users engage in argument styles that make it particularly difficult for the target of the criticism to respond. Examples include the use of incomplete references, referring to information that cannot be adequately verified, presupposition of position as opposed to assertion, and the use of rhetorical questions.[50] This creates what can be described as the "emperor's new clothes" effect—the content is obviously lacking but respondents may hesitate to criticize it due to its being steeped in intellectualism and convincing fallacies. Finally, additional insights to the adversarial style include frequent use of sarcasm and put-downs with significantly agonistic debating styles.[51] Reliance upon these linguistic behaviors can have the consequence of creating an environment hostile to constructive conversation, exchange, critical thinking, and meaningful dialogue.

Studies indicate a significant difference in feminine posting styles. Herring claims, "Women preferentially evoke an ethic of politeness and consideration for the wants of others, especially their desire to be ratified and liked . . . with the result that women with a politeness ethic must create and defend women-centered spaces online in order to carry out the kind of discourse they value."[52] In various studies, researchers have noticed a distinct pattern of women using rhetoric reflecting a concern with support and appreciation of others, using encouragement or polite language to criticize and disagree with others.[53] Additionally, some women users show a tendency to hedge their input, applying disclaimers to their posts or putting forth the statement as a question while seeking approval from other group members.[54] This extreme form of feminine online rhetoric clearly stands in stark contrast to the extreme version of masculine rhetoric, and clearly marks users as female/feminine to certain aggressive male users. Consequently, some female users are highly vulnerable to attacks from aggressive male users that can range from dismissive to silencing and even harassing. Due to the incompatibility of these two rhetorical styles, some women users report feeling uncomfortable in online forums and will often leave the group or seek women's only forums where they feel safer from masculinist intervention and aggressive rhetoric.

Herring notes that while the intimidation tactics used by aggressive men online can impact both male and female users, the patterns of response to such intimidation vary.[55] Men are more often comfortable with acts of aggression and intimidation, and are thus more likely to ignore certain posts or remain generally unfazed. Women, on the other hand, are more likely to feel personally vulnerable, insulted, and threatened in the face of such behavior. This could be a consequence of the fact that a large amount of extreme online harassment is targeted at women due to the simple fact that they are women. Herring defines gender harassment as unwanted contact that targets individuals with offensive content by reason of one's gender.[56] Such harassment often escalates when adversarial male users want to limit and discredit the participation of women in online discussions in order to preserve male control and increase masculine interest. While adolescent male users tend to harass women using crude, sexual, and direct language, older males will often steep harassment in intellectualism.[57] In both cases, however, the goal remains consistent. Similar to the forces informing Kimmel's "Guyland," this rhetoric serves to create and uphold masculine spaces that silence women, uphold male privilege, and shield men from responsibility for their aggression under the guise of gender essentialism and freedom of speech.

Herring describes six progressive stages of online harassment, referring specifically to gender harassment of women by adversarial men. The initial situation is often fueled by simple exclusion of males by female users or female users disagreeing with men in the forum. In cases of exclusion, some male users react strongly to women speaking only with each other, or women who are doing so and appear to be friends, affirming claims that men experience certain levels of insecurity in reference to female friendships.[58] In instances of supposed disagreement, Collins and Jarvis note that harassing or discriminatory behavior often arises in response to the increased participation of dissenting female users, but may also be a reaction to female users exhibiting individual agendas, independent views, or unimpeded talk. The researchers interpret the reactions of such male users as a response to equitable behavior by female users posing a threat to adversarial and/or hypermasculine contributors. This response then leads to the initiation of harassment, which often includes sexual or intellectually demeaning comments directed to female users.[59] Criticism of such comments is frequently accused of being an attempt at censorship. The third stage is resistance, in which female users might claim not to be bothered by such comments, denying being demeaned or derailed. Consequently, female users might continue to contribute at this point.[60] Following this stage is escalation, in which an adversarial male user increases harassment, demonstrating significant rhetorical reversals. Such reversals often include a denial of feminist concerns, accusations of oppression against feminism, and the use of power plays that discredit and intimidate the female targets.[61] The fifth stage is accommodation, where female users modify their participation to comply with male demands. Female rhetorical style might change, aligning with the masculinist conception of appropriate female rhetoric. Adoption of such style can be understood as coerced, and this style is often marked by behaviors such as flirting, silence, or an adoption of a masculine adversarial style. While the adoption of masculine rhetoric is not feminine, it is also cooperating with the tone set by male users, demonstrating a different form of accommodation. However, it should be noted that female aggressiveness is mostly ineffectual at best.[62] The sixth and final stage is silence from the female participant.[63]

The justification male users often give for this type of silencing is not simply put forward as masculine resistance or the desire for masculine space. Rather, the explanation given is often steeped in language concerning free speech and libertarian value systems. As Susan Herring notes, the values shaping the rules or expectations of online communication are often masculinist values reflecting commitments to individualism, complete freedom of expression, and a lack of concern for fostering community if such community creation conflicts with individual rights. According to Herring, male respondents often value freedom from censorship, candor, and debate in online interactions, arguing that individual autonomy is paramount in online contexts.[64] In her research, male respondents frequently claimed that these values override the feelings or responses of others, with the Internet functioning as the last bastion of expression totally free from interference due to political correctness, and so forth. Consequently, the aggressive behaviors and hypermasculine expressions often found online take on a moral and political justification, with some men arguing that such rhetoric reflects important rights and personal freedoms.

Overall, Kimmel's notion of "Guyland" has found a secure home in the Internet. Because of such values as a total freedom from censorship and personal autonomy, online platforms have both encouraged and provided safe spaces for masculine identity. These safe spaces are both created and maintained through the use of bullying language, intellectualism, silencing techniques, and the construction of online "boys clubs" such as gaming and message boards like Reddit and 4Chan. The combination of idealized masculine performance, politicized value systems, and male safe havens have made the Internet an ideal platform for the MRM. In the following section, I will argue that the MRM has co-opted essentialist masculinity and male space to create a political movement that, while pervasive in certain online contexts, isolates itself in the libertarian safe havens of online forums.

THE MRM AS AN ONLINE MOVEMENT

On the surface, the expansion and increased use of the Internet presents itself as a potentially helpful tool for democracy and the development of informed citizens. There is an almost endless amount of information easily and readily available for consumption online, along with discussion boards, blogs, social media outlets, and other venues for individuals to engage one another on almost any topic. However, this availability of information and platform does not guarantee that individuals will be exposed to multiple views or constructive debate. Cass Sunstein argues that the ability of individuals to precisely filter the information they receive and, consequently, the individuals they engage with online can, in fact, greatly compromise the political potential of online communities. According to Sunstein, this filtering results in the phenomenon of group polarization, causing individuals to become more entrenched in previous views as opposed to becoming well versed in wider political debates.[65] This phenomenon is quite visible in MRM online activity, and works as a persuasive explanation for the extremist political speech and opinions exhibited by these groups.

Sunstein points out that if diverse groups online are hearing very different points of view on very different topics without engaging other approaches, the ability of these groups to interact and converse becomes greatly compromised. This problem is attributed to group polarization, which he defines as:

> The idea is that after deliberating with one another, people are more likely to move toward a more extreme point in the direction to which they were previously inclined, as indicated, by the median of their predeliberation arguments. With respect to the Internet, the implication is that groups of people, especially if they are like-minded, will end up thinking the same thing they thought before—but in more extreme form.[66]

The intensity of group polarization is increased when individuals feel they share some sort of identity or basis of solidarity with others in the group. Sunstein points out that if group members think of themselves as similar along some social dimension or factor such as politics, geography, race, sex, and so forth, then the entrenchment and extreme nature of a given view is often heightened.[67] In his work on online communication, Mitch Parsell also notes this tendency, adding that individuals will frequently overemphasize a given shared characteristic or quality while downplaying differences between members in the group.[68] Consequently, as the group's polarization increases, the toleration for outside views and opinions decreases, often leading to an overwhelming amount of speech with very little variation in points of view.

Group polarization is a highly useful concept for analyzing the emergence of the MRM as an Internet based movement. First, given the level of frustration and anger certain men are experiencing (as evidenced by the "angry white men" Kimmel describes), the Internet offers an outlet for these frustrations through an ability to find like-minded men and other individuals to engage with. As these individuals share and communicate with one another in these contexts, it seems as though their suspicions are confirmed, and that men are truly suffering at the hands of women and feminism. This confirmation can then lead to the increase in extremism that Sunstein describes, resulting in the active, albeit scattered, MRM observed online presently. As individual views become more extreme and apparently universal, a mob mentality based on backlash to feminism and political correctness arises, creating a sense of urgency resulting in organized platforms, online organizations, and so on.

Furthermore, the sharing of certain experiences and emotions also contributes to the leveling of identity that is observed in the MRM. While men exhibit a variety of intersectional identities based on a wide range of sociopolitical factors, the shared anger and resentment expressed by men in the MRM result in a diminishing of these factors and an emphasis on shared "male" identity. The impact of group polarization combined with a lack of embodied interaction allows these men to create solidarity along the lines of extremist masculinity. Additionally, this extremism and polarization creates a sense of urgency to maintain hypermasculine online spaces in various online contexts that allow these men to express such gender views under the alleged principles of autonomy and freedom. As a consequence, male users come to dominate and maintain certain platforms such as Reddit or AVFM, or even to advocate a complete disassociation from women and femininity all together, as seen in the "Men Going Their Own Way" movement. The need to maintain such spaces results in eruptions of backlash online, as observed in phenomena such as the "Gamer Gate" controversy. While MRMs often complain the Gamer Gate is misrepresented as misogynist backlash when it was truly a matter of journalistic integrity, the extreme sexism of the incident (and the extreme sexism observed in gaming communities at large) is undeniable.

The MRM is also marked by the harassing and aggressive rhetoric that Herring describes, in an extreme form. MRM discussions are often marked by intellectualism, in the form of demeaning feminists' intelligence, praising male logic, and speaking in pseudo-scientific language steeped in statistics and so-called facts. The reliance upon cyberlibertarian values, combined with the claim of rational justification for the allegedly "political" outrage, make the MRM a rhetorically menacing and, at times, violent force on the Internet. These individuals have gained access to the idealized masculinity described previously, and vigorously defend this position in various ways online. Women and individuals the MRM view as oppressive or unfairly critical are often bullied, threatened, harassed, doxxed, and even run off of social media by MRAs. It can be argued that this violence is only heightened by the lack of embodiment online, because the moral claim of a human embodied person confronting the individual is erased. Thus, the gaps that Matthews describes only serve to heighten the politicized rage of the MRM movement.

Given these circumstances, one can conclude that the mere possibility of democracy online, combined with traditional liberal values, is no guarantee that collaborative or progressive deliberation will emerge from Internet interactions. In the case of the MRM, the potential for transcendent politics is obliterated by the prevalence of group polarization and the valuation of hegemonic masculinity. Although the MRM considers itself a political movement, its online context, isolationist policies, and leveling assumptions undercut its ability to function as a vehicle for liberatory social change.

Furthermore, its reliance upon violent rhetoric is only heightened by various online factors, making it a disturbing and threatening force of disruption as opposed to a transformational gender movement.

CONCLUSION

This chapter establishes the gender politics and methods of the MRM as a mainly online movement. Working within a mainly online platform results in various problematic interactions, belief systems, and expressions of self. This is not to say that the Internet is a bad thing—as Sunstein argues, while the Internet contributes to problematic politics at times, it also holds promise in its vast resources and information. Nonetheless, the MRM is an example of the dangers online movements and communications can entail. This is not to say that the Internet is solely responsible for the emergence of these beliefs and individuals, and one can readily observe "angry white men" in a variety of contemporary contexts. However, online communication has been usurped by the MRM as a conduit for its "movement" and voice, and works as a compounding factor for the rise of such belief systems as an organized platform of sorts.

NOTES

1. Marya Schechtman, *The Constitution of Selves* (Ithaca, NY: Cornell University Press, 1996), 73.
2. Schechtman, *Constitution of Selves*, 77.
3. Schechtman, *Constitution of Selves*, 81.
4. The concept of "second order desire" I refer to in this section is a term utilized by Schechtman, based on the work of Harry Frankfurt. Refer to: Harry Frankfurt, "Freedom of the Will and the Concept of a Person," *The Journal of Philosophy* (68).
5. Schechtman, *Consitution of Selves*, 83.
6. Generally, "catfishing" is the adoption of an online identity that is, to some degree, false. Such falsification may include faking pictures, personality, life history, and so on. More information can be found in Aisha Harris, "Who Coined the Term 'Catfishing'" *Slate*, January 18, 2013, http://www.slate.com/blogs/browbeat/2013/01/18/catfish_meaning_and_definition_term_for_online_hoaxes_has_a_surprisingly.html.
7. Susan Herring, "Gender and (A)nonymity in Computer Mediated Communication," in *Handbook of Language and Gender*, 2nd ed., ed. J. Holmes, M. Meyerhoff, and S. Ehrlich (Hoboken, NJ: Wiley-Blackwell Publishing, 2013), 5.
8. Herring, "Gender and Anonymity," 5.
9. Susan Herring, "Posting in a Different Voice: Gender and Ethics in CMC," in *Philosophical Perspectives on Computer-Mediated Communication*, ed. Charles Ess (Albany: State University of New York Press, 1996).
10. Herring, "Gender and Anonymity," 5.
11. Susan Bordo, *Unbearable Weight: Feminism, Western Culture, and the Body* (Berkeley: University of California Press, 2003), 165.
12. Michel Foucault, *Discipline and Punish: The Birth of the Prison* (New York: Random House, 1995), 136.
13. Foucault, *Discipline and Punish*, 170.

14. Judith Butler, *Giving an Account of Oneself* (New York: Fordham University Press, 2005), 22.
15. Judith Butler, *Gender Trouble: Feminism and the Subversion of Identity* (New York: Routledge, 1999).
16. Butler, *Gender Trouble*, 23.
17. Butler, *Gender Trouble*, 23.
18. Butler, *Gender Trouble*, 172.
19. Butler, *Gender Trouble*, 172.
20. Butler, *Gender Trouble*, 173.
21. Steve Matthews, "Identity and Information Technology," in *Information Technology and Moral Philosophy*, ed. Jeroen Van Den Hoven and John Weckert (New York: Cambridge University Press, 2008), 143.
22. Judith Butler, *Precarious Life: The Powers of Mourning and Violence* (New York: Verso, 2004), 20.
23. Butler, *Precarious Life*, 26.
24. Butler, *Precarious Life*, 27.
25. Matthews, "Identity and IT," 144.
26. Matthews, "Identity and IT," 145.
27. Butler, *Precarious Life*, 139.
28. Judith Butler, *Giving an Account*, 20.
29. Butler, *Giving an Account*, 149.
30. Matthews, "Identity and IT," 145.
31. Matthews, "Identity and IT," 147.
32. Matthews, "Identity and IT," 155.
33. Anita Superson and Ann Cudd, *Theorizing Backlash: Philosophical Reflections on the Resistance to Feminism* (Lanham, MD: Rowman and Littlefield, 2002), xiii.
34. Ann Cudd, "Analyzing Backlash to Progressive Social Movements," in *Theorizing Backlash: Philosophical Reflections on Resistance to Feminism* (Lanham, MD: Rowman and Littlefield, 2002).
35. Cudd, "Analyzing Backlash," 8.
36. James Gilligan, *Violence: Reflections on a National Epidemic* (New York: Random House, 1996), 231.
37. Gilligan, *Violence*, 233.
38. Kimmel, *Angry White Men*, 49.
39. Kimmel, *Angry White Men*, 49.
40. Michael Kimmel, *Guyland: The Perilous World Where Boys Become Men—Understanding the Critical Years Between 16 and 26* (New York: HarperCollins, 2008), 13.
41. Kimmel, *Guyland*, 19.
42. Kimmel, *Guyland*, 47.
43. Kimmel, *Guyland*, 15.
44. Laura Mulvey, "Visual Pleasure and Narrative Cinema," in *Film Theory and Criticism*, ed. Leo Braudy and Marshall Cohen (New York: Oxford University Press, 1999).
45. Herring, "Different Voice," 117.
46. Herring, "Different Voice," 118.
47. Herring, "Different Voice," 118.
48. Susan Herring, "Men's Language on the Internet," in *Norlyd* (28).
49. Herring, "Men's Language."
50. Herring, "Men's Language."
51. Herring, "Men's Language."
52. Herring, "Different Voice," 153.
53. See, Herring, "Different Voice," "Men's Language," and "Gender and Anonymity."
54. Herring, "Different Voice."
55. Herring, "Men's Language."
56. Susan Herring, "The Rhetorical Dynamics of Gender Harassment Online," in *The Information Society* (15), 153.
57. Herring, "Rhetorical Dynamics," 152.

58. Herring, "Rhetorical Dynamics," 156.
59. Herring, "Rhetorical Dynamics," 157.
60. Herring, "Rhetorical Dynamics," 158.
61. Herring, "Rhetorical Dynamics," 158.
62. Herring, "Rhetorical Dynamics," 159.
63. Herring, "Rhetorical Dynamics," 161.
64. Herring, "Different Voice," 126–127.
65. Cass Sunstein, "Democracy and the Internet," in *Information Technology and Moral Philosophy*, ed. Jeroen Van Den Hoven, John Weckert (New York: Cambridge University Press, 2008), 97.
66. Sunstein, "Democracy," 99.
67. Sunstein, "Democracy," 101.
68. Mitch Parsell, "Pernicious Virtual Communities: Polarization and the Web," in *Ethics and Information Technology* (10), 98.

Chapter Three

The Men's Rights Movement and Political Revolution

Once the agenda, methods, and membership of a given social movement have been established, it is necessary to examine the conditions under which such a movement arises, and to philosophically evaluate the status of a movement as progressive, liberatory, oppressive, and so forth. The previous chapters describe the nature of the MRM through a discussion of membership, ideals, and methods; this chapter will give a fuller philosophical analysis of the movement as a self-described political revolution rejecting social realities and norms that impact men. In order to complete this analysis, I will refer to progressive liberatory thinkers such as Herbert Marcuse to evaluate the worldview and methods proposed by the MRM, discussing the theories and norms that inform this group's concepts of gender, economics, personal liberty, and effective forms of social intervention. This discussion will indicate that while the MRM does in fact detect and illuminate various gender problematics, their methods and theories are not progressive or in the interest of liberation, but rather a creative retelling of and demand for traditional gender norms under the guise of political revolution.

SOCIAL FOUNDATIONS: GYNOCENTRISM AND ONE-DIMENSIONAL THINKING

Marcuse and Political Philosophy

The MRM claims that it has access to fundamental truths concerning gender and oppression in contemporary western society. In many ways, I will argue, the MRM justifies such claims using concepts analogous to those present in

Marcuse's discussion of repressive society and one-dimensional thinking. Namely, the MRM claims that men experience a total alienation of self in culture, and this alienation is achieved through unrewarding and exploitative work as well as the immersion of the individual in culture narratives and structures. However, unlike Marcuse, the MRM does not identify the source of alienating labor and existence as capitalism; rather, they argue, women and misandry are the true sources of men's societal woes. This is based on the notion that society is in fact "gynocentric"—based upon and revolving around women's needs and demands. This social centrism is obscured by misandric myths of patriarchy, which is established and entrenched by feminism. In this section, I will describe the MRM on its own terms in the context of Marcuse's political theories in order to theoretically unpack the MRM's self-conception.

Marcuse argues that western society is a society based upon repression. Borrowing from Freud's concepts of the life and death drives described in *Civilization and its Discontents*, Marcuse describes the ways in which these drives are repressed and sublimated in the establishment of working societies. The requirement of repression for the establishment of a given society is referred to as basic repression. While Marcuse will argue that the repressive society is one of unfreedom and oppression, he also admits that some degree of repression is necessary for cooperation and the survival of human communities. In contrast to basic repression, Marcuse defines surplus repression as: "the restrictions necessitated by social domination."[1] Surplus repression is determined by cultural, historical, and political norms working in the interest of oppressive and dominating societies. In Freudian theory, the reality principle is that which mediates the pleasure principle, allowing for the tempered attainment of pleasure by working within the realities of a given world. Marcuse adopts this concept in order to establish the performance principle, which is the historically prevailing form of the reality principle. Marcuse explains the performance principle within the context of western capitalism as follows:

> The performance principle, which is that of an acquisitive and antagonistic society in the process of constant expansion, presupposes a long development during which domination has been increasingly rationalized: control over social labor now reproduces society on a large scale and under improving conditions. For a long way, the interests of domination and the interests of the whole coincide: the profitable utilization of the productive apparatus fulfills the needs and faculties of individuals. For the vast majority of the population, the scope and mode of satisfaction are determined by their own labor; but their labor is work for an apparatus that they do not control, which operates as an independent power to which individuals must submit if they want to live. And it becomes the more alien the more specialized the division of labor becomes. Men do not live their own lives but perform pre-established functions. While

they work, they do not fulfill their own needs and faculties but work in *alienation*.[2]

Thus, surplus repression in the context of contemporary western capitalism requires a repression of Eros and Thanatos that supports an increasingly rationalized system of domination and exploitation. Because scarcity is no longer the driving force behind work, alternate schemas of justification and rationalization of labor must be dispersed in order to uphold power driven capitalist structures.

Taking into account the role of repression within the creation of an oppressive society, Marcuse argues that the total alienation of the individual becomes complete, such that the alienated individual becomes totally absorbed by the culture in which they exist. The result of this is what Marcuse refers to as one-dimensional thinking. In his discussion of one-dimensional thinking, he outlines the nature of what he terms "democratic unfreedom" in contemporary western society. According to Marcuse, liberation requires negative thinking, or two-dimensional thought, that negates current ways of being and thinking. Such negative thinking recognizes the contradictions that exist within a given society and the ways in which such contradictions contribute to structures of domination. Contrastingly, one-dimensional thought ignores such contradictions, rendering them invisible and thus removing any perceived need for change or revolution. He argues:

> Thus emerges a pattern of *one-dimensional thought and behavior* in which ideas, aspirations, and objectives, that, by their content, transcend the established universe of discourse and action and are either repelled or reduced to the terms of this universe. They are redefined by the rationality of the given system and of its quantitative extension.[3]

Under one-dimensional thought, the problematic and repressive modes of thought that present themselves are rationalized and incorporated into a seemingly coherent mode of thinking. Once the contradictions are obscured, the perceived need for challenge, revolution and liberation is erased or removed.

One-dimensional thinking creates a false sense of independence, individualism, and freedom within individuals of a given society. This is maintained through democratic unfreedom, in which individuals freely accept the oppressive conditions of society. Such acceptance is achieved and maintained through various methods. The acceptance of oppression is achieved in a general sense by the replacement of concrete authority figures with institutions, making domination into a form of administration.[4] Marcuse points out that the capitalist bosses and owners are losing their identity as individual oppressors as they are increasingly identified as bureaucrats in a capitalist, corporate machine.[5] The loss of individualized oppressive figures makes oppression overall less tangible, as exploitation seems to disappear behind the rationality of the sociopolitical system. Consequently, technological innovation is used as a tool to increase unfreedom for individuals, hidden behind the many comforts and liberties it simultaneously creates. The increase of unfreedom and one-dimensional thought is thus maintained by creating a false sense of freedom through certain liberties, access to comforts and goods, identification with oppressors, and the silencing of political discourse.

The adoption of false needs and liberties contribute to the individual's complicity with their own oppression. As these social and historical needs are internalized, the individual becomes indistinguishable from society. Additionally, the working of the media furthers this mimesis of individual and society, demonstrating the extent to which members of the population share these false needs and sources of satisfaction. Once such immediate identification between the individual and a society is achieved, the issue of alienation comes into question. Marcuse explains that the mimetic identification he describes is literal not figurative, as ideology is absorbed into culture. He argues, "The subject which is alienated is swallowed up by its alienated existence. There is only one dimension, and it is everywhere and in all forms."[6] Consequently, Marcuse points out that false consciousness is immune to its own falsity, due to the fact that the individual is completely absorbed by and identified with the dominant oppressive culture. Such mimesis is the source of one-dimensional thought, in which the individual cannot transcend the reality presented by repressive society. In such a context, liberation is prevented because it requires an awareness of one's servitude, and this awareness is prevented by the imposition of externally mandated false needs.

Politics and MRM Rhetoric

In some respects, the MRM appears to loosely mirror many of the concepts Marcuse describes, namely one-dimensional thinking, the importance of negative thinking, repression, and the import of the reality principle. However, while Marcuse points to exploitative western capitalism as the source of general oppression, the MRM redirects the source to gynocentrism and its related cultural tenets of misandry and the alleged myth of patriarchy. Starting with the reality principle, while Marcuse discusses the role of labor in reference to this principle, the MRM claims that the issue is not simply labor but labor imposed on men to be performed in the interest of women. According to Warren Farrell, the exploitation of masculine labor, both economically and emotionally, is obscured by the myth of male power. While contemporary progressive movements point out women's relative disadvantage to men in the context of interpersonal relations, social autonomy, and economic power, Farrell points out that men are actually powerless, but we translate that powerlessness into deceptive descriptions seeming to imply power. For instance, he argues, we call "male killing" on battlefields, and so forth, "glory," call on men to be unpaid bodyguards while referring to such behavior as properly masculine or respectful, and focus only on the amount of money an individual makes as opposed to the who is spending the money and how. The last point Farrell refers to as the spending gap—essentially the notion that women make the overwhelming majority of choices concerning how money is spent while men merely provide the funds. Such a gap is an example of how Farrell conceptualizes power overall, namely, the notion that power consists in the control one has over their life. MRAs like Farrell argue that men have significantly diminished power because the work they perform in a given society is in the interest of maintaining the respect and approval of women while providing the means for women to purchase and invest in a wide variety of cultural goods. In other words, men are deprived of choices because of the need to make money, and this money has the opposite impact on women since it gives them the freedom to spend it as they see fit.

Consequently, the MRM often focuses on the idea that men are economically exploited and used, however, the source of this exploitation is not capitalism itself. Rather, the actual issue is the fact that society is structured in the interest of catering to and giving advantages to women, referred to as gynocentrism. Generally, the definition provided states that gynocentrism is a dominant or exclusive focus on women theoretically or practically, and such gynocentrism has its historical roots in chivalry and courtly love.[7] However, a mere focus on women does not imply an injustice or harm. Thus, Adam Kostakis expands the definition, arguing, "Gynocentrism, whether it went by the name honor, nobility, chivalry, or feminism, its essence has gone unchanged. It remains a peculiarly male duty to help the women onto the lifeboats, while the men themselves face a certain and icy death." The point of such arguments is to demonstrate that gynocentrism persists in the allegedly commonly enforced demand that men sacrifice for women, whether it be economically, emotionally (families and romantic relationships), or bodily (going to war, working dangerous jobs, etc.).

Gynocentrism (in the sacrificial model outlined above) is marked by misandry, or an oppressive dislike/hatred of men and masculinity. According to Kostakis, feminism is a current outgrowth of gynocentrism, furthering misandric tendencies within a given society. Kostakis argues that feminism does not create misandry but rather attracts women with some level of misandric tendencies. He explains feminism as follows:

> Feminism is the most recent, and presently the most culturally dominant form of Gynocentrism. It is a victim ideology which explicitly advocates female supremacy, at every facet of life in which men and women meet; it does so in

> accordance with its universalizing tendency, and so it does so in each sphere of life, including but extending beyond the political, social, cultural, personal, emotional, sexual, spiritual, economic, governmental and legal. By female supremacy, I refer to the notion that women should possess superiority of status, power and protection relative to men. It is the dominant cultural paradigm in the Western world and beyond. It is morally indefensible, although its adherents ensure that their hegemony goes unchallenged through the domination of societal institutions and the use of state violence.[8]

In other words, feminism furthers the reach and entrenchment of gynocentrism through a politicized naturalization of feminine superiority, supported by the instilling of the myth that patriarchy exists and structures the majority of a given society.

According to MRAs such as Kostakis, the instilling of the myth of patriarchy is what keeps gynocentrism firmly entrenched, because the notion of patriarchy obscures the reality of the cultural forces at play. He explains:

> Feminism is a victim ideology which freezes women perpetually in *Struggle*; it cannot afford to indulge in *Liberation*, else the game is up. To continue playing, feminists must imagine that they are under the control of external forces which are responsible for every fate that befalls them. They have a name for this mass delusion: *The Patriarchy*.[9]

Consequently, feminists allegedly instill this myth over and over again through complete and consistent indoctrination, one method being the persecution and/or silencing of anyone who disagrees. This message is apparently so pervasive and entrenched that it commits a sort of brainwashing for women, and they consequently grow to despise men, disrespect masculinity, and demand services from men that they are not morally or practically entitled to. This brainwashing takes form in what Kostakis refers to as a "dehumanization campaign," consisting of three distinct tactics.[10] This involves the portrayal of men as innately violent and inhuman, turning men against one another, and normalizing brutality against men.

A survey of these arguments reveals an important and pervasive theme in MRA rhetoric, namely the idea that the MRM is able to perceive the "truth" about what is actually going on in society in terms of normative convention, power, and oppression. The MRM sees itself as having taken a sort of "red pill" concerning gender and feminism, meaning they have become conscientious of the fact that women run the world without bearing any of its responsibilities while men must suffer silently in support of this gynocentric system.

Marcuse and Progressive Criticism of the MRM

Returning to Marcuse, it is in this sense that the MRM relates to his concepts of two-dimensional thought, or negative thinking. According to the MRM, society has become distinctly alienating due to the fact that it is completely gynocentric, and patriarchy has become a mimetic force within western culture, as men internalize, accept, and enact the stereotypes concerning masculinity as presented within the myth of patriarchal power. This myth is pervasive, and it is maintained through a silencing of dissent combined with other violent emotional appeals, as executed by feminists and other misandric individuals. In other words, the MRM sees the current state of affairs as completely irrational, but this irrationality is obscured by total absorption and alienation within the culture at large. The reaches of feminism touch on all points of life, and its claims are maintained and furthered through a total control of state, political, economic, and media apparatuses. However, as mentioned previously, the issue is not capitalism or exploitative labor overall, but the control of women on labor and women's oppressive impact on current capitalist systems. The MRM has taken the "red pill," however, and as such engages in what they allege to be a form of negative thinking—transcending the realities of contemporary oppression to examine the possibilities existing outside the limits of a dominating, oppressive culture.

Notably, the MRM does not generally express any criticisms of capitalism nor do they assert support or reference to socialist cultural theories. In fact, they appear to do the opposite, as many blogs and websites provide scathing critiques of Marx while promoting the alleged goods of a capitalist system. This being the case, the problem seems to be not labor per se or alienation in terms of the selling of one's labor, but rather the performance of labor and gaining of capital when that capital is diverted to spending on pleasing women, in one way or another. It is not the capitalist or the bourgeoisie who stand as the villains or source of suffering for the worker; rather all men, regardless of class and income, suffer equally under the demand that their hard earned money be turned over to women for spending.

Additionally, the MRM repeatedly and overtly refuses to engage with other social movements or issues, translating other social problems such as race or class into broader issues concerning masculinity and the so-called gender war. There is no recognition of the ways in which various aspects of identity and social realities interlock to create unique standpoints and experiences of oppression. Rather, in order to uphold the claim that feminism, misandry, and gynocentrism are the most pervasive and damaging forces impacting men, the MRM consistently ignores other aspects of oppression or argues that these other forces (race, class, sexual orientation, etc.) are secondary to or originate in sexism directed against men. Such a refusal to engage in complex social realities results in a flat social movement that fails to meaningfully transcend current social realities, thus upholding certain privileged modes of perception and knowledge in creating an explanation for male experiences. The obsessive focus on feminism as the culprit behind most if not all male suffering, combined with an essentialist account of masculinity creates a movement with no momentum for change. Meaningful political struggle requires deep forms of negative thinking resulting from a consciousness of a culture indebted to domination on all levels, impacting human identity and experience in diverse and pervasive ways.

Thus, while the rhetoric of a "red pill" seems to suggest negative thinking in the form of transcending current social realities and one-dimensional thought, there are significant and disturbing issues with MRM thought patterns. First, the identification of "women" as the problem, along with the accompanying description of women/femininity, seems at best a misogynistic straw man, ignoring complex issues of oppression while relying on highly stereotypical and dichotomous concepts of gender. Second, the use of an essentialist form of masculinity works to erase the impact of racism, classism, homophobia, and other oppressive forces on individual males, creating a narrative based squarely in the experiences of privileged individuals. Third, the ideals upheld within the MRM are consistently deeply libertarian, such as freedom of speech, individuality, and so forth, and the noticeable lack of criticism concerning these basic ideals suggests that the MRM does not escape the democratic unfreedom Marcuse describes in his discussion of one-dimensional society, since their political critique rests fully on attacks on women, gynocentrism, and femininity. Finally, their consistent use of violent rhetoric, abusive language, and refusal to engage with meaningful debate indicates that this movement persists in working within the oppressive realities currently manifested in western culture, regardless of their claims that they reject the system all together, or do not want to engage with current culture but "break it."[11]

THE WAR OF THE SEXES:
MASCULINE/FEMININE CONFLICT IN MRM RHETORIC

Contemporary thought and social theory has no shortage of theories concerning the nature and ontological status of gender. While theories on gender vary, there seems to be a general consensus that a significant part of gender identity is socially constructed, as opposed to innate, essential, or merely biological. The nature of such social construction is controversial, with explanations ranging from psychoanalytic to performative. For the purposes of this discussion, I will be relying on a broad concept of gender that views masculinity and femininity as cultural artifacts, dictating various forms of external behaviors, relationships, and internal conceptions of self. Understood as artifacts, one need not assume that there is any essential "truth" to gender, or that masculine and feminine genders are clearly demarcated and/or binary cultural concepts. Furthermore, these categories of gender cannot be understood in isolation from other social concepts, nor is gender to be understood as a primary mode of identification that determines other aspects of identity. Rather, gender works in an interlocking system of social categories creating unique standpoints for individuals in a given culture. Using this schematic, I will address and critique the concepts of femininity and masculinity that repeatedly arise in MRM rhetoric, discussing the limits and problems of the typically dichotomous, stereotypical and simplistic presentations of gender frequently found in MRM writings and discussions.

MRM Models of Gender: Masculinity and Femininity

Attempting to locate a clear or coherent theory of gender in the massive amounts of writing by the MRM is no easy task. While the MRM has a significant amount of data (reliable or not), examples, anecdotes, mission statements, and points of concern, most sites and authors avoid the assertion of a clear theory of what gender truly means. In other words, the discussion of gender stays mainly in the realm of praxis. There could be several reasons for this, perhaps relating to the recent commitment on the part of certain MRM sites such as "A Voice for Men," (AVFM) to avoid universalizing positions if possible. However, while no clear theoretical commitments emerge in these writings, patterns of gendered assumptions do make themselves clear in the rhetoric and points of concern expressed by prominent MRAs. Namely, gender is presented as dichotomous, pervasive, and in frequently stereotypical terms. This section will attempt to analyze the way gender functions within the identity politics of the MRM, how this concept of gender reflects one-dimensional thinking, and the consequences this has on the MRM claim to progressive or liberatory politics.

Notably, many MRAs on AVFM are quick to point out that men are very different in terms of social location, certain experiences, and so forth, and consequently emphasize the importance of individualism and self-determination. However, while this movement claims to desire a respect for multiplicity and diversity, it is also quick to assert that men share certain experiences within a given culture qua men. According to the MRM, these experiences are overwhelmingly oppressive, and thus these experiences are a large aspect of what it means to be a "man" in contemporary western society. AVFM links a particularly comprehensive list, including facts concerning high homicide and suicide rates for males, statistics claiming that men are the overwhelming number of rape victims in the United States, issues concerning low numbers of men receiving full custody of children, high rates of paternity fraud, and male experiences of domestic violence.[12] In addition to being comprehensive, this list of concerns is fairly typical, covering a host of issues commonly addressed in MRM writings. Consequently, the initial impression one gets from these sites is that what men have in common is a base of experience that is generally harmful, and this experience is determined by male identity alone.

Analogously, some MRM sites avoid asserting a universal or general schema of women/femininity as well. In fact, Paul Elam from AVFM points out the number of women who write for their site and who align themselves explicitly with the MRM.[13] The problem, according to sites like AVFM, is with feminism, and to a lesser degree, "trad-con" (traditional conservative) women. Starting with feminism, as pointed out in the discussion of gynocentrism above, MRAs, such as Elam and Kostakis, argue that feminism does not create misandry, but rather misandrists are attracted to feminism as an outlet for their male-directed spite. The general claim is that feminism fuels and maintains itself through the perpetuation of a false victim identity, and the construction of an "enemy" group (read: men) used to sustain the victim identity in order to allow women to maintain their power over men.[14] Thus, feminists contribute to gynocentrism through the maintenance of victim rhetoric levied against men. This victim identity is then further enforced by feminist fueled representations of men as innately flawed and deviant. Kostakis argues, "The solution, as feminists found, is to play Dr. Freud and posit some subconscious, underlying motivation—a dark, sexual, deviant, violent mentality, which acts as a universal explanation for male behavior."[15] Thus, it is feminists who are responsible for the damaging representations of masculinity within our culture.

AVFM also condemns misandry stemming from traditional women and gender arrangements, shortened for reference to "trad-cons." Discussions of gynocentrism frequently point to the fact that the historical basis of gynocentrism is chivalry and courtly love.[16] Contemporarily, MRAs argue that traditional nuclear families, in which the mother stays home and the father works and provides economic support, is a new form of gynocentrism and hence source of male oppression. Dean Esmay argues that "traditional" women call for a return to a family structure that is a fairly recent invention, shrouding its contemporary post-war emergence in the language of nostalgia.[17] However, this plays against men and their interests, because:

> But modern-day "tradcons" tend to view this as "the way things ought to be," because that's what they perceive to somehow be in the interests of women—never mind how body-and-soul crushing it might be on a man. They sell that self-sacrifice as "being a real man" rather than what it really is: dehumanizing reduction of a man to nothing but a utility to be cast aside if he fails.

In other words, Esmay is arguing that traditional family structures force men into becoming economically producing objects whose humanity is degraded and ignored in the context of being used merely for their productive capacities.

The overall issue AVFM seems to have with gynocentric women can be encapsulated in a description of the theory that women use the position of "damsel in distress" to manipulate men into a variety of exploitative situations. This can be understood as a more specific explanation of what MRAs refer to as "victim feminism." To summarize:

> In all of these accounts the behavior being described is *damseling*, a practice feminists have been at the forefront of preserving from the medieval canon. Evoked in conjunction with claims of male brutality, rapiness, depravity and insensitivity, the ultimate purpose of damseling is to draw chivalric responses from men.[18]

Thus, according to this author, feminist women position themselves as helpless victims, garnering sympathy and support via complaints about sexism, harassment, and so forth. However, instead of soliciting support and intervention from individual chivalrous males, feminists have gone to the government and state institutions to have their demands fulfilled. This also spirals out to businesses, clubs, organizations, and so on, that sponsor "women only" spaces, positions, safety measures, and the like.

An examination of these arguments demonstrates that, while AVFM claims to avoid making universal statements about gender, the site does, in fact, rely upon outdated and reductionist models of gender that neglect standpoint, interlocking oppression, and complex systems of power and identity. Rather, they simply reverse the dichotomy of the "gender war," claiming that it's really a war women declared on men to further their own interests and sadistically punish men. The problems contained in these discussions can be highlighted through the various binary-based stereotypes that often serve as a basis for a variety of MRM arguments.

One of the most common stereotypes presenting itself on sites like AVFM is the issue of intellect and logic. According to the MRM, they are using "bricks of logic" to defend themselves from the hysterical oppression of uninformed feminists.[19] According to authors such as Kostakis, feminists fear logic, because it threatens to undermine their ideology, expose the truth, and help individuals to think for themselves. He argues, "That is to say, *it cannot be reasoned with*. It is a waste of time trying to get feminists to see sense, and every MRA soon learns that he will more easily squeeze blood from a stone."[20] These kinds of passages are telling. To be clear, this is not to say that all women or feminists make good arguments, or that some feminists do not, in fact, make irresponsible claims. However, Kostakis seems to be implying that not only do feminists refuse to use logic, but also none of them do. Furthermore, not only do they not use logic, but also such usage is an impossibility. This sets up a simplistic binary conception that assigns women to the negative prong of a binary, and this assignation is a long-standing female stereotype. It allows for a dismissal of female intellect (unless the female parrots the views of the MRM), maintenance of masculinity's claim to allegedly calm rationality, and also an entrenchment of male intellectualism that justifies the dismissal of or refusal to engage with intellectual women or feminist theory.

The second telling cluster of stereotypes involves the issue of honesty or transparency. According to the tenets outlined above, AVFM argues over and over that feminism is dishonest about oppression, violence, rape, and patriarchy. Using a victim identity allows these women to manipulate men and the society at large for greater privileges and power. The notion of women as manipulators and liars is not a new stereotype either. Our culture is rife with stories and images of female liars and manipulators, ranging from the myths of Pandora and Eve, to the contemporary manifestations of the femme fatale, the tease, and the con-woman. Films, stories, and websites with warnings against these sorts of "black widows" and users are abundant. Thus, these accusations coming from AVFM come across as a new telling of an old story. There is not a lot of explanation as to how feminists are achieving such levels of mastery, but more of an indication that no other explanation is available, fallaciously relying upon a lack of information to prove a point.

Finally, the theme of women as being consuming, demanding, and overbearing is pervasive. According to AVFM, women will take everything from you, and it will never be enough. Women overwhelm, overbear, overconsume, and suffocate. Once again, this is a familiar story based on old and culturally pervasive stereotyping. Susan Bordo argues that there are a variety of cultural expressions that reflect the fear of women being "too much," often revolving around conceptions of female sexuality. Bordo identifies the trend of devouring and insatiable women in mythology and ideology, arguing, "Anxiety over women's uncontrollable hungers appears to peak, as well, during periods when women are asserting themselves politically and socially."[21] Consequently, Bordo argues that these images and stereotypes represent a backlash to feminist progress, casting feminists and their demands as aggressive, suffocating, and voracious. Given that AVFM is targeting feminists with these claims, Bordo's analysis is telling. If Bordo is correct, the issue is not women invading or taking over, but rather feminism's disruption of a status quo and the resulting uncertainty over masculine identity and value.

The fact that AVFM relies heavily upon dichotomous gendered stereotyping suggests, once again, that they are engaging in one-dimensional thought. If there is indeed a "war of the sexes," AVFM is doing little to stop it. Bell hooks argues that early waves of white privileged feminism did indeed contribute to the creation of said war, failing to show men that they too could benefit by working for the end of sexist oppression. However, hooks points out, "Feminist movement can end the war between the sexes. It can transform relationships so that alienation, competition, and dehumanization that characterize human interaction can be replaced with feelings of intimacy, mutuality and camaraderie."[22] What hooks suggests reflects Marcuse's call for negative thought—progressive action and rhetoric in the interest of totally altering society to create a new existence in which individuals can thrive. Even if the MRM is right to some extent about certain feminist approaches, it fails to be progressive in its response. Reversing the "truth" about the "war of the sexes," demonizing feminists, becoming reactive, and refusing to recognize liberatory potential creates a movement that looks more like backlash than social justice. Furthermore, the recreation of problematic gender constructs and stereotypes in this reversal creates an even deeper failure to transcend the present oppressive reality that we currently inhabit.

ESSENTIALIST MASCULINITY

One of the most notable tendencies in MRM rhetoric is the promotion of essentialist masculinity. AVFM will claim to be sympathetic to issues concerning race and sexuality, but it also makes it clear that men experiencing these forms of oppression can come to see that masculine oppression is the most basic aspect of all other forms of oppression. The idea that gender is the most "fundamental" aspect of oppression was a pervasive idea in second wave feminism, and persists in certain contemporary theories. However, given the criticisms provided by people of color, global feminists, GLBTQ activists, and so forth, many feminists have worked to give an account of oppression that recognizes the complex interactions involved in the creation of identity and experiences of oppression. Essentialist theories of gender work to erase other aspects of oppression, compromise individuality, and promote arrogance in the legislation of others' identities.

Elizabeth Spelman provides an in-depth critique of what she refers to as the "ampersand problem" in feminist theory. According to Spelman, an additive analysis of oppression is one that assumes gender can be discussed in isolation from other aspects of identity, including race and class. Spelman argues that such an additive analysis distorts oppression because it fails to recognize the implicit differences in the experience of gender for individuals due to their standpoint in terms of race, class, sexual orientation, and so forth.[23] In other words, women do not experience a uniform femininity, and men do not experience a uniform masculinity—various aspects of identity work together to create unique experiences of gender that cannot and should not be equivocated or essentialized.

Spelman claims that separating individuals into parts may create a very misleading concept of the person, and can also work to promote a privileged point of view as "objective" or central. The extraction of gender as a category can work to hide the identity of privileged women at the center of the theory: "The particular race and class identity of those referred to simply as 'women' becomes explicit when we see the inapplicability of statements about 'women' to women who are not of that race or class."[24] Spelman further argues that such essentialism results in claims of common oppression amongst women that allows for the usurping of feminism by bourgeoisie white women to further their own interests.[25] Thus, non-white, non-heterosexual, non-privileged women are erased, alienated, and sometimes used to further an agenda that is not their own.

One important effect of this type of essentialism is what Spelman refers to as arrogance. She explains, "This reminds us that the claim of commonality can be very arrogant indeed: the caller may be attempting to appropriate another's identity."[26] Thus, the arrogance that occurs involves a declaration that we are the same, and the declarer of this sameness then asserting what this means for both of us. Such arrogance creates a presumption of the ability to legislate identity for other people. Spelman recognizes this arrogance and discusses further implications, arguing that privileged feminists acted as though gender oppression was a new revelation of their own finding, imposing what they saw as "the" analysis of gender on all women, and centering the focus of discourse on their experiences.[27] Such legislation of identity, essentialist rhetoric, and theoretical arrogance works to erase individuals and individuality. Spelman points out that if gender is a separable and essential property, then it creates inessential individuals. This is due to the fact that if gender is static and monolithic, then we do not need individual experiences and voices to understand it.[28]

The reliance upon essentialist masculinity in MRM rhetoric creates the same harms as essentialist feminism. Although repeatedly accused of being racist and homophobic, AVFM has attempted to reach out to gay men and men of color under the auspices of shared masculine gender oppression. However, the notion that masculinity can be extracted from other aspects of identity works to create a concept of masculinity based in white heterosexual experience, imposing this experience onto other individuals and erasing their unique intersectional identities. While not necessarily intentionally racist or homophobic, this essentialism works to uphold heteronormative and white supremacist frameworks, eliminating the possibility for a progressive reworking and understanding of gendered realities.

Heteronormativity, Homophobia, and the MRM

Feminists and other critics have repeatedly accused the MRM of homophobia, a claim that is not unfounded. Examples of explicit homophobia are abundant on Red Pill and ROK, with ROK warning men against the dangers of homosexuality to masculine identity and stating that homosexuals are discouraged from posting on the site. The homophobia and essentialist masculinity of a site like ROK is so explicit that I argue (as in the masculinity/femininity section) it does not necessitate further analysis in this work, however, understanding the allegedly inclusive views of groups like AVFM is slightly more complex. I will argue that while AVFM claims to be welcoming and understanding of gay men and their experiences, the general rhetoric presented on AVFM is a view based on hegemonic masculinity and erasure of intersectionality, thus representing oppressive one-dimensional models of thinking.

On AVFM, Paul Elam discusses the issues that arise between "gay men" and the MRM, arguing that the rift between the two groups can largely be explained by gay men's alignment with the feminist movement.[29] According to Elam, gay men have developed a victim mentality through their work with feminism, causing them to misidentify the "real enemy" as heterosexual men. The problem then, he alleges, is that gay men are not considered men in contemporary culture, and they are persecuted in spite of the fact that gay men have contributed and advanced society in a multitude of ways. While the feminization of gay men appears to be a relatively progressive stance, Elam adds, "But of course, they did not do these things because they were gay. They did these things because they were *men*. Solving problems and making advances is what men do, and there is no evidence to suggest that gay men are any less proficient at it than straight men."[30] Elam then concludes the blog by stating that it is his hope that gay males will join the ranks of the MRM as men, not "gays."

A second example from the AVFM website features Dean Esmay's article, "Gays against Feminism: Because Gay People Are Not Your Property, Feminists."[31] This article contains many of the same general points that Elam provides, but it also includes language use that tells an important story. In the first paragraph, Esmay refers to himself as a "moralfag," telling readers to look it up.[32] The term refers to an individual expressing moral opinions, often in an inhospitable environment, and Esmay seems to be looking to reclaim the term as a positive label within the context of this article. Further on, Esmay provides an anecdote about "saving" a licentious gay male from a mob-style beating, taking him home and offering him shelter.[33] While the article calls for a welcoming of gay members and a call for individuals to become aware of the true dangers of feminism, it is also peppered with terms that are often perceived as offensive or derogatory—the words "fag" and "dyke" both appear more than once.

There are many more examples of blogs and discussion boards concerning these issues on the site, however, I believe that Elam and Esmay's pieces are fairly representative, thus, I will utilize these two posts as examples of the general stance presented on AVFM.[34] The first issue is the repeated insistence that the primary focus of identification for individuals is gender. Although AVFM seems willing to recognize diversity in experience, and so forth, to at least some extent, they repeatedly emphasize that the overriding source of suffering and oppression for men is gender identity. This insistence on prioritizing gender as a category of oppression, coupled with the subtle (and at times, not so subtle) references to hegemonic masculinity work to erase the intersectional nature of individual experiences of identity. Furthermore, both pieces reference hegemonic, monolithic masculinity in different ways. Elam directly claims that men are, by nature, innovators and cultural advancers, which is a direct reference to masculine gender essentialism. Esmay, on the other hand, helps himself to the stereotypical masculine identity of savior and tough-talking truth teller—a man so confident in his masculinity that he can refer to himself as a "moralfag," be hit on by a gay man (because gay men, it is implied, are overly sexual), and as a defender of "the gays" in all platforms without hesitation. He is, in fact, apparently so comfortable and welcomed in queer communities that he is welcome to reclaim and use traditionally derogatory slang. In either case, stereotypical forms of masculinity are upheld, the impact of sexual identity on gender identification is downplayed, and the essentialism of men is reinscribed by stating over and over that men can bond simply over the righteous hatred of feminism.

In spite of these direct addresses to gay men, sites like AVFM rely heavily on a heteronormative framework for understanding gender and men's alleged oppression at the hands of women. For instance, in the discussions of gynocentrism, various authors repeatedly point to the fact that this cultural norm arose as an entrenchment of the demands made on males in the name of courtly love and/or chivalry. Over and over, AVFM's authors discuss the ways in which misandrist women take advantage of men economically in the context of marital and romantic relationships. Consequently, it seems fairly clear that many of the contributors at AVFM see the problems men face as a direct result of heterosexual interactions, ranging from economics support, rape, domestic abuse, divorce, and custody. This reliance upon heteronormative frameworks then deeply impact concepts of gender, as suggested above.

Judith Butler argues that gender is a performative act, and that heterosexuality contributes to the naturalization of gender as essential, as well as the dichotomous division of gender roles. According to Butler, the compulsion to identify homosexual and queer identities as derivative or imitative of heterosexual identity works to construct heterosexuality as some form of naturally existing prior or original. However, the way in which heterosexuality constantly needs to assert its essential nature or reenact its ideals are evidence of the fact that heterosexuality itself is constantly in danger of being exposed as performative, constructed, and compromised. Butler argues, "That heterosexuality is always in the act of elaborating itself is evidence that it is perpetually at rise, that is, that it 'knows' its own possibility of becoming undone: hence, its compulsion to repeat which is at once a foreclosure of that which threatens its coherence."[35] Thus, heterosexuality becomes an incessant, panicked imitation that works to conceal its performative nature while asserting its central role in identification and sexuality.

Butler's analysis provides a compelling framework of interpretation in creating an analysis of arguments such as Esmay's and Elam's. First, the reliance upon hegemonic masculinity and masculinity as a basic and primary mode of identification works to naturalize and centralize the implicit heteronormative bias in such discussions. The dismissal of intersectionality in the name of masculinity erases the complexity of human standpoint, and reinforces masculine assumptions and stereotypes. Second, the primacy of heterosexual relations in the discussion of gynocentrism, and so on, is merely reworked in different terms when applied to the experiences of non-heterosexual males: if the issue is not a heterosexual relationship, then the issue is described in that same framework, with women capitalizing on men in specific ways (castrating, demanding, etc.). Finally, rhetoric such as Esmay's serves to cast non-heterosexual males in typically feminized roles—individuals in distress and in need of saving, hypersexualized, and so forth. This reflects Butler's claim that homosexual identities are often perceived as inversions of heterosexual identities.

Consequently, AVFM does not provide a significantly revolutionary or progressive platform for gay men. Rather, it represents restrictive modes of one-dimensional thought, relying upon existing forms of masculinity and heteronormative frames of social understanding. Heterosexual males such as Elam and Esmay arrogantly legislate what masculinity means, inform gay males about the "truth" of their experiences, hand wave the unique masculinity experienced by non-heterosexual males as inconsequential in the larger schemata of gender, and usurp the voices of non-heterosexual men in the promotion of their own interests. Once again, this does not promote transcendence or negative thought, but merely rewrites cultural dominance in allegedly progressive rhetoric. While the oppression of non-heterosexual males is not the intention, such essentialist rhetoric illustrates a devastating blind spot in the MRM conception of masculinity.

Race and Masculinity in the MRM

As in the case with homophobia, AVFM makes a pronounced effort to establish the fact that it is not racist, distancing itself from the explicitly racist rhetoric that can be found on sites like ROK. Much like the writing on gay men, the pieces on AVFM addressing race call for recognition of shared oppression amongst all men, often claiming that focusing on difference serves only to create divisions that further entrench racism. In order to make this point, writers on AVFM frequently attempt to create comparisons and analogies between the experiences of black and white males, arguing that while not always identical in nature, the oppression at its basis is the same. Thus, white and black males have suffered equally, and feminists and other progressives have worked to create victims out of black males in order to hide the true source of their suffering—misandry, gynocentrism, and the like. This argument generally involves a redefinition of racism, appeals to equality, and equivocations of experience.

Sage Gerard discusses the problem of racism in his post, "Dissecting the New American Racist," on the AVFM site.[36] According to Gerard, the new racism is disguised as anti-racist activism on the part of whites and blacks alike. The new white racist has black friends merely as status symbols, and patronizingly coddles black persons with politically correct speech and so forth. Gerard rejects the notion that black persons cannot be racist, arguing:

> When I hear a black person say that (s)he can't be racist because there is no systemic backing for black bigotry, then I take that as seriously as a drunk saying they can't actually be drunk until they get in a car. Drunks are still far more dangerous once they get behind the wheel, but to say that you can't be drunk *unless* you are behind the wheel?[37]

Thus, the new black racist manipulates terms such as "white privilege," in order to impose guilt on whites while apparently preventing any possibility of white persons understanding or relating to black experience. Gerard claims that accusations of privilege shame whites into submission, and those theories such as standpoint theory prevent genuine empathy, interaction, communication, and compassion. The solution, he suggests, is to dismiss the emphasis on difference and privilege, and focus on seeing one another as fundamentally human beings.

Other articles point out specific issues concerning men of color, such as Dre Morrell's post, "Black Men and Men's Rights: Where Do We Fit?"[38] According to Morrell, the MRM must recognize certain issues that impact men of color in order to become a working movement. However, while Morrell presents astute observations concerning the specific challenges men of color face, he frames the problem in terms of the same oppressive issues faced by all men impacting men of color more deeply or frequently. Once again, the foundational concept of essentialist masculinity coupled with the bogeywoman of feminism remains intact. Similarly, Walter Preysler in his post, "Why Black Men Need the MHRM and Not Feminism," further emphasizes these alleged connections, pointing out that issues like police shootings are *men's* issues that disproportionately impact black *men*.[39] Preysler argues that race movements have aligned themselves with feminism, creating victim mentalities for black males, and that black men must liberate themselves from this rhetoric through an alignment with the MRM. The overarching message of such posts is that men, at their base, are equal and the same, and that difference only creates divisions.

In the attempt to create a sense of unity with men of color, sites like AVFM frequently highlight allegedly "shared" experiences with black men. One experience that persistently comes up is the issue of slavery. Gerard points to this issue, claiming that the problem of white slavery in the colonial United States was a comparable issue to black slavery.[40] While he admits to difference in scope, Gerard points to indentured servitude as an example of how history has been distorted or ignored in order to further distance black and white persons in U.S. American society. Thus, according to Gerard, the example of white "slavery" is just as bad as black slavery, although less people were involved—a harm is a harm, regardless of scope. Consequently, black and white people must stop using slavery to indict one another, and recognize shared experiences.

Warren Farrell, a noted MRM, writes about slavery as a powerful analogy to gendered experiences in his work, *The Myth of Male Power*. Farrell argues that feminists have long referred to black slavery in the United States as a model for the oppression of women; however, he counters that both sexes enslave one another. He then provides a long list of experiences that he views as commonalities between black slaves and male experiences: slaves risked their lives in the field while men risk their lives in the draft/wars; both men and slaves share the experience of having their children taken from them; men, like slaves, are forced into hazardous jobs; slaves were subservient and men are subservient to women through politeness; both men and blacks are more likely to be homeless, end up in prison and experience an early death; men and blacks are both less likely to attend college.[41] Applying this to current gender conditions, Farrell reaches the following conclusion: "Among slaves, the field slave was considered the second-class slave; the house slave, the first-class slave. The male role (out in the field) is akin to the field slave—or the second-class slave; the traditional female roles (homemaker) is akin to the house slave—the first-class slave."[42] This argument allegedly accomplishes two things: first, to show that male and black experience have much in common; and second, to show that while the feminine role is not always desirable it is far better than what men experience.

The above arguments are littered with disturbing fallacies and rooted in what bell hooks terms "white supremacist thinking." Gerard's piece moves the locus of concern from the experiences of black U.S. Americans to the experiences of white (male) citizens. The narrative centers on white experiences of racism, from the fact that black individuals commit racism to the ways in which privilege accusations damage white psyches. Finally, the equivocation of black slavery to indentured servitude erases the experiences of black chattel slavery while upholding a theory that has repeatedly been used by racist white supremacist groups to dismiss "white guilt" or to deny the need for slavery reparations in the United States. This theory, or myth, of white slavery in the United States has been examined and identified as inaccurate revisionist history multiple times, but since it lines up with white supremacist narratives and the desire for everyone to "get over it," it persists in popular culture under the guise of factuality or truth.[43]

The comparisons or analogies arising in these arguments are also troubling. For instance, the analogy of being drunk and driving a car to racism seems strange at best—racist thinking and actions are significantly more complex than an alcohol-induced state, as are social institutions to driving. The simplistic nature of these comparisons demonstrates a one-dimensional, single-minded thinking about race and racism: that you are either racist or you are not, and anyone who reacts negatively to someone based upon racial identifications is a racist. Additionally, Farrell's discussion reflects a similar problem with simplistic comparison, although his comparisons are significantly more offensive and dismissive in terms of the realities of black slavery. Ignoring the details of suffering, torture, and exploitation involved in slavery, Farrell chooses to focus on extremely broad themes of harm in order to create a false sense of similarity between slaves and men. Notably, Farrell in no way sees himself as racist—quite the opposite. His view as a white heterosexual man of means allows him to insert himself into the center of any experience or narrative, shoe horning the experiences of blacks and black men into his own perceptions of exploitation and suffering. His inability to recognize this aspect of white supremacist thinking allows him to believe that he is not a racist, but merely a sympathetic observer of shared suffering between groups.

According to bell hooks, white supremacist thinking lies at the heart of U.S. American culture, shaping the way all of us think, perceive one another, perceive ourselves, and our concepts of reality. No one is immune to this sort of thinking—it impacts and shapes individuals of all races, although its impact varies with certain social positions. One aspect of white supremacist logic that contributes to its persistence in discourse and action is its fluidity; it can alter according to different circumstances or needs.[44] White supremacist thought can alter narrative about race and identification in line with the current needs or desires of the dominant social group. This type of thinking cannot be counteracted with simplistic models of diversity that merely call for an inclusion of more people of color without a radical alteration in thinking. Hooks explains that these models of diversity do not remove or alter white supremacist thought—the addition of difference does not alter what is at the center. She argues:

> Diversity could not and cannot have meaningful transformative significance in any world where white supremacy remains the underlying foundation of thought and practice. A huge majority of unenlightened white folks believe that the mere presence of "difference" will change the tenor of institutions. And while no one can deny the positive power of diverse representation, representation alone is simply not enough to create a climate supportive of sustained diversity.[45]

Thus, the MRM rhetoric above reflects white supremacist thinking in its arrogance—the assumption that these men can legislate and describe the experiences of men of color. This arrogance leaves white narratives and perspectives at the center of black experience, whether through the legislation of identity or the simplistic comparisons made to slavery, and so forth. Merely claiming to be inclusive or allowing black men to post on your site is not progressive diversity, and reflects a nonrevolutionary additive analysis of race relations.

Hooks also describes the problematic nature of "blame culture" and racism. In blame culture, individuals are more focused on and energized by practicing blame as opposed to transformation. She explains, "Our attachment to blaming, to identifying the oppressor stems from the fear that if we cannot unequivocally and absolutely state who the enemy is then we cannot know how to organize resistance or struggle."[46] This mode of dualistic thinking stems from what hooks terms as "dominator thinking," which separates people into dichotomous groups of good/bad, oppressor/oppressed, victim/victimizer. Dominator thinking creates a simplistic worldview, however, hooks argues that there is no straightforward way to identify oppressed and oppressors, and so forth. What is needed is accountability: "Accountability is a more expansive concept because it opens a field of possibility wherein we are all compelled to move beyond blame to see where our responsibility lies."[47] Accountability requires us to recognize interlocking systems of oppression, and such an interlocking system creates a level of indictment and responsibility for every member of a society—it becomes impossible for anyone to always identify as a victim, oppressed, and so on. Rather, it calls for mutual recognition, self-awareness, and a move toward partnership and mutuality as opposed to dualism and dominator thought patterns.[48]

The MRM discussions of race reflect the dualistic, dominator thought patterns that hooks describes. Instead of examining the complex ways in which contemporary culture positions gender and race in a way that implicates and impacts all individuals, the MRM chooses to identify a war of the sexes in which they are the hidden victims. The insistence upon maintaining a monolithic view of feminism combined with a refusal to engage in accountability with race relations nor recognize the impact of dominant voices or perspectives makes it impossible for the MRM to identify as a legitimate or progressive social movement. Mocking standpoint theory, dismissing critical race theory, maintaining myths of individualism, and calling for equality in unsophisticated, leveling terms allows individuals in the MRM to convince themselves of their progressiveness and ignore their own racism and homophobia by allowing privileged men and men informed by white supremacist thought to write and discuss without recognizing their own positions or accountability. Their status as oppressed within their dualistic thought patterns relieves these individuals of any responsibility, since they are not "intentionally" racist, homophobic, and so forth. This line of thought also impacts senses of diversity, allowing token black writers on AVFM to work as "evidence" of the fact that the site itself is in no way racist or engaging in white supremacist thought patterns. In conclusion, while AVFM is significantly better than the overtly racist rhetoric of a site like ROK, it is deeply problematic in its rhetoric and views on race, and should be criticized for its arrogance and unrecognized, unnamed dominance-laden rhetoric.

POLITICAL SPEECH AND TACTICS

The above sections demonstrate the problems in identifying the MRM as a progressive gender movement. Although at times highlighting troubling or harmful aspects of masculine gender codes, the MRM fails to evolve beyond one-dimensional thought, and does not create legitimate suggestions or theories of oppression that would contribute to the creation of new liberatory social codes. Some critics have noted that the MRM reflects what are often perceived as libertarian values—independence, freedom of speech, equality, and individualism. In response, MRM leaders such as Paul Elam have argued that the MRM does not reflect a unified political approach or party, although libertarian values are not antithetical to many of the MRM's spirit or goals.[49] Either way, the values that the MRM claims to support and uphold are the values informing many progressive movements, specifically in reference to the goals of free expression and equality. In this section, I will argue that in spite of an asserted support of freedom and equality, the MRM reflects oppressive one-dimensional thought due to its reliance upon these values in the context of democratic unfreedom, coupled with the MRM tactic of disengagement from direct modes of activism.

One of the most persistent ideals represented on MRM sites is the notion of equality. The source of much MRM ire is the perceived inequitable distribution of social benefits and burdens to men and women in society, combined with the (alleged) fact that men are shouldering significantly more of the burden. Countless articles point to men's draft requirements, overrepresentation in dangerous jobs, perceived obligation to sacrifice/pay for/protect women at all costs, and lack of respect/rights as fathers. Thus, the arguments tend to conclude with a discussion of why feminism, which claims to work in the interest of equality, repeatedly ignores these issues and contributes to the further oppression and disabuse of men everywhere. The mission statement of AVFM claims that equity must be achieved for both genders; in fact, it is time for the good of humanity as a whole and its accompanying needs to transcend the individual concerns and privileges attached to one gender or another. This reasoning leads Elam to claim that the MRM is actually an investment in humanism, simply defined as an individual who is concerned with the welfare of other humans.[50]

One result of this commitment to humanism is that AVFM refuses to align itself uniformly with any political party, political ideology, or religion. Thus, in some respects, AVFM can be difficult to characterize; however, the one principle that is uniformly upheld is a rejection of gynocentric culture. In this rejection of gynocentrism, authors appearing on AVFM often encourage men to recreate their own senses of self, and to leave behind culturally dominant narratives of masculinity to create new identities.[51] Images of self-reliant, independent, and freethinking men are common on AVFM, a reality that is promised by a rejection of gynocentrism and the oppressive limitations of feminism. Such rejection is expressed in a variety of ways, with some men going on "strike" against the alleged oppression of heterosexual marriage, with some men going as far as to avoid interactions with women all together. Men rejecting such relationships with women refer to themselves as "Men Going Their Own Way," or MGTOW.[52] This movement captures broader themes of rugged individualism, autonomy, and independence that regularly appear on MRM websites.

In addition to the values of equality and independence, MRM sites frequently discuss the importance of free speech, often arguing that free speech is in great peril due to the silencing forces of political correctness. Generally speaking, the MRM characterizes political correctness as dogmatism upheld by pressure to conform and policing of thought and action. Deviations from political correctness can cause an individual to be labeled a racist, sexist, homophobe, and so forth, a label that can kill careers or invalidate an individual's body of work.[53] Furthermore, individuals in the MRM emphasize that an obsession with political correctness leads to censorship and silencing, which directly contradicts liberal values of speech, expression, and freedom of thought. At the center of this silencing political correctness, according to the MRM, are feminists.

The claims of oppression through inequality combined with a perceived violation of individual rights to freedom of thought and expression obviously require some sort of reaction or intervention on the part of the MRM. Elam argues that the first step to self-healing for men is to change the cultural narrative informing their senses of self. In order to do this, one must become aware of gynocentrism, extract its supposedly toxic impact on internal narratives and identity, and then create a new independent sense of self, based upon life affirming and individualistic principles.[54] Moving beyond individual senses of self, Elam then explains that the MRM (as he sees it) is not attempting to break into mainstream culture or to change the currently existing system; rather, the MRM is working to provide a counterculture. Elam explains:

> We are not changing the mainstream by changing law or customs, though, as with all countercultures before, those things will happen. We are changing the mainstream by changing ourselves, by openly ridiculing their foolhardy ways, and by simply providing a place to exist for the countless victims they have created with their raw stupidity. All we have to do to grow is to *be*. These mindless fools will do the rest for us.[55]

Elam states over and over that lobbying and legal intervention is not the purpose of AVFM. The purpose is to change the cultural narrative. Elam believes that this change will occur via the MRM doggedly exposing the lies of feminism, a practice encapsulated by the "fuck their shit up" or FTSU method. One particularly notable aspect of this method was the "register-her" site, which was claimed to be a registry of female criminals.[56] The crimes in question were false rape accusations, child abuse, and domestic violence, just to name a few. The site regularly posted pictures of such "criminals" along with personal information, including telephone numbers and addresses. The original site was taken down in 2014, but there were plans to replace it and no recanting of that particular aspect of the FTSU methodology.

The problem with the MRM as expressed through AVFM is the fact that while it recognizes legitimate issues in masculinity and the toxicity of masculine gender codes while supporting liberatory core values, the source of these issues is deeply misidentified. The obsessive targeting of feminism as the sole or main source of all men's supposed suffering positions the MRM as a symptom of backlash more than as a progressive liberation movement. As Marcuse points out, real social change requires negative thinking, while one-dimensional thought fails to recognize the degree of oppression an individual in a given society experiences. While the MRM claims to engage in negative thinking through its revelations concerning the "truth" about feminism, it actually fails to see the complex sources of men's experiences of harm and privilege—gender, race, class, capitalist exploitation, and globalization, just to name a few.

Furthermore, Marcuse points out the ways in which liberatory concepts or ideals can be co-opted in the name of oppressive movements. In his essay, "Repressive Tolerance,"[57] Marcuse argues that concepts such as tolerance have come under the service of one-dimensional thinking in certain contexts. According to Marcuse, a repressive society can cause progressive movements to turn oppressive when they rely upon political rights that, ideally, are progressive and liberatory, but when used to strengthen political administration become limiting and reinforcing servitude. Relating this to the concept of democratic unfreedom, the problem is that true freedom cannot be found in the freedom to choose between administratively determined and limited options. For example, voting is a democratic free choice, but when voting is limited to choosing between pre-determined, power laden, administrative elites, that choice is not one of true self-determining freedom. However, the existence of "choice" creates the illusion of freedom in the context of deep unfreedom.

The example of tolerance in terms of one-dimensional thought and democratic unfreedom is particularly compelling. Marcuse argues that in a completely liberated and truly equal society, universal tolerance can be practiced as an end in itself; however, if such idealistic conditions do not prevail, the nature of tolerance is weighed down and directed by institutional inequalities. Thus, oppressed groups must tolerate the practices of repressive and/or administrative forces in a given society, which further oppressive conditions under the guise of the liberatory ideal. The practice of tolerance then takes on two general forms: (1) passive tolerance of damaging established attitudes, and (2) the tolerance of both liberatory and aggressive, damaging political movements. Tolerance can become destructive when it is indiscriminately equal in its expression and application. Because the telos or purpose of tolerance is the finding of the truth, indiscriminate tolerance that curtails the truth and allows for the promotion of damaging untruths has no progressive or liberatory value.

Because the MRM refuses to acknowledge the complexity of repressive society by focusing solely on feminism and refusing to recognize the impact of capitalism and administration on individuals, it ultimately fails to recognize legitimate contradictions in current cultural contexts and social rule. The values it claims to seek will continue to promote democratic unfreedom without the use of genuine negative thinking. It creates false dichotomies of choice: recognize the lies of feminism or live a lie; reject women and marriage or continue to be a "slave;" call feminism out as brutally as possible or continue to suffer its consequences. In each case, the MRM presents its followers with a freedom in choice, but the choices are distressingly limited and destructive. By placing women and feminism firmly in the enemy camp, the MRM destroys the opportunity for the genuine communal bonds needed for liberation. Furthermore, by not questioning capitalism or other structures, the MRM creates a limited set of anti-feminist choices within a set of choices already deeply limited by the administrative forces of white supremacist capitalist patriarchy (to borrow a term from hooks).

The promotion of the liberal values of individuality, free speech, and equality by the MRM is vulnerable to the criticisms Marcuse levels against tolerance. Without a truly non-repressive, non-authoritarian society, the indiscriminate use of these concepts contributes to existing oppressive structures, giving momentum to a deeply problematic and misogynist movement. The call for tolerance and even a respect for aggressive, sexist, and even violent speech from men in the MRM under the guise of anticensorship politics works to neutralize the progressive potential of free expression and tolerance itself. It warps the call for tolerance into a politicized demand for a lack of criticism concerning repressive rhetoric—in other words, the MRM is adept at taking the progressive left's values and methods and turning these against them. Additionally, the constant demands for a leveling form of equality ignore the ways in which distributions of benefits and burdens in a given society work across complex and interacting social structures. Like tolerance, indiscriminate equality only makes liberatory sense if individuals are outside of repressive society completely. The uncritical adoption of this construct allows for the MRM to perpetuate a narrative of deprivation and harm that works to reinforce the villainizing of feminism to undermine its gains and demands. For example, the consistent complaint that men are overwhelmingly put into dangerous jobs is based on a simplistic notion of equality. It conveniently ignores the analogous occurrence of "pink collar" work for women, and the ways in which gender creates limiting and oppressive work choices within a system of overall capitalist exploitation. In fact, the issue of low pay and exploitation as a result of capitalism is ignored all together, focusing only on a bafflingly simplistic call for "equality."

The so-called rejection of society by movements such as MGTOW is also not progressive or liberatory. In *An Essay on Liberation*, Marcuse discusses the nature of what he terms the "Great Refusal" of the student protests of the 1960s. According to Marcuse, such a refusal rejects multiple aspects of repressive society, embracing life instincts over aggression. Subjectivity will change if this refusal systems of dominance are displaced and replaced with liberatory understandings of self and others. While in some respects this seems to echo the goals of the MRM and specifically MGTOW—the desire to create one's own sense of individual self through the rejection of certain social systems and norms. However, the problem with the refusals of the MRM and MGTOW is that the refusal can hardly be characterized as "great"—the refusal is limited to rejecting women and feminism. This narrow conception of focus fails to adequately identify the nature of dominance and repression, creating a straw man of feminism as a target of anger and frustration. Furthermore, the refusal to engage in other political struggles, to address social issues, and the promotion of aggressive language and strategies further demonstrates the fact that the MRM is not a progressive movement. It's an isolated, narrowly focused, misdirected source of rhetoric that fails to create a promising, radical reconceptualization of masculine gender. Rather, it simply seems to repeatedly request an upholding of traditional masculinity without the incoming guilt or hassle from feminism.

CONCLUSION

This chapter attempts to provide a reading of the MRM as a political movement. It is certainly true that the MRM gets some things right—there are plaguing issues concerning masculinity, men are harmed by current models of gender, and sometimes feminism is irresponsible. However, what it does with these insights is where the trouble begins. Instead of engaging with the wider culture, questioning the multiple and complex forces that distribute social goods and create cultural identities, it chooses to focus solely on feminism and its alleged "damage" to men. Such singular focus combined with its lack of scope causes this movement to collapse into a deeply conservative and generally misogynist conglomeration of blog writers and angry online interactions. However, I also argue that we cannot simply hand-wave the MRM away as simple backlash. Its use of indiscriminately applied liberal values such as equality and freedom of expression are not unique to the MRM, but rather resemble distressing cultural trends in political rhetoric. Furthermore, its frustration with feminism and resistance to progressive movements is also not unique. While the MRM is certainly not a progressive or political movement, it does symbolize an important movement for men and masculinity in the twenty-first century, reflecting the stress, resentment, and sense of loss men have experienced in the face of social change. As old social promises and roles fade away, some men feel lost in a world that feels hostile. The solution is not to ignore or dismiss this sense of loss and anger, but to critically reevaluate gender and masculinity in a way that values life-affirming forces and liberatory potential.

NOTES

1. Herbert Marcuse, *Eros and Civilization* (Boston: Beacon Press, 1955), 35.
2. Marcuse, *Eros and Civilization*, 45.
3. Herbert Marcuse, *One Dimensional Man: Studies in the Ideology of Advanced Industrial Society* (Boston: Beacon Press, 1964), 12.
4. Marcuse, *One Dimensional Man*, 98.
5. Marcuse, *One Dimensional Man*, 32.
6. Marcuse, *One Dimensional Man*, 11.
7. "About Gynocentrism," last modified July 14, 2013, https://gynocentrism.com/2013/07/14/about/.

8. Adam Kostakis, "Gynocentrism Theory Lecture Series: Pig Latin," last modified May 24, 2014, https://gynocentrism.com/2014/05/24/pig-latin/.

9. Adam Kostakis, "Gynocentrism Theory Lecture Series: Chasing Rainbows," last modified May 24, 2014, https://gynocentrism.com/2014/05/24/chasing-rainbows/.

10. Adam Kostakis, "Gynocentrism Theory Lecture Series: The Eventual Outcome of Feminism, Part II," last modified May 24, 2014, https://gynocentrism.com/2014/05/25/the-eventual-outcome-of-feminism-part-ii/.

11. Overview of AVFM mission: Paul Elam, "Preparing for the Next Conquest," last modified July 30, 2015, http://www.avoiceformen.com/a-voice-for-men/preparing-for-the-next-conquest/. Discussion of engagement with wider culture: Paul Elam, "Counterculture," last modified October 22, 2013, http://www.avoiceformen.com/mens-rights/counterculture/.

12. Ray Barry, "The Facts About Men and Boys," last accessed November 14, 2016, http://www.avoiceformen.com/the-facts-about-men-and-boys/.

13. Paul Elam, "Welcome to AVFM," last modified June 5, 2014, http://www.avoiceformen.com/a-voice-for-men/welcome-to-avfm/.

14. Kostakis, "Chasing Rainbows," https://gynocentrism.com/2014/05/24/chasing-rainbows/.

15. Adam Kostakis, "Gynocentrism Theory Lecture Series: Old Wine, New Bottles," last modified May 24, 2014, https://gynocentrism.com/2014/05/24/old-wine-new-bottles/.

16. "About Gynocentrism," https://gynocentrism.com.

17. Dean Esmay, "Breaking the Pendulum: Tradcons vs. Feminists," last modified March 26, 2014, http://www.avoiceformen.com/gynocentrism/breaking-the-pendulum-tradcons-vs-feminists/.

18. Peter Wright, "Damseling, Chivalry, and Courtly Love," last modified July 17, 2016, http://www.avoiceformen.com/feminism/damseling-chivalry-and-courtly-love-part-two/.

19. "Defending Freedom with Bricks of Logic," last modified September 28, 2013, http://www.avoiceformen.com/updates/news-updates/defending-freedom-with-bricks-of-logic/.

20. Adam Kostakis, "Gynocentrism Theory Lecture Series: False Consciousness & Kafka Trapping," last modified May 24, 2014, https://gynocentrism.com/2014/05/25/false-consciousness-kafka-trapping/.

21. Susan Bordo, *Unbearable Weight: Feminism, Western Culture and the Body* (Berkeley: University of California Press, 1995), 161.

22. bell hooks, *Feminist Theory: From Margin to Center* (Cambridge: South End Press, 1984), 35.

23. Elizabeth Spelman, *Inessential Woman: Problems of Exclusion in Feminist Thought* (Boston: Beacon Press, 1988), 125.

24. Spelman, *Inessential Woman*, 114.

25. Spelman, *Inessential Woman*, 9.

26. Spelman, *Inessential Woman*, 139.

27. Spelman, *Inessential Woman*, 11–13.

28. Spelman, *Inessential Woman*, 125.

29. Paul Elam, "The Problem with Gay Rights," last modified September 1, 2010, http://www.avoiceformen.com/mens-rights/the-problem-with-gay-rights/.

30. Elam, "The Problem with Gay Rights," http://www.avoiceformen.com/mens-rights/the-problem-with-gay-rights/.

31. Dean Esmay, "Gays against Feminism: Because Gay People Are Not Your Property, Feminists," last modified June 26, 2015, http://www.avoiceformen.com/feminism/gays-against-feminism-because-gay-people-are-not-your-property-feminists/.

32. "moralfag," last modified July 28, 2016, https://en.wiktionary.org/wiki/moralfag.

33. Conveniently, Esmay claims not to know the name or location of this man, claiming to be a sort of Good Samaritan.

34. Other such articles include a four part series on gay men and feminism: "Why Gay Men Don't Need Feminism: Part One, Challenging Assumptions," last modified July 13, 2015, http://www.avoiceformen.com/feminism/why-gay-men-dont-need-feminism-part-1-challenging-assumptions/.

35. Judith Butler, "Imitation and Gender Insubordination," in *The Lesbian and Gay Studies Reader*, ed. Abelove, Barale, and Halperin (New York: Routledge 1993), 314.
36. Sage Gerard, "Dissecting the New American Racist," last modified December, 28, 2015, http://www.avoiceformen.com/featured/dissecting-the-new-american-racist/.
37. Gerard, "Dissecting the New American Racist," http://www.avoiceformen.com/featured/dissecting-the-new-american-racist/.
38. Dre Morrell, "Black Men and Men's Rights: Where Do We Fit?" last updated June 16, 2015, http://www.avoiceformen.com/art-entertainment-culture/black-men-and-mens-rights-where-do-we-fit/.
39. Walter Preysler, "Why Black Men Need the MHRM and Not Feminism," last modified February 19, 2016, http://www.avoiceformen.com/mens-rights/why-black-men-need-the-mhrm-and-not-feminism/.
40. Gerard, "Dissecting the New American Racist," http://www.avoiceformen.com/featured/dissecting-the-new-american-racist/.
41. Warren Farrell, *The Myth of Male Power: Why Men Are the Disposable Sex* (New York: Simon and Schuster, 1993), Kindle edition, 842–844.
42. Farrell, *Myth of Male Power*, 867.
43. For more information, refer to: Alex Amend, "How the Myth of 'Irish Slaves' Became a Favorite Meme of Racists Online," last modified April 19, 2016, https://www.splcenter.org/hatewatch/2016/04/19/how-myth-irish-slaves-became-favorite-meme-racists-online.
44. bell hooks, *Writing Beyond Race: Living Theory and Practice* (New York: Routledge, 2013), 5.
45. hooks, *Writing Beyond Race*, 27.
46. hooks, *Writing Beyond Race*, 29.
47. hooks, *Writing Beyond Race*, 30.
48. hooks, *Writing Beyond Race*, 37.
49. Dean Esmay, "Is Libertarianism the Undercurrent of the MHRM?" last modified August 18, 2014, http://www.avoiceformen.com/mens-rights/is-libertarianism-the-undercurrent-of-the-mhrm-politics-mra/.
50. The mission statement links the following definition of humanism: "Humanist," last modified August 20, 2014, https://reference.avoiceformen.com/wiki/Humanist.
51. "Authoring Your Own Life," last modified May 31, 2015, http://www.avoiceformen.com/men/mens-issues/authoring-your-own-life/.
52. "Men Going Their Own Way," last modified November 14, 2016, https://en.wikipedia.org/wiki/Men_Going_Their_Own_Way.
53. B. J. Gallagher, "The Problem of Political Correctness," last modified February 25, 2015, http://www.huffingtonpost.com/bj-gallagher/the-problem-political-correctness_b_2746663.html.
54. "Authoring Your Own Life," http://www.avoiceformen.com/men/mens-issues/authoring-your-own-life/.
55. Elam, "Counterculture," http://www.avoiceformen.com/mens-rights/counterculture/.
56. Dave Futrell, "Register Her Was a Fake 'Offenders Registry' Run by Misogynists, Designed to Vilify and Intimidate Women," last modified December 17, 2016, https://manboobz.com/2012/12/17/register-her-is-a-fake-offenders-registry-run-by-misogynists-designed-to-vilify-and-intimidate-women/.
57. Herbert Marcuse, "Repressive Tolerance," in *A Critique of Pure Tolerance* (Boston: Beacon Press, 1969).

Chapter Four

Oppression, Harm, and Masculinity

The MRM does not merely argue that men experience harms due to gender constructs or feminism. Rather, they claim that men experience systemic oppression as a result of their gender identity, and that this oppression is both furthered and maintained by feminists. Notably, the MRM does not refer to intersectional masculine identity in its discussions, but promotes the notion that men experience oppression on some level as an entire group based solely upon the fact that they are men. It is this shared oppression that MRAs claim bond men together in the fight against infringements against men's rights in a given culture. The charge of oppression must be addressed on several levels. First, a basic understanding of social groups, including social institutions, must be established in order to determine whether or not oppression is occurring. Next, oppression must be clearly distinguished from other types of harm, and the social relations involved, including but not limited to, power, must be highlighted. Finally, the multiple aspects of power must be demonstrated, and the interactions between distributive and psychological oppression clarified. This chapter will attempt to create a philosophical framework to address these issues, thereby establishing a theoretical system for testing the extent, legitimacy, and nature of the harms/oppression the MRM claim regularly impact men's lives.

GROUP IDENTITY

One of the necessary conditions of oppression is the existence of social groups. Philosophers and other social theorists have emphasized the fact that oppression is not an individualized phenomenon; rather, oppression is a social injustice that creates harms to voluntary and involuntary social groups.[1] Thus, in order to understand and evaluate the claim that men are oppressed qua men in a given society, men must constitute a legitimate social group. Furthermore, the oppressive harm to men must benefit some other social group(s) in a society, namely women and/or feminists according to MRM arguments. This section will discuss the nature of social groups, as well as the ways in which social groups interact within a culture along the lines of power and social organization.

Sociological definitions of social groups emphasize that members of such groups must recognize themselves as members of a distinct social unit, and such recognition often results in identification and attachment between members. However, the basis of such unit formation can vary widely within cultures. For instance, families, political parties, clubs, and the like, can all be the basis of social groups. Thus, the mere creation of or identification with a social group does not necessarily entail the conditions for oppression or power-laden interactions. The question then becomes, what kind of social groups are involved in social power relations and oppressive interactions? Clearly, who is oppressed and who is in power changes over time, thus the specific identities of groups need not be sufficient for oppressive situations. Rather, the issue of interest is the type of groups that become involved in such power-driven interactions.

Iris Young offers a compelling account of social groups that culturally operate in terms of power and oppression. Young argues that social groups are not simply collectivities or aggregates of individuals. Rather, social groups differentiate themselves from other groups via cultural practices and lifestyles, and this differentiation impacts the ways in which such groups interact with other social groups.[2] This definition helps avoid certain arbitrary social groupings that may have little to no impact on one's life style or core identity. The cultural importance of social groups, according to Young, is the fact that a social group provides individuals with a sense of self. She argues:

> A social group is defined not primarily by a set of shared attributes, but by a sense of identity. . . . Though sometimes objective attributes are a necessary condition for classifying oneself or others as belonging to a certain social group, it is identification with a certain social status, the common history that social status produces, and the self-identification that define the group as a social group.[3]

Thus, the self emerges from (at least in some part) from a relational group identity, a notion that challenges the atomistic concepts of self often found in classic liberalism and distributive theories of justice. This view of identity is compelling because, while individuals have unique qualities and perspectives, social group membership deeply impacts an individual's understanding of the world and the way in which that individual interacts with others in that world.[4]

Young further points out that in many ways we experience a sense of "throwness" in regards to our identification with a given social group. In other words, we emerge into a world in which social groups already exist, and the norms, identities, and so on, governing such social groups are established prior to any individual's existence. The concept of being thrown into a world not of one's choosing does not imply that group membership is always nonvoluntary. In fact, many social groups are voluntary, and identification with a given group may alter with shifts in individual identity.[5] One prominent example of voluntary group membership is adult choices in religious affiliation, and these affiliations may change over time. This is not to say that voluntary social groups do not deeply impact individual identity, but there is a greater sense of agency in terms of identity creation within these contexts. However, the issue of throwness persists in these groups as well, due to the fact that, while there is some sense of choice present, the choices are established prior to the individual and beyond direct control.

Nonvoluntary social groups also have some unique properties, and these types of social groups are particularly relevant because sex/gender is often considered to be the basis of culturally important nonvoluntary social groups. Ann Cudd elaborates on the nature of such groups, arguing:

> Membership in a nonvoluntary social group is socially not individually determined. . . . Social groups are formed not by the intentions of the individuals in them to join together and shape a particular project, but by the actions, beliefs and attitudes of others, both in the group and out, that constrain their choices in patterned and socially significant ways.[6]

In other words, membership in a nonvoluntary group seems to amplify the sense of "throwness" that Young describes. This description serves to emphasize the relational aspects of identity, pointing to the ways in which other persons mediate, shape, and contribute to individual senses of self. Notably, Cudd points out that individuals in such groups need not recognize membership in the group in order to be a member of it. For instance, individuals may live in denial, or reconceptualize various experiences that impact the group as lying in individual faults or failures.[7] On the other hand, individuals in such nonvoluntary groups may embrace the identity, gaining a sense of self-worth, identity, and/or solidarity with others through the recognition of this social membership.

Identifying gender as a social group has been a notoriously difficult task. In some respects, the identification of gender as a nonvoluntary social group seems straightforward—the division of the world in to "male" and "female" is a basic and pervasive social categorization. Nonetheless, gender has been (rightly) deeply contested, criticized and questioned in contemporary feminist theory, exposing binary and essentialist models of gender to extremely damaging criticism. The way in which feminists and other scholars have approached gender is to problematize the concept, challenge its foundations, and to suggest that gender must minimally be understood as a culturally informed, intersectional, fluid, and fractured concept of identity. In other words, it is commonly accepted that one's gender identity is highly mediated and informed by other aspects of identity, including race, class, sexual orientation, ethnicity, and so forth. Further, if gender is in fact a cultural construct, it seems as though certain aspects of gender are not "real," and may in fact be performative. This then entails that gender cannot be understood as two poles of identification, but rather as a constantly changing and evolving set of cultural rules distributing individuals along a complex spectrum.

These challenges to normative gender reject gender essentialism, gender binaries, and universal experiences of gender regardless of race, ethnicity, class, sexual identity, and other social groupings. Thus, the question becomes how we can talk about "women" and "men" coherently in the context of oppression and social identity. While it is clearly the case that such categories are deeply troubled and fractured, there is also some sense in which we know what one "means" when they refer to such categories. The reference, I argue, is to hegemonic concepts/constructs of gendered identity that order individuals across binary heteronormative frameworks. In other words, even if gender is a fiction or social construction, there are still agreed upon rules and identifiers that mark gendered identity and performance in a given culture. There are, then, widely spread and deeply entrenched norms concerning gender that individuals are shaped by and respond to in the creation of an intelligible gender identity. Consequently, within current gender frameworks there are sets of behaviors, preferences, appearances, bodily markers, and so forth, that carve out the general concept of "masculinity" for male identified individuals within this construct. While this concept may be hopelessly inadequate for addressing the gendered experiences of individuals falling under its umbrella, the term is coherent, pervasive, and constitutive of identity.

Marilyn Frye addresses the challenges of identity politics when it seems like social identities like gender fail to reflect universal truths or experiences. In other words, if we are talking about "men" or "women," how can such categories make sense as unifiers if the individuals in these categories vary so greatly in terms of identity, experience, and perceptions of oppression? Frye argues that feminists must search for patterns, explaining, "Our experience has been one of discovering, recognizing, and creating patterns—patterns within which experience made a new kind of sense, or in many instances, no sense at all . . . pattern recognition and construction open fields of meaning and generate new interpretive possibilities."[8] Hence, patterns within a social group need not be reductive, universal, or as Frye puts it, totalitarian. Rather, the existence of the pattern gives us insight to both individuals who fit the pattern and those who do not. The patterns or norms are generalities that impact our interactions and understandings of others and ourselves. Fry encourages feminists to think of patterns like metaphors, providing frameworks for the creation of meaning while also containing limits.[9] The image of a pattern then impacts the way a group might conceive oppression. Frye argues that discovering patterns of norms and oppression create an epistemic community based upon a common but not homogenous oppression.[10]

Taking comprehensive stock of the philosophical insights presented in this section allows for a clear sense of "men" as a social group. It seems obvious that "male" is a coherent nonvoluntary social group presenting both biological and social criteria for successful membership. While the biological/anatomical criteria are at the base of the category, the social aspects that impact and shape identity are significantly complex and central to identity formation. Individual males may well reject certain aspects of this identity and can embrace others, experiencing both stress and affirmation from the internalization and identification with certain masculine norms. Because men vary deeply in experiences and relationship to various norms and demands related to this identity, one can easily search for the patterns Frye describes in her piece in order to establish certain commonalities (but not homogeneity) within the group.

If men qualify as a social group under the criteria and discussion provided here, there is no clear objection to the MRM assertion that men make up an important social group culturally, and that this group shares certain patterns of experience, pressure, and difficulty. What is controversial is how we can come to identify these patterns of experience—are the difficulties this social group engages with oppression? Is it possible for men to be oppressed only on the basis of gender? What would such an experience look like? In order to work toward such answers, the following section will provide an explanation of power, identity, and coercion in terms of gender that will provide a more detailed picture of what forces impact and shape the masculine standpoint.

SOCIAL GROUPS AND POWER

Oppression is something that occurs between social groups, creating unjust burdens on one group for the benefit of another. The nature of this injustice can function in terms of distribution of social goods, psychological harm, or some complex overlapping of the two. These issues will be examined in detail later in the chapter. However, if oppression impacts the relationship between groups in the interest of creating unjust disparities, then the relationship at work in such instances must be one concerning power. However, the concept of power is far from simplistic. While liberal theories engaging with oppression frame power as a resource an individual or group of individuals have or can wield over others, contemporary authors such as Michel Foucault challenge this conception of power as something one can have or as something that merely constrains or limits. Rather, Foucault argues that power is a type of relation, involving complex interactions between individuals, institutions, and cultural constructs. Due to its ability to capture this complexity, I will be defending the Foucaultian concept of power, and explicating its impact on oppression in general, and relating it to the concept of power utilized in MRM discourse.

Young argues that models of power that are distributive, namely, those models that treat power as an object possessed by individuals, are deeply flawed. To make this point, she establishes five points concerning power in the context of social groups cultural institutions. First, Young rejects the notion of power as an object that can be possessed in favor of an understanding of power as a relation. Second, Young claims that distributive models of power treat power as a transaction between individuals as opposed to a complex interaction involving various individuals, groups, institutions and social forces. Third, Young argues that the distributive model of power treats power as a static pattern when power is actually a dynamic interaction that is inherently active. Finally, Young explains that distributive models of power portray power as being the possession of a select few when power is something that is diffused and dispersed widely throughout a society.[11]

Framing power as an active relation that is diffused throughout a given society reflects the Foucaultian influence on Young's theory. She explains that we must go beyond sovereignty or simplistic exchanges of power in a given society, analyzing instead allegedly liberal and humane practices found in institutions such as education, medicine, punishment, and so forth.[12] According to Foucault, "Power is not an institution, and not a structure; neither is it a certain strength we are endowed with; it is the name that one attributes to a complex strategical relationship in a particular society."[13] Consequently, power creates asymmetrical relationships within a given context, and these relationships allow for an analysis of power's movement. For Foucault, power is multidirectional and productive, thus, power is invested in and impacts all individuals and relationships within a culture, creating various forms of knowledge and identities.

Hence, power as fundamentally productive creates not just reality and knowledge, but subjects as well. To become a subject, one must be subjected to power relations that shape the individual into an intelligible and docile subject. In *Discipline and Punish*, Foucault describes disciplinary power as a modern form of power generally concerned with the individual fulfillment of certain standards. Using the prison as a model, Foucault discusses the various ways in which surveillance and correction discipline individuals into docile bodies that are not only subject to but reflect the law itself. In the internalization of the law, individual subjects incorporate the law into their bodies through the correction of so-called deviant behavior. Consequently, individual bodies become the actual signification of the law through the inscription of the law onto the body through disciplinary mechanisms, namely hierarchical observation, normalizing judgment, and the examination.

However, as Foucault discusses in *The History of Sexuality*, individuals are not controlled merely as objects of discipline but as self-scrutinizing, self-policing subjects. In other words, becoming a subject necessarily involves emerging through and being subjected to power relations. Judith Butler takes up this theory of subject formation, arguing juridical power produces what it claims only to represent, thus politics must concern itself with both the juridical and productive aspects of power. She explains, "Foucault points out that the juridical systems of power *produce* the subjects they subsequently come to represent . . . subjects regulated by such structures are, by virtue of being subjected to them, formed, defined, and reproduced in accordance with the requirements of those structures."[14] Applying this to the problem of gender, Butler claims that persons only become intelligible by conforming to recognized gender standards. Foucault points out that the truth of sex is produced through regulatory practices contributing to the creation of coherent identity; thus, sex is an artificial concept extending and disguising power relations.[15] In line with this, Butler claims that the demands of gender (among other socially constructed norms) create normative structures that function not only to discipline the subject and elicit intelligible behavior, but also critically function in the creation of consciousness and subjectivity. Consequently, no subject exists in a vacuum—all individuals in a given society are produced in great part by normative expectations concerning identity, and these normative structures are so pervasive that they take on the appearance of universal, innate, and/or natural aspects of one's socially determined group identity.

Power, then, is a complex and multiple manifested strategy or relationship functioning within society to attain certain levels of control through disciplinary methods and the creation of socially intelligible, self-normalizing subjects. This understanding of power also adequately captures the previous definitions of oppression outlined in this chapter. First, the Foucaultian concept of power can account for distributive disparities while also looking toward the institutional and cultural contexts operating within the creation of such inequalities. Further, this model of power addresses the complex interactions between groups, individuals, political/legal/social institutions, normative standards, and so forth, in a given community that creates the conditions for certain unjust deprivations for groups of individuals. Finally, the emphasis on power in the creation of subjects can be used to analyze psychological oppression as well as the importance and function of norms in the creation of social groups, and the resulting impact those group identities have on individual subject formation.

This model of power in the context of oppressive cultural interactions does not suggest a simplistic relationship between two groups where one side has all the power and one side does not. On the contrary, this model of oppression recognizes the importance of power and the related role of domination in power, while avoiding identifying oppression as simply the domination of one group over another. Hubert Dreyfus and Paul Rabinow summarize Foucault's conception of dominance, explaining, "Dominance, then, is not the essence of power . . . power is exercised upon the dominant as well as on the dominated; there is a process of self-formation and autocolonization involved."[16] Certainly one cannot argue that dominance does not occur in power relations—Foucault does not deny that certain individuals/groups in given context wield greater advantage and privilege. Rather, the point is that all groups are enmeshed in matrices of power, meaning that all individuals are involved in some way in power relations.

Consequently, the act of claiming gender oppression need not involve an argument demonstrating the complete domination of one gender by another. Rather, one must show that gendered individuals are subjected to normative influences that impacts subjects in various ways—socially, politically, culturally, and psychologically. If these norms create advantages for one gender over another, creating observable patterns of unjust deprivations and damaging psychological concepts, then there is a case for establishing oppression. This suggests that simplistic complaints concerning distribution or arguments involving "victim" competitions will not be adequate to establish the presence of oppression. Thus, if the MRM is to establish the oppression of men, they must do more than state that not all men are guilty of misogyny and so forth, or that women really run the world and men must sit and suffer.

MODELS OF OPPRESSION

The problem of oppression for social and political philosophy is historically prominent, and is an issue that philosophers have been engaging with far before the advent of feminist philosophy or philosophy of race (just to name a few). Oppression became an issue of interest in philosophy with the emergence of liberalism and the ensuing notions of individualism and equality. This trend is particularly notable in the modern era, focusing on oppression as the illegitimate imposition of unjust laws on citizens by the government. While this was certainly an important concern in various historical contexts, social movements in the 1960s and 1970s shifted this definition from an injustice imposed by tyrannical power to one imposed by the everyday practices of a liberal society—in other words, oppression is structural as opposed to being the result of a few people's actions or policies.[17] Consequently, the view of oppression as structural indicates the importance of examining the practices and institutions of society as a whole, as opposed to focusing on a narrow scope of practices and individuals. The structural concept of oppression also integrates the model of power defended in the previous section.

Ann Cudd presents a concise definition of oppression, stating, "As I will use the term, 'oppression' names a harm through which groups of persons are systematically and unfairly and unjustly constrained, burdened or reduced by any of several forces."[18] For Cudd, oppression is a normative term implying a moral wrong that can never be justified. She further points out that oppression is systematic in the sense that it starts in one sphere, namely economic, political, or legal contexts, and comes to permeate the consciousness of oppressors and oppressed alike.[19] Cudd's emphasis on both institutions and psychology highlight an important aspect of oppression, namely its dual yet intertwined mechanisms impacting distribution and consciousness. This distinction leads Cudd to make a variety of important distinctions concerning the nature of oppression, including objective and subjective facts of oppression, as well as direct and indirect forces of oppression. Objective oppression consists in the facts of one's oppression while subjective oppression concerns one's feeling of oppression, which may or may not be accurate.[20] In each case, the importance of social realities and facts combine with a form of oppressive phenomenology to create a complete picture concerning the reach and impact of oppression on groups and individuals.

Beginning with distribution, Young argues that various distributive paradigms of justice utilize a single model referring to justice in terms of an equitable distribution of goods between individuals. Such a model implies that individuals are to be understood atomistically, with little attention paid to internal relations among people.[21] However, if oppression is a culturally complex phenomenon, such an explanation of oppression will be inadequate in the following ways: the distributive paradigm presupposes and ignores institutional contexts, and the distributive paradigm tends to overextend itself, namely in terms of nonmaterial goods and resources.[22] While Young points out that distribution is an important issue in a culture exhibiting vast differences in material goods, she also argues that many issues or appeals to justice do not feature distribution as a primary concern. Consequently, focusing solely on distribution inappropriately restricts the scope of justice, obscuring questions concerning decision-making structures, division of labor, and culture.[23] The second objection concerning overextension refers to the seeming ability of distributive paradigms to accommodate any justice issue. However, Young points out that the distributive model fails to recognize its own limits, namely the inability to extend the logic of distribution to certain social goods that are not material or measurable.[24] Examples of such goods include rights, self-respect, and opportunity.

Young's discussion of distribution demonstrates that while distribution is certainly an important aspect of justice and element of oppression, it is not the sole or necessarily even the primary point of interest. Rather, distribution of goods happens within a wide social context constructed by various social relationships, subjects, norms, institutions, and workings of power. Thus, Young offers the following definition of oppression: "Oppression consists in the systematic institutional processes which prevent some people from learning and using satisfying and expansive skills in socially recognized settings, or institutionalized social practices which inhibit their feelings and perspectives on social life in contexts where others can listen."[25] Thus, oppression involves both external factors, such as distribution and relationships, as well as internal factors such as feelings and perspectives.

The internal, or psychological, impact of oppression can take various forms. As Cudd points out, oppression impacts the consciousness of individuals in deep and unavoidable ways. Sandra Bartky defines psychological oppression as follows:

> To be psychologically oppressed is to be weighed down in your mind; it is to have harsh dominion exercised over your self-esteem. The psychologically oppressed become their own oppressors; they can come to exercise harsh dominion over their own self-esteem. Differently put, psychological oppression can be regarded as the "internalization of intimations of inferiority."[26]

Bartky points out that this sort of oppression is also institutional and systematic because it creates conditions where individuals suffering from oppression have internalized damaging norms, lessening the likelihood for resistance. Consequently, oppressive norms reinforce the notion of docile subjects shaped by disciplinary mechanisms, and such discipline can be both internally and externally experienced. This creates psychic stress, as well as the creation of self as oppressor through the internalization of unjust and limiting norms.

Reviewing the various insights and theories provided above, there are various conditions for determining whether a group in a given culture is oppressed. First, there will be some sort of distributive inequality in terms of access to material goods, economic gains, and so forth. Second, these distributive inequalities will interact with various institutions within a given culture to create other forms of injustice, such as diminished respect, rights, and opportunities. Third, external aspects of oppression such as distribution and relationships will have a psychological impact on individuals of oppressed groups, creating a diminished sense of subjective worth through various means relying upon the functions of fragmentation and mystification. Finally, oppression can impact various types of social groups, and individuals in these groups may be voluntary or involuntary members. Individuals in a given group need not subjectively recognize or admit to being oppressed in order for oppression to function.

POWER, OPPRESSION, AND THE MRM

This section will analyze the MRM's charge of oppression within the framework of power established in previous sections. It might be objected that analyzing MRM arguments with feminist theory is a hopeless project, or minimally one that is problematically biased. However, the definitions offered by feminist philosophers such as Sandra Bartky, Iris Marion Young, and Ann Cudd are easily applied to a wide range of oppressive phenomena, including but not limited to race, class, and gender. Thus, although the MRM rejects feminist claims as biased, I believe these theories are philosophically sound and universally applicable, making them appropriate sources for discussing whether or not men experience oppression. In fact, many of the general criteria involved in these theories reflect the concerns and goals stated by the MRM (exploitation, violence, etc.), making an even more compelling case for utilizing these theories in this context.

Men and Power

A centerpiece MRM claim is that men lack power socially and culturally. This lack of power is argued to be the result of gynocentrism, the demand that men sacrifice physically, emotionally, and economically for women. The alleged problem is that this imbalance of power is misrepresented in the wider culture, and men are portrayed as powerful while feminists argue that women are oppressed. Most MRMs argue that women are in fact the power group in a given society, and that men are overwhelmingly the victims of feminist oppression. This section will use the Foucaultian model of power to address these claims, arguing that the MRM generally relies on concepts of power that are simplistically distributive, causing a troubling neglect of the complex workings of power in the creation of social subjects.

Warren Farrell suggests that power is having the ability to control one's own life.[27] However, he argues, men do not have the ability to control one's own life, as evidenced by the fact that men commit suicide at higher rates, lack spending power, experience more violence, and are drafted for the military (just to name a few). This lack of control is obscured by the cultural rewards men gain from such actions, for instance, honor, heroism, and being viewed as desirable. Such minimal rewards make oppression even more problematic, because men and other individuals in a society may not be aware of its presence or effects. Overall, this understanding of power is generally a liberal distributive view, arguing that individuals have a basic right to reasonable noninterference. The imposition of cultural, social, and economic demands on men by women violates this basic right.

Other sources such as AVFM make further claims concerning the nature of power, arguing that feminists actively consolidate power for women at the expense of men. For instance, Ken Gallagher argues that feminism is simply theft, and should be understood as a cultural scam aimed at taking wealth and resources from men.[28] He uses the rhetoric of emasculation frequently throughout the article, pointing out that feminism wages a constant war on overall male worth, wearing away at various social institutions such as proper education and the family unit. Other videos on the site point out that feminism is dishonest about its calls for equality, because feminism strategically ignores men's issues as well as women's privilege.[29] Additionally, it is argued that feminism is a tool of the government that is used to undermine freedom and control subjects.[30]

The impact this form of power has on the creation of subjects is not creative but limiting. Many MRAs rely upon essentialist notions of gender, referring to natural or singular masculinity.[31] There are an abundance of references to innate, biological, and evolutionary gender traits, further contributing to the notion of a singular masculine concept.[32] Men are described in traditional terms, such as rational, provider, and patriarch. Feminists, on the other hand, are called hysterical, scheming, and undermining. There are some calls to leave traditional, older styles of masculinity behind, but this is not a call to reject masculinity completely. Rather, it generally consists of recognizing innately gendered traits that must be directed at better aims and individuals.[33]

One must admit that, in some respects, the MRM does focus on certain troubling issues. Anyone living in current society can rightly be concerned about violence, inequality, and so forth. However, the mode of analysis found within the MRM is disturbingly unsophisticated, relying upon archaic gender essentialist models of masculinity. Beginning with the general notion of power, arguments that one group has power and privilege simply at the cost of another paints the issue in far too broad of strokes. As Foucault argues, power is not something one can possess and is not mainly repressive or negative in its effects. Rather, power works across various individuals and institutions in the creation of subjects. However, the MRM persists in arguing that the suffering of men can be reduced to the limitations placed upon their innate nature by external forces, namely feminism.

The MRM's reliance upon overly simplistic distributive models of power has several important consequences. First, it creates a complete neglect of other social and cultural forces impacting various aspects of men's lives. For instance, blaming women for economic exploitation completely ignores the complex oppressive aspects of contemporary capitalism. This prevents the development of progressive responses to social issues, and rather creates a two-sided gender war with no real solution in sight. Additionally, the arguments concerning innate masculinity completely ignore the important ways in which group identity impacts senses of self, and how social institutions work in the creation of docile subjects. This contributes further to the suspicion that this movement is a male reaction to losses in privilege or based on some kind of nostalgia, even though its members vehemently deny this. Finally, treating power as an object that one can "have" allows for consistent references to equality as something being a matter of mere distribution. Thus, if women "have" anything that men don't, this is immediately referred to as a deficiency in equal distribution. However, simple distribution is not sufficiently complex to address power and oppression, as was previously argued.

In conclusion, the MRM does not utilize adequately nuanced or sophisticated concepts of power and identity to address masculinity's complex issues. While they frequently refer to legitimate issues of social concern, the analysis inevitably falls back into a simple distributive concept of power that supports the demonization of feminism coupled with refusals to critically engage. Furthermore, the reliance upon an innate model of masculinity that mirrors in many ways stereotypical, hegemonic masculinity further damages any opportunity the MRM has to be truly progressive. The refusal to recognize the ways in which masculinity is mediated by other aspects of identity, such as race, results in writing that consistently comes off as outmoded, overly simplistic, and culturally tone deaf.

Men and Oppression

Although the modes of analysis used by the MRM seem largely ineffective, this does not necessarily mean that men are not oppressed in some way. This section will examine some general themes in allegations of men's oppression, relating them to the psychological and distributive aspects of oppression discussed in earlier sections. Conditions for male oppression will be specified, creating another lens of analysis for a more in-depth discussion of specific issues in later chapters. Generally, since men meet the criteria of a social group, it must be shown that men are constrained in certain ways within the contexts of social institutions. Ann Cudd argues that constraint consists in facts that impact the structure of one's life or shapes one's attitudes. These facts include legal obligations, stereotypes, economics, social status, and norms.[34] Social institutions are, then, broad social entities impacting individuals as members of social groups in a given culture. Cudd explains, "A social institution sets constraints that specify behavior in specific recurrent situations, that are tacitly known by some nontrivial subset of society, and that are either self-policed or policed by some external authority."[35] Based on this definition, oppression can then be understood as a form of institutional unjust harm existing in unequal and unjust social constraints. These constraints may be external, impacting choices, and so on, or internal, impacting background beliefs, and the like.

Psychological Oppression

The MRM claims that men are oppressed psychologically, due to the emasculation men and boys experience in current society. Additionally, this psychological oppression is not something that all men are currently aware of, and this may cause men to contribute to their own oppression by internalizing emasculating norms. These arguments reflect Bartky's discussion of psychological oppression, explaining why most men are complicit in or minimally do not resist their own oppression. Bartky further argues that psychological oppression generally falls into three categories: stereotyping, cultural domination, and sexual objectification.[36] Within each category, Bartky claims, the mechanisms of fragmentation and mystification operate to varying degrees. Fragmentation involves the splitting of a person into parts; while mystification refers to a systematic obscuring of psychological oppressive forces in order to make the inferior sense of self appear unavoidable or innate. Notably, the MRM relates much of oppressive male experience to similar or analogous phenomenon.

Starting with stereotypes, Bartky claims that stereotypes are both morally reprehensible and psychologically reprehensible. She argues:

> First, it can hardly be expected that those who hold a set of stereotyped beliefs about the sort of person I am will understand my needs or even respect my rights. Second, suppose that I, the object of some stereotype, believe in it myself—for why should I not believe what everyone else believes? I may then find it difficult to achieve what existentialists call an authentic choice of self, or what some psychologists have regarded as a state of self-actualization.[37]

This explanation captures and expands on Cudd and Young's points concerning distribution and oppression. The nature of oppression is multidirectional and manifested within a variety of relationships and institutions. It is not only the fact that oppressed people may be denied appropriate access to certain social goods, but also the fact that oppressed people experience psychologically wounding stereotypes, labels, and assumptions that they may internalize to create an inhibited inauthentic subjectivity.

The MRM frequently complains of the ways in which men are culturally represented and stereotyped. In general, it is alleged that men are portrayed as hapless losers, butts of jokes, bad fathers, and violent.[38] These stereotypes lead men to believe damaging untruths about themselves and others, such as the myth that men are inferior to women as parents. Thus, instead of making informed choices to construct a self based in self-respect and esteem, men will rely on problematic masculine constructs. This creates feelings of frustration and worthlessness in men across various cultural locations, according to the MRM.

Cultural domination refers to a dominant culture whose norms and objects serve to uphold the dominance of certain groups while oppressing and degrading others. For example, a sexist culture would be one in which the majority of items in the general life of individuals are sexist, upholding the supremacy of one gender over another.[39] Bartky points out that mystification works in the context of the male supremacist culture of exclusion—for instance, the historical lack of women in science and mathematics is mystified and explained away by stereotypes concerning women's intellectual abilities. Fragmentation occurs when an oppressed individual must maintain a sense of self while conforming that self to the culturally determined abstract self for whom cultural artifacts are manufactured to express cultural values.[40] These forces reflect a culture of domination and exclusion, in which individuals cannot find authentic reflections of self or ability, and these lacks are reflected as natural or inevitable in terms of group identity. The absence of reinforcing or empowering cultural images, norms, history, and so forth, serve to further diminish the capacity for developing and empowering sense of self.

For the MRM, cultural domination takes the form of gynocentrism and the total absence of authentic masculinity in cultural representations. One alleged manifestation of this tendency is the control women assert over consumer spending. In other words, even if men make more money in terms of salaries, women spend significantly more money as consumers, impacting television programming, advertising, and so forth.[41] Furthermore, some MRAs point out that historically men have been told to always put women and their needs first, as is evidenced by such things as chivalry codes. In all of these cases, the MRM claims that men experience cultural erasure and marginalization as a result of these practices.

The final aspect of psychological domination is objectification, namely sexual objectification. Bartky explains, "A person is sexually objectified when her sexual parts or sexual functions are separated out from the rest of her personality and reduced to the status of mere instruments, or else regarded as if they were capable of representing her."[42] This is not to say that the recognition of an individual as a sexual being is necessarily problematic—it may well be a desired and positive experience. Rather, objectification becomes oppressive when it extends into the majority of an individual's experiences, independent of what that individual wants or desires. Notably, if the occurrence of such objectification appears to involve at least two actors—the objectifying person(s) and the objectified person. However, Bartky argues, a person might also objectify herself. Using the example of beauty standards, Bartky points out that there is often something obsessional about women's relationship to their bodies and perceived attractiveness, and cultural norms create such obsession through the suggestion that women are not good enough the way they are.[43] This results in a self-defeating cycle of insecurity and personal devaluation that creates a diminished sense of self and furthers internal feelings of alienation.

While men can certainly be sexually objectified, the MRM tends to focus on different types of objectification, namely treating men like economic and violence objects. Starting with economic objectification, MRAs point out that men are often used for their income, and that women tend to treat men like ATMs. For example, Farrell points to a spending obligation gap, arguing that men feel an obligation to pay for women in certain contexts, an obligation women do not experience.[44] Furthermore, MRAs often argue that men are required to put themselves in harm's way in order to protect women and others, functioning as a sort of "unpaid body guard" working within culture.[45] Not only is this a general expectation, but also it is argued that men experience more violence than women, their experiences are often silenced or disregarded, and men are forced into physically dangerous military service. To conclude, women then treat men as objects or as a means to an end, and this objectification alienates men from their own selves, sense of self worth, and other people in a society.

One important point emerges throughout this discussion: masculinity as a gendered identity creates psychic stress and alienation in individuals. However, the problem that presents itself is whether or not these experiences constitute oppression or merely harm. First, I would argue once again that the MRM consistently misidentifies the source of masculinity problems and issues as women and feminism. Additionally, in accusing women and feminists of stereotyping men, the MRM inappropriately stereotypes women as frivolous spenders, hysterical harpies, and so forth. Second, as Marilyn Frye points out, in order to determine if certain sorts of constraint qualify as oppression, one must examine what is being constrained, who maintains the constraint, and in whose interest the constraint works. Thus, if it is accurate to say that the MRM has a weak justification for blaming women and feminists for male cultural suffering, it's very possible that certain portrayals of men in culture or the use of men as economic objects, for example, is an identity that men actively contribute to, continue, and benefit from. In conclusion, psychological oppression in men will be considered in the context of violence, sexuality, and parenthood in future chapters. For each case, harms against men in these contexts will be carefully considered, and an assessment of oppression presented within the constraints of legitimate psychological oppression outlined here.

Faces of Oppression

In addition to psychological oppression, the MRM argues that men experience oppression in terms of general constraint within the context of various social institutions. Young argues that there are five faces of oppression, which are a family of concepts that describe the injustice of oppression in different contextualized manifestations. These five conceptual categories all involve issues of distribution but also point to additional sources of injustice: exploitation, marginalization, powerlessness, cultural imperialism and violence.[46] In order to utilize these criteria in an assessment of oppression, Young explains, "The presence of any of these five conditions is sufficient for calling a group oppressed. But different group oppressions exhibit different combinations of these forms, as do different individuals in the groups."[47] Consequently, the presence of certain oppressive categories may not be uniform, and certain categories may interact in important ways. In any case, if men are indeed oppressed, it must be demonstrated that they suffer institutional damage in at least one of these categories consistently based solely upon gender.

The first category, exploitation, has its roots in a Marxist understanding of the capitalist exploitation of workers. However, Young points out that the Marxist framework for exploitation neglects the normative aspects of such injustice. She argues that the injustice of capitalism is that certain people are required to work or exercise certain capacities for the benefit, control and purposes of other people.[48] Consequently, this diminishes the power of workers in terms of material deprivation, a loss of control and a resulting potential loss of self-respect. Exploitation cannot be understood as a simple matter of distribution, because it involves important relationships between social groups as well as contributing to internal senses of identity and self. Young argues that these social relations consist in what counts as work, what constitutes adequate compensation, and the ways in which labor is utilized to form and reinforce certain positions of power within a cultural system.[49]

While many feminists have argued that women suffer from exploitation as a form of oppression, many individuals in the MRM argue that men are exploited as workers and providers, contributing to significant oppression of men qua men. These arguments are generally based upon unfairness in terms of providing economic income to families, as well as the high monetary costs to men following divorce. If this is to count as male oppression, MRAs must demonstrate why this oppression is unique to men as opposed to a phenomenon attributable to exploitative capitalism in general. Furthermore, there must be more evidence that men's work contributions are somehow more degrading to senses of self as well as resources compared to other types of gendered labor. Male labor and income must be done for the advantage of others in order for this to count as oppression, but it certainly seems as if income benefits men directly as a social group in a wide variety of ways.

Young's next category is marginalization, referring to individuals that the system cannot and/or will not use, creating dangerous sorts of invisibility and deprivation.[50] While this is an important aspect of oppression, it does not have significant relevance to the MRM allegations of oppression. Men may be marginalized on the basis of other aspects of identity, but as a whole, men are a highly visible social group.

The third category is powerlessness, which suggests a lack of authority, status, and sense of self as a member of a given society. As discussed previously, the MRM argues that men are actually disempowered as members of society, and that the concept of patriarchy is a myth. Thus, any situation in which men are claimed to be powerless suggests oppressive conditions. The way in which the MRM discusses power is deeply problematic in some respects, but if the understanding of powerlessness implies overwhelming constraint that damages self-determination, the MRM may have a more convincing argument. For example, there may be some legitimacy to the claim that men sometimes feel powerless in the context of families, specifically in terms of custody or divorce. Additionally, some MRAs argue that men are powerless in regards to the fact that they are automatically assumed to be violent or dangerous, or that women can vindictively ruin men's lives through false rape claims. Importantly, these instances of powerlessness cannot merely be loose patterns operating mainly on the individual relationship level to qualify as oppression. Thus, the MRM must demonstrate that the dominance of men in leadership positions, certain careers, and general gendered perception is not only false or misleading, but that the powerlessness they describe is a universally constraining phenomenon imposed externally in the service of external interests.

Next, is the category of cultural imperialism. This category has a significant amount in common with Bartky's description of cultural domination. According to Young, this process occurs when the dominant group's cultural artifacts are widely distributed and saturate the culture so completely that these norms become universalized. Once this occurs, individuals or groups not meeting or varying from these norms are marked as deficient in some way, and come to constitute what it referred to as Other. Feminists and other social theorists have argued that white privileged heterosexual masculinity has been the dominant source of cultural imperialism in western culture, creating a sense of double consciousness for women and other minorities existing in this social framework. Double consciousness occurs when an oppressed individual is defined simultaneously by two cultures: the dominant culture and the subordinate culture of one's group identification.[51] Thus, Young's definition covers both distributive and psychological aspects of the phenomenon. MRA arguments concerning gynocentrism reflect this face of oppression, and issues concerning spending power, and so on, relate to the distributive issues Young describes. Responses to the MRM analysis here will be very similar to the discussion of Bartky previously.

Finally, Young argues that oppressed groups will suffer from systemic violence. In this systemic form, violence will be targeted at an individual simply because they are a member of a certain social group, and this violence often consists of random and unprovoked attacks with the intention of humiliating and damaging the victim.[52] Young explains, "The oppression of violence consists not only in direct victimization, but in the daily knowledge shared by all members of oppressed groups that they are *liable* to violation, solely on account of their group identity. Just living under such a threat of attack on oneself or ones family and friends deprives the oppressed of freedom and dignity, and needlessly expends their energy."[53] Social theory arguments detailing the nature of violent hate crimes and assault as committed against racial groups, the LGBTQ community, and women are many and varied.

The MRM argues that men suffer from systemic violence, claiming that while men perpetrate violence, they are exposed to violence in systematic and unfair ways, often being the victims of certain assaults, encouraged to engage in physical violence, and exposed to violence and death through male-only military drafts. In addition to these problems, MRAs indicate that the suicide rate for men is disturbingly high. In general, these arguments tend to portray men as unrewarded violence fodder, forced to act to protect women at the cost of their own well-being. The issue of violence and masculinity is complex. In some ways, violence does reward men in addition to the obvious risks involved. Furthermore, the violence perpetrated against men is often by other men, a point that merits analysis if male oppression is due to women and feminism. The case for male oppression based on violence is not clear.

CONCLUSION

To assess the possibility of male oppression, I will be utilizing general claims concerning oppression in reference to exploitation, cultural imperialism, powerlessness, and violence. In addition to these criteria, the psychological impact of gender norms and the possibility of psychological oppression for men will be addressed. At the center of these arguments lies the distinction between oppression and harm. Authors such as bell hooks and Marilyn Frye point out that men may be able to make a case that certain gender norms harm them in certain ways, but that such harms do not constitute oppression. Frye points out, "Human beings can be miserable without being oppressed, and it is certainly perfectly consistent to deny that a person or a group is oppressed without denying that they have feelings or suffer."[54] Keeping these parameters in the analysis, I will be discussing two major issues for the MRM: violence and family roles. For each, I will assess the ways in which these umbrella issues impact men, MRM conceptions of these issues, the possibility of oppression in relation to these issues, and the nature of harm and power.

NOTES

1. Ann Cudd, *Analyzing Oppression (Studies in Feminist Philosophy)*, 1st ed. (New York: Oxford University Press, 2006), 53.
2. Iris Marion Young, *Justice and the Politics of Difference* (Princeton, NJ: Princeton University Press, 1990), 43.
3. Young, *Justice and the Politics of Difference*, 44.
4. This relational model of self is utilized in a variety of works, notably Judith Butler's *Giving an Account of One's Self*, New York: Fordham University Press, 2005.
5. Young, *Justice and the Politics of Difference*, 46.
6. Cudd, *Analyzing Oppression*, 44.
7. Cudd, *Analyzing Oppression*, 45.
8. Marilyn Frye, "The Possibility of Feminist Theory," in *Women, Knowledge, and Reality*, ed. Ann Garry and Marilyn Pearsall (New York: Routledge, 1996), 39.
9. Marilyn Frye, "Oppression," in *Gender Basics: Analyzing Women and Men*, ed. Anne Minas (Belmont, CA: Wadsworth Publishing, 2000), 42.
10. Frye, "Oppression," 43.
11. Young, *Justice and the Politics of Difference*, 30.
12. Young, *Justice and the Politics of Difference*, 41.
13. Michel Foucault, *The History of Sexuality, Vol. 1: An Introduction* (New York: Routledge, 1990), 93.
14. Judith Butler, *Gender Trouble: Feminism and the Subversion of Identity* (New York: Routledge, 1999), 4.
15. Foucault, *History of Sexuality*.
16. Hubert Dreyfus and Paul Rabinow, *Michel Foucault: Beyond Structuralism and Hermeneutics*, 2nd ed. (Chicago: University of Chicago Press, 1983), 186.
17. Young, *Justice*, 41.
18. Cudd, *Analyzing Oppression*, 23.
19. Cudd, *Analyzing Oppression*, 10.
20. Cudd points out that one may be oppressed and not be aware of one's oppression, or one may feel oppressed when they are not actually oppressed at all. This subjective error will be important in the discussion concerning male oppression vs. harm in following sections. See Cudd, *Analyzing Oppression*, 23.
21. Young, *Justice and the Politics of Difference*, 18.
22. Young, *Justice and the Politics of Difference*, 19.
23. Young, *Justice and the Politics of Difference*, 22.
24. Young, *Justice and the Politics of Difference*, 25.
25. Young, *Justice and the Politics of Difference*, 38.
26. Sandra Bartky, *Femininity and Domination: Studies in the Phenomenology of Oppression* (New York: Routledge, 1990), 22.
27. Farrell, *Myth of Male Power*, 687.
28. Ken Gallagher, "Feminism for Beginners," last updated April 19, 2015, http://www.avoiceformen.com/feminism/feminism-for-beginners/.
29. "The Reality of Feminism," video, last updated December 19, 2015, http://www.avoiceformen.com/feminism/the-reality-of-feminism/.
30. Paul Elam, "The X%: What Feminism is Really About and Why Anyone Who Values Freedom Should Fight Against It," last updated November 19, 2013, http://www.avoiceformen.com/feminism/the-x-what-feminism-is-really-about-and-why-anyone-who-values-freedom-should-fight-against-it/.
31. J T, "On Masculinity," last updated May 16, 2016, http://www.avoiceformen.com/men/on-masculinity/.
32. Travis Scott, "The Role of Masculinity," last updated August 15, 2016, http://www.avoiceformen.com/feminism/the-role-of-masculinity/.
33. Paul Elam, "The Plague of Modern Masculinity," last updated July 1, 2010, http://www.avoiceformen.com/men/the-plague-of-modern-masculinity/.
34. Cudd, *Analyzing Oppression*, 50.

35. Cudd, *Analyzing Oppression*, 51.
36. Bartky, *Femininity and Domination*, 23.
37. Bartky, *Femininity and Domination*, 24.
38. Nikita Coulombe, "Portrayal of Men in the Media: Why There Needs to Be a Reverse Bechdel Test," last updated May 27, 2015, http://www.avoiceformen.com/art-entertainment-culture/portrayal-of-men-in-the-media-why-there-needs-to-be-a-reverse-bechdel-test/.
39. Bartky, *Femininity and Domination*, 25.
40. Bartky, *Femininity and Domination*, 26.
41. Warren Farrell, *The Myth of Male Power: Why Men Are the Disposable Sex* (New York: Simon Schuster, 1993), Kindle edition, 747.
42. Bartky, *Femininity and Domination*, 26.
43. Bartky, *Femininity and Domination*, 28–29.
44. Farrell, *Myth of Male Power*, 761.
45. Farrell, *Myth of Male Power*, 829.
46. Young, *Justice and the Politics of Difference*, 40.
47. Young, *Justice and the Politics of Difference*, 64.
48. Young, *Justice and the Politics of Difference*, 40.
49. Young, *Justice and the Politics of Difference*, 50.
50. Young, *Justice and the Politics of Difference*, 53.
51. Young, *Justice and the Politics of Difference*, 60.
52. Young, *Justice and the Politics of Difference*, 61.
53. Young, *Justice and the Politics of Difference*, 62.
54. Frye, "Oppression," 51.

Chapter Five

Fathers' Rights, Parenting, and Power

The MRM argues that pervasive misandry has had a significant impact on men as fathers. MRM evidence for the oppression of men in the context of fatherhood is presented as: disparities in reproductive choices between men and women; economic demands placed on fathers; unjust custody and alimony payments in divorce; and the negative impact these factors have on children. This section will present these arguments alongside other data concerning parenting, custody, and economics in order to assess such claims. Overall, the arguments presented by the MRM imply that men experience oppression in the context of the family along the following faces of oppression Young describes: exploitation, powerlessness, and cultural imperialism. I argue that while men can potentially experience harms, both psychological and material, in the context of the family, these harms fail to meet the conditions of gender-based oppression. If men do experience oppression, this oppression is due to the workings of exploitative capitalism and interlocking aspects of oppression, as opposed to oppression by women, misandry, and/or gynocentrism.

FATHERS' RIGHTS

Parenting is a centerpiece issue for the MRM. Traditionally, feminists have argued that women experience oppression in the context of motherhood. The focus of these discussions vary, and can cover distributive issues such as mothering and housework as unpaid labor, as well as psychological oppression through the devaluation of mothers and mothering activities. Furthermore, the expectation for women to be mothers is often considered an oppressive and limiting force impacting many women, and becoming a mother can jeopardize women's careers or create unreasonable workloads. However, the MRM dismisses these concerns, arguing that women have significant control over parenting in terms of reproductive decision making, parenting, and custody, and that women often enjoy a free ride from hardworking men through economic support in marriage, or by alimony and child support payments during divorce. These cultural trends are then identified as major sources of oppression for men, creating both economic exploitation as well as psychological and emotional harms. Consequently, the MRM suggests that men experience oppression through powerlessness in the context of reproduction, paternity, and parenting roles, and that such powerlessness is reinforced through cultural portrayals of fathers as failures.

Paternity and Reproduction

One of the most basic issues presented in fathers' rights arguments concerns the decision to have a child, as well as the potential for false paternity claims. In each case, MRAs commonly complain that men have a complete lack of agency concerning decisions about whether or not to have a child, and that this lack of agency is unjust and dehumanizing. Furthermore, this agency is allegedly further compromised by women lying about being pregnant in one context or another, or being dishonest about the paternity of their children after cheating on a partner. According to the MRM, this powerlessness results in unjust inequality in reproduction, oppressing men through a violation of basic rights.

One aspect of such denial of choice involves the claim that men are coerced into fathering children who are not biologically theirs by way of paternity fraud. According to MRAs, paternity fraud is a very common occurrence, resulting in both psychological harms and economic exploitation. AVFM regularly cites studies that indicate high levels of deception on the part of women. One example of such evidence is a study published in *That's Life!* magazine, and shared on AVFM, that polled 5,000 women on various questions concerning honesty.[1] Notable results from this survey include: 50 percent responding that if they became pregnant by another man and wanted to stay with their partner, they would lie to their partner about paternity; 42 percent stating that they would lie about contraception if they wanted to get pregnant, regardless of the wishes of their partner. The poll asked a variety of questions covering many different types of dishonesty, resulting in the headline, "96% of Women Liars, Honest." Such studies and resulting headlines reinforce the MRM perception of paternity fraud as epidemic, causing AVFM to regularly warn men to get DNA paternity tests on all children at birth.[2] According to AVFM, the high frequency of women's dishonesty in the context of paternity makes such testing a necessity for men who want to protect themselves from the emotional pain and financial exploitation that false paternity creates.

The MRM perceives the alleged prevalence of paternity fraud as a symptom of women's inherently deceptive and manipulative nature in gynocentric culture. On the AVFM website, Robert Estephe addresses the issue of female deception as an overlooked problem in society, arguing:

> Instances of female sociopathic personality disorders are, it is well known, underrepresented in statistics due to the fact that the behavior which is considered normal for women (superficial charm, manipulativeness, predilection of indirect rather than direct communication, relational aggression, histrionics) is similar to that which, in men, would be considered noticeably abnormal and problematic. Yet, when you're a woman, living in a land ruled by the principle of female privilege, many allowances are given.[3]

Thus, gynocentric culture protects women from the consequences of immoral and even illegal acts, creating a certain freedom for women to take advantage of and use men for their own immoral ends. According to Estephe, the climate of political correctness arising out of misandric culture has caused us to neglect or ignore the fact that women can be, and often are, both physically and emotionally violent. Rather, men are portrayed as the only possible perpetrators of violence, exploitation, and oppression, specifically in the context of interpersonal relationships. The projection of such tendencies onto men, while portraying women as innocent or victims, works to further obscure the abuses women commit against men and children, effectively erasing supposedly widespread female enacted harms such as paternity fraud.

While the MRM often emphasizes the economic exploitation that paternity fraud creates, it also points to the coercion involved in paternity fraud as a symptom of a larger problem concerning men's lack of agency in reproductive decision making. Across multiple political contexts, the right to autonomously make choices concerning one's reproduction is framed as a basic human right. The World Health Organization (WHO) includes the following in their definition of reproductive freedom:

> Reproductive health, therefore, implies that people are able to have a responsible, satisfying and safe sex life and that they have the capability to reproduce and the freedom to decide if, when and how often to do so.
>
> Implicit in this are the right of men and women to be informed of and to have access to safe, effective, affordable and acceptable methods of fertility regulation of their choice, and the right of access to appropriate health care services.[4]

Janet Bloomfield uses this passage to argue that while there is a claim that individuals of all genders have a right to make choices concerning reproduction, men are often denied reproductive choices in various situations, suggesting a significant violation of basic individual rights.[5] Her discussion focuses on men's reproductive rights after birth, pointing out that women are able to dissolve all parental rights of a child through adoption without notifying the father of such action or even of the existence of the child. Furthermore, Bloomfield points out, men are not legally able to dissolve their legal obligation to a child at will in the way that women can. Consequently, Bloomfield argues, these conditions violate the ethical demand for equity in parental responsibility as well as in rights concerning access to children. Combining such concerns with the charge of widespread paternity fraud, it appears that men have little choice in parenting responsibilities across the board; whether through coercion/deception or the inability to voluntary choose (or not choose) to uphold parental responsibility after the birth of a biological child.

Arguments concerning voluntary parenting relate to situations in which a child is already born, but the issue of pregnancy and abortion also arise in many MRM arguments. While Bloomfield is clear that she believes men have no right to say when a woman should or should not have an abortion, this view is not necessarily the most common amongst fathers' rights activists and MRAs. Some fathers' rights advocates claim that abortion without the consent of the father violates men's rights through the resulting loss of a child/baby.[6] Relying on antiabortion rhetoric concerning the personhood and moral rights of a fetus, some sites advocate the prevention of abortion as a moral imperative, claiming, "When you try to prevent your wife or girlfriend from getting an abortion, you are being a good dad. Good dads stand up for their children and don't stand by passively while someone kills their child."[7] Such groups generally recommend interpersonal strategies for intervening with women seeking abortions, but also state that legal recourse, while rarely effective, can be used. The resource cited above recommends legal organizations such as the Alliance Defending Freedom, the Thomas More Law Center, the Christian Law Foundation, and the Life Legal Defense Foundation. In general, these antiabortion arguments construct fathers as the saviors of unwanted children, rescuing "children" from demise at the hands of irresponsible, uncaring, or selfish women. The argument rests on the assumption that a desire on the part of a potential father to assume such a role overrides the desire/rights of a woman to terminate a pregnancy.

While there is significant discussion concerning the economic exploitation of fathers in the context of false paternity or involuntary fatherhood, MRM arguments concerning paternity and reproduction are consistently based mainly upon the claim that men are denied appropriate agency in making the autonomous decision to become a parent. Utilizing the values of equality and self-determination, the MRM frames reproductive choice as something that men and women should have symmetrical control over. The arguments against false paternity are somewhat compelling, since deception clearly is immoral and undermines basic human and moral values. However, the claims concerning adoption, parenting and abortion are more controversial. There is little to no discussion concerning women's bodily autonomy or reproductive labor in these arguments. Rather, the lack of complete equality in decision-making power is emphasized as a strategy for establishing men as powerless, and hence oppressed, in the context of assuming parental roles and responsibility.

Marriage and Divorce

The institution of marriage is often touted by the MRM to be one of the most exploitative and personally damaging institutions men can be exposed to.[8] MRM discussions of marriage are generally two-pronged: the first focusing on the exploitation and harms involved during marriage, and the second focusing on the harms experienced as a result of divorce. In both discussions, the problems generally refer to economic exploitation in terms of income, alimony, and child support, or to psychological harms such as degradation, emasculation, and the prevention of fathers' interaction with or care for children. This section will discuss both the economic/distributive harms as well as the psychological harms that the MRM argues men experience as a result of marriage.

Starting with the economic/distributive harms, the MRM consistently argues that men are exploited as economic providers to women and families. Warren Farrell argues,

> Although male heads of households have higher gross incomes and assets, they have much higher spending obligations. They are much more likely to support wives [or ex-wives] than wives are to support them and thus their income is divided among themselves, a wife, and children—not only for food and housing but for tuition, insurance, and vacations.[9]

Farrell then argues that women end up with higher net worth than men, in spite of the fact that men have higher incomes than women overall. This, he claims, is due to the fact that women have higher spending power but lower spending obligations. The issue with spending power is the notion that the reality of wealth is that it is not based simply on what one earns, but rather on what one can spend on themselves at their own discretion.[10] Women's power comes from the fact that women control consumer spending by a wide margin in almost every market.

In addition to this, Farrell points to the reality of what he terms the "spending obligation gap." This gap is the cultural expectation that men should pay for women in a variety of contexts. Such spending obligations, Farrell argues, pushes men into jobs they do not like or want that will make them more money, which is required to uphold the expenditures that women expect or require. Consequently, high paying jobs result in a form of powerlessness, because of the lack of agency in selecting the job combined with the resulting female expectations for monetary support. In addition to this, many MRAs point out that men work in more dangerous jobs, for longer hours, and spend far less overall than women in western economies. Thus, MRAs conclude that authentic economic power resides in being provided for, not in the ability to generate capital or revenue.

In the context of divorce, the MRM levels a variety of complaints concerning child support, custody, and alimony. Robert Estephe argues that women's economic oppression is a myth leading to the further elevation of women, and that alimony is a form of slavery, referencing Judge Joseph Sabath's 1939 determination that alimony is an "easy money racket."[11] In other articles, Estephe continues to highlight alleged scams in alimony, referring to cases in which women married men only to divorce them and collect rich alimony sums.[12] In terms of child support, a common complaint from MRAs and other fathers' rights advocates is that child support is based upon a father's income rather than a child's need, often requiring men to pay far more than necessary. This is coupled with the fact that men's paying of child support does not in any way guarantee custody or even visitation, reducing the man and father to a mere object or resource for financial gain.[13]

In addition to economic exploitation, the psychological and personal harms of marriage, fatherhood, and divorce also contribute to male oppression, according to MRM arguments. Starting with marriage, many MRMs argue that men have become the butt of jokes as opposed to respected family figures in recent times. Helen Smith claims, "A couple of generations ago, a man wasn't considered fully adult until he was married with kids. But today, fathers are figures of fun more than figures of respect: The schlubby guy with the flowered diaper bag at the mall, or one of the endless array of buffoonish TV dads in sitcoms and commercials."[14] Smith goes on to point out that marriage for men results in diminished sexual activity, freedom, and personal space. Farrell adds to this analysis, pointing out men in marriages often feel neglected by their wives, and alienated from their own children, due to work and the female-controlled household.[15] Overall, these types of analyses concerning marriage portray the experience as castrating and personally destructive.

In terms of fatherhood, many MRAs argue that men are forced to miss out on a large amount of their children's lives due to demanding work schedules, and lacked input in the home due to the dominance of the mother in the family unit. One blog entry on AVFM, titled "21st Century Fatherhood," argues, "That which men gained through power they lost in the personal connection with those around them, like their own children."[16] While feminism allowed women to enter the workforce, it allegedly changed very little for men, the majority of whom still worked outside of the home. The blog quoted above continues the argument, claiming that financial servitude continues to limit men's options and deny them interpersonal connections with children. Additionally, many MRAs argue that, not only do men work outside the home, but also men's contributions to housework are indeed significant, in spite of feminist claims to the contrary.[17] Consequently, men are overworked both outside and inside the home, providing for spouses and children with whom they have almost no time to bond with, creating a life of labor that is absent of care and relationality. Overall, these analyses point to the conclusion that men are highly marginalized within the context of heterosexual marriage and family structures, and are consistently denied the emotional care provided by meaningful interpersonal relationships.

Many of these personal harms become heightened within the context of divorce. Farrell argues, "When divorces occurred, women's greatest fear was financial privation. Men's was of emotional privation."[18] Authors such as Farrell argue that divorce serves to exacerbate the alienation and economic objectification that men experience in the context of marriage. Furthermore, due to the fact that women retain custody of children far more frequently than men, men are unable to defend themselves against the potentially damaging and devastating rhetoric and narratives angry ex-spouses relate to the children concerning fathers. In extreme circumstances, fathers' rights advocates and MRAs argue that angry ex-wives will attempt to goad men into violent altercations and behaviors, in order to create false domestic violence charges or institute unjust restraining orders.[19] This damages men not only in terms of legal issues and fines, but also marks men permanently as criminals, dangers, and social pariahs.

The demands that fathers' rights activists and MRMs make in light of these criticisms vary along different organizations and sites, but retain general threads throughout. First, a call to end alimony entirely seems almost universal. This demand often couples with a criticism of women's financial input into the household overall and a restructuring of economic responsibilities. Second, the shift in work responsibilities should be coupled with an overall shift in family and parenting roles. Men should be more involved in parenting and included in household decisions. This should extend to situations concerning divorce, implying that women should not be favored in custody agreements, with joint custody being the preferred method of childcare distribution. Finally, in situations of divorce, men who have children should only provide monetary child support in proportion to need, if at all. In fact, if men had equal custody child support would become obsolete, requiring both parents to put in equal time and resources. In summary, the MRM and fathers' rights movement demand a flattening form of equality, both in terms of material goods as well as emotional and psychological.

Children

In addition to claiming that marriage and divorce harm men, the MRM and fathers' rights movements also argue that denying custody to fathers has a significantly negative impact on children. The MRM argues that single parent households are bad for children psychologically and emotionally, and that keeping children from their fathers results in generalized harms. Further, some individuals in these movements have gone as far as to identify a disorder, parental alienator syndrome, that occurs as a result of keeping children from their fathers following divorce and/or separations. The denial of visitation and custody that allegedly results in such a syndrome occurs as a consequence of isolation from the father combined with the slandering of the absent father by an ex-wife as an act of revenge. Overall, the MRM uses the alleged damage to children caused by unequal custody arrangements to further support arguments concerning the injustice of denying fathers custody and access to children.

The MRM claims that children growing up in homes without a father are vulnerable to a variety of social and economic harms. According to AVFM, single mothers fail children in a multitude of ways.[20] Bloomfield points out that children growing up with a single mother are more likely to live at or below the poverty line, and have trouble moving up the economic ladder later in life. Boys growing up with single mothers are more likely to be incarcerated, and girls are five times more likely to experience teenage pregnancy. Furthermore, Bloomfield argues that children benefit academically from having a "natural father" in the home, because only natural fathers consistently provide guidance and assistance for children in terms of homework and other academic pursuits. Her discussion ends with the following warning:

> Single women under the impression that raising children without a father in the home is a value neutral choice should perhaps consider whether they consider pregnant daughters, incarcerated sons and blighted futures for both also value neutral, because those are likely outcomes for children raised without their natural fathers.

These arguments against single motherhood and absent "natural fathers," are common on MRM sites.[21] Such arguments frequently claim that even if women are good mothers, they simply cannot replace the role of the father, and that the lack of a present father figure harms children in significant ways. The inability for women to fulfill such paternal roles suggests an essentialist concept of gender that entails certain stereotypical abilities on the part of men and women in heteronormative family contexts.

In addition to these potential harms, MRAs often point to the existence of parental alienator syndrome as the most severe possible consequence of divorce and absentee fathers. On the AVFM site, a full discussion of this syndrome, its causes, and effects, is provided in several posts. One post explains the reality of the situation, arguing:

> The root cause of the syndrome is when a custodial parent indirectly or deliberately thwarts the relationship between the non-custodial parent and his/her child, causing the child to wish no longer to spend much or any time with the non-custodial parent. This is done through a number of manipulative tactics by the custodial parent, usually as a form of revenge, to turn the child(ren) away from the non-custodial parent. The majority of alienated parents are fathers, which comes as no surprise since mothers are usually given greater legal custodial rights over their children, than fathers.[22]

According to the AVFM site, this syndrome has reached the level of epidemic, and can be understood as the result of children being treated like bargaining chips in divorce as opposed to persons with needs. The site encourages men to be vigilant about the emergence of this syndrome in children that they have become alienated from in the context of divorce.

The post quoted above goes on to describe three tiers of severity relating to parental alienation. It urges men to be prepared at all times to combat such issues, comparing the having of information to a boxer getting ready by knowing his opponent. The first tier is referred to as "naïve alienator," in which the alienator has a laissez faire approach to parenting, and encourages the child to treat the father as simply a taxi service and cash provider. "Active alienators" compose the second tier, and involve more aggressive alienation tactics. The site describes these individuals as: "typically angry, vengeful and could be categorized as narcissistic." Consequences of this type of alienation include children coming to view fathers as enemies. The final tier is the "obsessive alienator" and is characterized as the most dangerous form of alienation. These individuals allegedly often have narcissistic personality disorder, and will stop at nothing to destroy their ex-husbands. Such destruction often takes place through "bankrupting" men in the court system over and over, while causing children to despise the absent father due to feelings of abandonment. These children do not recognize that the abandonment was not voluntary.

AVFM characterizes this syndrome as emotional abuse, and argues that the courts must recognize it as such. However, they also acknowledge that it is extremely difficult to diagnose, making the battle for alienated fathers even more challenging. Other authors confirm these actions as child abuse, and argue that this syndrome is pervasive in divorce scenarios. Edward Kruk claims that 11–15 percent of children in divorce situations experience this syndrome, and 1 percent of children in North America overall.[23] Symptoms of this disorder include low self-esteem, lack of trust, and substance abuse. Because of the trauma of such alienation, Kruk claims that reunification with the alienated parent must proceed with great caution, due to the possibility of the child experiencing post-traumatic stress disorder.

Three points are consistent and central in MRM arguments concerning custody and children. First, the absentee father is generally portrayed as involuntarily absent. The MRM denies the reality of "deadbeat dads" as a common occurrence.[24] Next, the MRM claims that the forced absence of fathers creates psychological/emotional harm for children, a harm that is encapsulated by the so-called parental alienation/alienator syndrome. Finally, children experience harm in social/personal/economic goods in being raised by a single mother. In addition to these issues, such arguments reinforce the notion of women being "sociopaths" or naturally deceptive, lending more credence to arguments made concerning paternity fraud. As in paternity fraud and reproductive arguments, MRM arguments concerning custody claim that society constructs men as immoral/neglectful/abusive and women as innocent/caring/victims, an arrangement that the MRM vehemently rejects, claiming that the situation may, in fact, be quite the opposite.

EVALUATING FATHERHOOD AND MALE OPPRESSION

Having outlined the MRM views on men's oppression in family and parenting contexts, I will now examine the legitimacy in portraying such experiences as male gender oppression. Before outlining my strategy, it is important to note the specific content of MRM arguments concerning families generally, because these arguments contain highly stereotypical conceptions of marriage and family. MRM arguments on the whole relate to heteronormative family structures, focusing almost exclusively on heterosexual marriage and relationships. There are several possible reasons for this. One might be the fact that the MRM believes that women are the source of male oppression, and this may entail that homosexual male relationships may simply not require analysis due to the absence of oppression resulting from the lack of female presence. However, this still does not address the absence of discussion relating to the very real multiplicity of familial possibilities and relationships, such as transgender identity and relationships, lesbian relationships, and extended communal family structures, just to name a few. Thus, it seems likely that the reliance upon heteronormative concepts reflects, first, the predominance of heterosexual men in the MRM, as well as a deeply conservative and traditionalist sense of marriage and family. Both of these tendencies undermine the MRM's claim of being a source of progressive or radical politics, instead supporting criticism that views the MRM as a deeply nostalgic and conservative movement.

While I believe the above observation is significantly damaging to MRM arguments in this area, the prevalence of fathers' rights movements requires an engagement with the arguments and concerns described in previous sections. Thus, I will assume a heteronormative framework in addressing MRM arguments, restricting the field of analysis to the context set by the MRM. While this restriction is inherently problematic, the outcry of groups that have traditionally held privileged cultural positions must be addressed in order to locate the sources of frustration, and to determine what aspects of such group concerns hold legitimacy. Thus, the following sections will combine facts, data, and theory to assess the claims made by the MRM, allowing for a determination of oppression as distinguished from personal and group harms.

Fathers and Exploitation

This section will evaluate the charge that men experience oppression as fathers through financial and economic exploitation. As Iris Marion Young argues, exploitation involves more than a mere disparity in the distribution of economic goods, relating the phenomenon to worker alienation and labor that unjustly contributes to the benefit of others. Thus, exploitation involves both psychological and distributive oppression, and the MRM claims that the exploitation of fathers and husbands is created and maintained by women and feminists. I will argue that men as workers are exploited in the context of white supremacist patriarchal capitalism, and this system serves as the source of oppression, not women or feminists. While all individuals participating in exploitative capitalism as workers can arguably be said to experience oppression, there do seem to be oppressive experiences in this context that mainly impact men. Nonetheless, the sources of such harm are complex and overlapping. I will argue that while the MRM arguments fail to adequately address exploitation as a capitalist phenomenon, the impact of capitalist oppression, work, self-esteem, and emotional damage on men create serious harms meriting a more complex analysis.

The Myth of Meaningful Work

Capitalism in the United States has made promises that go far beyond financial gain, security, or even wealth. The appeal, in some instances, is far more personal. Men frequently report feeling a sense of identity and self-worth through their jobs and employment, making unemployment a devastating personal experience for men across a variety of contexts. As bell hooks argues, many men in our culture believe that the ability to provide for themselves and their families is a critical aspect of their identity as men.[25] Thus, when work becomes demeaning, difficult to come by, or financially unrewarding, men may experience a deep sense of personal crisis impacting self-esteem and worth. Furthermore, if work is unable to fulfill these psychic needs, men often lack other outlets or resources to maintain a healthy or complete sense of self.

Michael Kimmel argues that men in the United States are experiencing feelings of betrayal, anger, and grief in current economic contexts. If the hallmark of masculinity is the ability to provide, failure to do so results in men perceiving themselves as useless, discarded, and, consequently, humiliated.[26] This is particularly impacting for middle class men, who have noticeably felt shifts in the workplace due to economic downturns, the entrance of women and minorities into professional fields, as well as a growing disparity between the upper and middle classes. The stress this creates is impacting men at earlier and earlier ages, Kimmel argues, pointing out that young men in their late teens and twenties are avoiding professional commitment as long as possible due to their having unrealistic expectations concerning the nature of work and career. According to Kimmel, young men have an expectation that jobs must be emotionally and financially fulfilling, making the search for an appropriate career a life changing sort of decision. However, given the level of job instability in recent economic climates, these expectations do not always match reality, resulting in volatile job trajectories.[27]

These feelings of rejection and humiliation in the context of work are often not alleviated in the family environment. Hooks argues, "Work stands in the way of love for most men then because the long hours they work drain their energies; there is little or no time left for emotional labor, for doing the work of love."[28] Combined with the fact that men are often not socialized to express themselves emotionally, this lack of fulfillment can have serious consequences, resulting in depression or even violence. However, hooks points out, while work keeps men from families, men also use work as a place to hide from emotions and emotional labor, freeing themselves from such pressure by constructing work as an emotion-free environment, basing friendships on superficial hypermasculine bonding, and promoting daydreams about playboy type lifestyles. These issues create a troubling cycle for some men. Because of the exploitative nature of much work, men feel castrated in this environment, but they are also unable to meaningfully engage in emotional contexts via family and other relationships. Consequently, men cannot find a sense of masculine identity at work, and there is no alleviation for this insecurity in personal contexts due to long working hours combined with the emotional limitations resulting from masculine socialization. Thus, men find self-worth elsewhere, investing in surface relationships that are often contingent on engaging in stereotypically masculine behaviors that can become extreme, negatively impacting personal relationships.

The source of the problem, however, is not simply women or feminism. First, the expectation that work in an exploitative capitalist system with severe class disparities will be self-affirming and uplifting verges on impossible. Thus, such expectations set up men to fail. Second, women who work long hours also report similar feelings to men in terms of exhaustion, inability to emotionally engage, and feelings of exploitation.[29] If this is true, it is the demands of the economy and employment that diminish capacity for emotional labor, not the refusal of women to allow men to participate in family life. Finally, MRAs have misidentified the "enemy" or source of psychological and emotional harm. Kimmel explains, "The enemies of white American men are not really women and men of color. Our enemy is an ideology of masculinity that we inherited from our fathers, and their fathers before them, an ideology that promises unparalleled acquisition coupled with a traditionally impoverished emotional intelligence."[30] Consequently, while women may in fact participate in the continuance of toxic masculine stereotypes, this is not a conspiracy. Rather, it demonstrates the pervasive nature of patriarchal gender norms that both men and women perpetuate in a given culture. Men are certainly damaged by unrealistic expectations of work and emotional disempowerment, but the reductive explanation of feminist refusal and castration is far too simplistic to unpack the reality of the problem. MRM conceptions of women as enemies only serves to further remove men from the possibility of caring relationships and interactions with others, creating an additional sort of "boys club" that, although it claims to be liberatory, serves to further the emotional damage of hegemonic masculine constructs.

Capitalist Exploitation

The MRM does not often engage with capitalist criticism, redirecting complaints to the barriers women and feminists put up to prevent their success within the given system. However, the issues and anger they refer to can be more adequately explained in terms of alienation as a result of a culture based in a white supremacist capitalist patriarchy. Instead of looking to create new possibilities or options for gender and work, the MRM consistently recycles existing norms, relying upon oppressive and limiting models of masculinity and economy to suggest better options for men. This tendency reflects what Marcuse refers to as one-dimensional thinking, or the refusal to transcend oppressive cultural realities based upon total alienation of a subject resulting in complete identification with one's culture.

To be clear, this is not the way in which the MRM views itself. On the contrary, the MRM sees itself as refusing culture all together, or as breaking the wheel of society instead of turning it. Nonetheless, this is a claim that is difficult to accept. First, the MRM does not demonstrate any coherent interest in altering the nature of labor, work, or class structures. The problem, as the MRM frames it, does not seem to be capitalism, but rather the simple distribution of capital, namely, the demand that men be seen as economic providers. In turn, some solutions proffered are that women should work as much as men, or men should be allowed to stay home while women work.

Absent here is any consciousness of the false needs that create the demand for greater amounts of earning and labor, or the fact that U.S. Americans work far longer hours than many other western peoples.

However, the most emphasized point of contention is the idea that women take men's money thoughtlessly, using up resources as frivolous consumers and expecting that men will finance their exploits. According to the MRM, women regularly exploit their husbands and fathers of their children economically, while preventing men from participating as full members of the family unit. Men become nothing more than an ATM machine, emotionally cut off and ignored, and further punished for any perceived failure in ability to provide. This narrative does indeed sound like an unfortunate state of affairs for men. However, it also helps itself to some extraordinarily oppressive and sexist gender stereotypes portraying women as superficial, ornamental, fiscally irresponsible, and vindictive.

There are pervasive cultural stereotypes that portray women who stay at home as lazy, living in extravagance, lacking responsibility, and reveling in ornamental/decorative pleasures such as shopping. One can only assume that such gendered narcissism is what Farrell means when he refers to the "spending gap"—men earn and women shop. However, such stereotypes of women as narcissists do not necessarily reflect female privilege, and rather relate to feminine experiences of cultural alienation, as opposed to a female financial scheme. Sandra Bartky argues that the phenomenon of feminine narcissism involves the estrangement from one's bodily being as a reaction to the fashion-beauty complex.[31] The fashion beauty complex, a capitalist driven network relying upon women's physical insecurities, offers its products as solutions to the anxiety women feel over appearance. The result is endless investment in products and items that result from false needs generated by oppressive capitalism. As Marcuse points out, one-dimensional thought causes individuals to come to see the capitalist demands of a society as the innate needs of ones own.[32] Such superficial investments reflect the internalization of problematic gender norms in women, often enacted in the interest of pleasing men, resulting in capitalist investments women feel are required to meet certain gendered standards and expectations. Consequently, if women are spending, it is not simply for the pure joy of using up male resources. Rather, it is a response to complex capitalist gender norms that create a compulsion to spend money in order to meet certain cultural standards that create a dubious, externally dependent sense of self worth. In such an alienating capitalist framework, it seems as though neither gender wins.

Additionally, the notion that women stay at home, lack financial input into the family, and revel in such narcissistic behaviors also shows a complete lack of awareness to the diverse experiences of women along the lines of race and class. As bell hooks points out, "From slavery to the present day, black women in the United States have worked outside the home, in the fields, in the factories, in the laundries, in the homes of others. That work gave meager financial compensation and often interfered with or prevented effective parenting."[33] Thus, once again, the MRM comes off as tone deaf to intersectional experiences of work and family. Without recognizing their own privileged standpoint, the MRM asserts various "facts" that are, in reality, stereotypes of white middle class experiences in the United States. Stereotypes that, under scrutiny, fail to fairly represent women in any context, due to their essentialist and misogynist underlying assumptions about feminine frivolity and consumption.

In any case, the feeling of being used as an ATM machine is based on a misdirected source of blame in women. In order to discern the locus of concern as well as in an effort to clarify the error in blame assignment, a more detailed look at capitalism and alienation is required, because these concepts relate directly to an impoverished sense of self and control in capitalist contexts. As Karl Marx argues, the more workers produce the more they become impoverished in capitalism, because such exploitative labor commodifies workers, the products of labor, and the process of labor. In capitalism, the product of labor confronts the worker as an alien entity, an objective realization of labor that has become estranged from an individual. Marx argues, "For on this premise it is clear that the more the worker spends himself, the more powerful becomes the alien world of objects which he creates over and against himself, the poorer he himself—his inner world—becomes, the less belongs to him as his own."[34] Such alienation is compounded by an estrangement not just from the object of labor but from the process of labor itself, making work a tedious and unhappy experience. Furthermore, such alienation also causes individuals to become estranged from their essential human nature, and as such, from other persons.

This classic notion of alienation can then be applied to more contemporary capitalist contexts. As Marcuse points out, contemporary western society must consistently justify its capitalist framework, because technological advances have made the possibility of human liberation from economic demands a real possibility. Economic freedom would then be freedom from the control of economic relationships and forces.[35] However, the problem of alienation and economic exploitation persists, indicating that, as Marcuse argues, the irrational society must work to make it appear rational. False needs are perpetuated in such a society, manifested in products requiring repression and the maintenance of a euphoria in unhappiness. The pursuit of needless luxury becomes central to human life, pushing individuals to earn more and more capital in the name of satisfying these false and irrational desires. Marcuse points out: "The extent to which this civilization transforms the object into an extension of man's mind and body makes the notion of alienation questionable. The people recognize themselves in their commodities."[36] In other words, having material objects, such as the ones demanded by systems of false capitalist needs, becomes the determinant of individual senses of self and self-worth. Thus, individuals become mimetic with the world around them, losing inner private space to the status quo. This state of affairs does not indicate a new form of alienation, but a new level, one in which individuals are completely consumed by alienated existence. This results in the one-dimensional society Marcuse describes.

These concepts can be helpful in understanding men's experiences in capitalism, and the frustrations emphasized within the MRM. If work is alienating, then the lack of power and fulfillment men experience is unsurprising. However, if we accept the new level of alienation that Marcuse describes, then men truly identify themselves with commodities, including women as commodities, in line with the analysis Bartky provides. However, they also lack meaningful inner lives due to all-consuming alienation, and other men are perceived as competitive threats in the context of work. This presents the individual with a deeply superficial existence with unfulfilling relationships that is only alleviated by the accumulation of more and more commodities. However, these luxuries serve little purpose for someone who is always at work, creating increasing resentment.

Furthermore, as women's roles change, the female commodity begins to confront men as hostile. The accumulation of capital is not sufficient for recognition of the male as he sees himself. As women become less commodified and dependent, men's anxiety about masculinity increases, because the traditional concept of masculinity is becoming unstable and challenged. Furthermore, as the acceptance of work on the basis of masculine privilege becomes less tenable, men become more and more frustrated by work, lack of respect, and the lessening rewards of producing commodities. The perception that women create anxiety and the nature of one-dimensional thought allows some men to identify with other men via the superficial channels that Marcuse describes. This creates false bonds between men, and shifts the focus from the problem of irrational capitalism to the straw man of invasive feminism.

The MRM captures this tendency in an extreme way. They complain about servitude but misidentify the source. As Marcuse points out, "All liberation depends on the consciousness of servitude, and the emergence of this consciousness is always hampered by the predominance of needs and satisfactions which, to a great extent, have become the individual's own."[37] The problem with the MRM is that they expend significant revolutionary energy in all the wrong directions. Kimmel, in line with Marcuse, points out that the ability of MRAs to sound off angrily yet impotently on blogs and other online formats can actually serve oppressive power structures.[38] Instant communities allow MRMs to vent frustrations to one another, blow off steam, and return to work as a docile disciplined subject. In the context of capitalism, identifying women as the problem allows men to direct their anger at some visible source, without requiring them to participate in negative thinking, rejecting the one-dimensional system that is the actual source of their alienated and impoverished state of being.

In conclusion, the MRM is right in some limited sense. Certain men are being exploited economically in western culture. However, it is not all men, since this exploitation does not occur as a result of women oppressing all men, but by men participating in an oppressive, alienating, irrational capitalist system. While it is certainly arguable that all individuals are harmed by such limited one-dimensional thought, economically privileged individuals certainly suffer far less than most. In any case, oppressive powers benefit from men's willingness to project their insecurities, fears, and anger onto women, distracting them from the true source of exploitation. Furthermore, the propaganda of rewarding work and equal opportunity contribute to the continued maintenance of docile subjects and laborers. By ignoring these complex social structures and systems of exploitation, the MRM inadvertently works to contribute to the maintenance of men's exploitation, not to its end.

Fathers and Powerlessness

The charge of powerlessness is at the center of the MRM discussion of paternity, birth, and custody. In each instance, the MRM argues that women wield all of the power and men do not have comparable say, and this, it is argued, violates certain basic principles of equality. Such violation results in powerlessness for men, a source of oppression that creates a lack of status, sense of self, and diminished authority, according to Iris Marion Young. However, if we accept that power is productive as Foucault argues, the deprivation men may feel in terms of certain aspects of parenting is not necessarily oppressive. Rather, power itself is distributive, placing individuals in certain relationships along various cultural matrices. This concept works to undermine claims of baseline equality, requiring an examination of the underlying mechanisms informing such distributions and autonomous decision-making structures. I will argue that the MRM complaints concerning agency in terms of paternity, pregnancy, and custody reflect a highly problematic concept of responsibility and agency, and thus do not indicate any sort of blanket sense of oppression as powerlessness for men as a social group.

Paternity

Starting with the question of paternity, the MRM claims that paternity fraud is a rampant problem, citing disturbingly high rates of such deception. However, a closer examination of the statistics gives a far less clear picture. In a

2005 study performed by Bellis et al., the conclusion was reached that available data on false paternity was misleading due to its sources.[39] Most available statistical data on paternity has been the result of data collected for other purposes, and these purposes tend to over- or underestimate false paternity based on the nature of their investigation. For instance, one source of this data is people seeking genetic testing because of suspected false paternity, meaning that the results will most likely demonstrate a high rate of false paternity. On the other hand, other studies performed for genetic screening, and the like, may show a low rate of paternity fraud, due to certain subjects avoiding such testing due to fear of exposure. Mark Joblin and Turi King support these findings, claiming that in families without prior suspicion of paternity, the rate of false paternity is at a value of 1–2 percent.[40]

The experience of false paternity or paternity fraud is unquestionably devastating. It can have profound negative effects on the father's emotional and social well-being, as well as on the child and the mother.[41] In cases of accidental or mistaken paternity, it must be argued that women should proceed with due diligence and caution in the assessment of paternity, in order to avoid such emotionally traumatizing results for herself and others. Further, in cases of paternity fraud, the woman is obviously acting in a morally reprehensible fashion, using deception to impose certain emotional demands and expectations on another individual that deeply compromise the future health and happiness of her child and other persons. Overall, the MRM is correct to say that paternity fraud is a great harm against men.

The error that the MRM makes is claiming that paternity fraud is a widespread, oppressive experience for men as a group. This claim is dubious. The statistics they frequently refer to are not adequate, as argued above. There is no evidence that this is a widespread, pervasive phenomenon. This entails that there seems to be little evidence that women as a group are using this strategy to oppress men through disempowerment, because oppression is not an individual phenomenon. Unless clear evidence emerges that paternity fraud is such a widespread abuse, the charge of oppression cannot hold, and such issues should be considered and analyzed as interpersonal moral harms.

Pregnancy

Some MRAs complain that they lack any power in the decision making about whether or not a woman carries a pregnancy to term. While this lack of power may be an accurate description, there is no evidence that it constitutes harm. In fact, many feminists have argued that having such power violates a woman's bodily autonomy and is thus morally and legally prohibited. However, the language of equality regularly emerges in MRM discussions of this issue, specifically in terms of how it relates to their perceived loss and lack of autonomy in determining the future of what they commonly refer to as a child or baby. I will argue that the MRM uses a problematic concept of equity that effectively avoids issues of bodily autonomy and the labor of pregnancy for women.

The MRM regularly frames access to and distribution of various social goods in terms of a basic, dichotomous, evenly split model where everyone should receive the exact same amount of all resources. What such a model neglects is the unique experiences of individuals in cultural, biological, medical, and other contexts that are deeply informed by the workings of power. So, if we strip pregnancy of all of its contexts, reducing the issue to nothing more than the existence of an embryo receiving equal genetic input from two individuals, then the claim to equitable decision making seems reasonable. However, it verges on ludicrous to dismiss the fact that women are the ones who are pregnant, perform the labor of pregnancy, and act as what some feminists have called "good Samaritans."[42] Consequently, the base equity model that the MRM appears to be using dismisses the experience of pregnancy, treating women as mere incubators for fetuses.

Susan Bordo argues that the issue of abortion for fathers' rights activists cannot be based upon equality, since the father and mother in such scenarios have goals that are mutually exclusive.[43] In other words, if the mother wants an abortion and the father does not want her to do so, only one person can have his or her desires prevail, and MRAs suggest that it should be the father in such cases. She then relates this to the historically based notion that fathers are the "true" parents of children, as manifested in laws referring to children as the property of a father or biological descriptions emphasizing the active role of male sperm and genetics in the creation of children. In any case, the notion of patriarchal authority emerges in these contemporary contexts as well, suggesting that men's desires can override women's in cases of abortion. The fact that this fulfillment of desires on the part of the father is not met cannot be construed as a lack of power overall or oppression.

Interestingly, Bordo notes that fathers' rights activists in these cases will sometimes argue that they would have the child if they could, emphasizing their ability to nurture and fulfill caregiving roles. While the ability to emote and nurture is certainly admirable and often not associated with masculinity, the way that this is expressed in the context of the MRM is often, if not always, at the expense of women. Bordo explains:

> In fathers' rights cases, every assertion of male feeling has been accompanied by a corresponding denial of *female* sensibility; every attempt to prove that men can be nurturers, too, has involved an attempted discreditation of the *woman's* nurturing capabilities. . . . While the men describe themselves as tender flowers, easily bruised and damaged, the women are portrayed as cold, ruthless destroyers of fetal life, running roughshod over paternal sensibilities.[44]

As usual, women are framed as the enemy, taking away men's choices and ability to participate in meaningful caring relationships. The problem with this is that such arguments do not suggest a progressive approach to gendered interactions and relationships, and reinstate adversarial approaches that keep men and women separate, demonizing women in the process.

Theories of female autonomy and abortion are well established and argued for throughout philosophical literature, thus I will not provide a comprehensive overview of these discussions here. However, the point of this section is to demonstrate that the MRM arguments concerning the interest men have in women continuing a pregnancy do not establish any rights on their part to intervene with or decide on the continuing or termination of pregnancy. While men may want a woman to continue a pregnancy, which is a legitimate desire, this desire cannot override any desire a woman has to continue or not continue a pregnancy. As Bordo points out, cases of conflicting desire cannot be solved with appeals to simple equity. Rather, it is imperative that women's investment in pregnancy through physical and emotional labor combined with her right to bodily autonomy prevents men from intervening or imposing their desires onto her. The male physical contribution to pregnancy is not comparable to a woman's, and while some men feel as though this is a deprivation, such deprivation cannot reasonably be framed as a moral or personal harm. Men might experience disappointment or any other range of emotions in reaction to women's decisions during pregnancy, but the decision to become or remain pregnant must remain with the woman. Any other demand is a violation of rights that cannot be overridden by competing desires.

Custody and Parenting

There are several aspects of custody that the MRM criticizes and I will focus on two major areas in this section: first, custody decisions involving women who do not desire custody shortly after giving birth, and second, custody issues arising in the context of divorce. In both scenarios, the MRM points out that custody consistently defers to the mother, with fathers lacking any power to influence access to their biological children. According to the MRM, courts consistently side with the mother in both forms of custody cases, depriving fathers and children of important relationships and access to family members. The alleged denigration of fathers also is argued to occur in general parenting activities, with children suffering as a result. In this section, I will argue that there are systemic issues that damage men in terms of masculinity and fatherhood. However, the MRM and fathers' rights groups misattribute these harms to feminism and angry women, distorting the nature of parenthood by emphasizing base notions of equality and rights over care and relationships.

One aspect of custody occurs in situations where the mother and father are not in a relationship, and all decisions concerning custody fall to the mother. Mary Shanley discusses the gender issues impacting such cases, focusing on cases of biological mothers surrendering children for adoption without consulting or offering custody to the biological father.[45] In such cases, biological fathers have argued that they have a right to be given the opportunity for custody prior to any other adoption proceedings. The MRM uses such cases as further examples of the harms that fathers endure at the hands of women who despise men, do not trust men due to misandric prejudices, and a system that operates in the favor of women as opposed to men. Utilizing the language of equality, the MRM and fathers' rights groups demand that fathers have an equal and symmetrical right to determine the future care of a child, based upon biology alone. Additionally, the MRM and fathers' rights groups extend this demand for equality to all cases of custody, using such liberal principles to create a demand for default joint custody combined with a dismissal of alimony and child support.

In all cases of custody, the MRM consistently uses and repurposes liberal feminist language concerning equality and rights. While these are undeniably important political virtues, they are not adequate principles for examining the complex nature of parent-child relationships, especially within the context of custody issues. As Michael Kimmel points out, fathers' rights arguments problematically emphasize rights over relationships and responsibilities.[46] Instead of analyzing the challenges of family relationships, overall family goods, and models of care, the MRM consistently holds views that emphasize sheer access and unanalyzed equity in terms of distribution. Kimmel argues that this approach often involves targeting male rage and frustration at women and ex-wives, as opposed to properly dealing with emotional pain and criticizing a possibly unjust legal system.

Starting with issues of early adoption, Shanley argues that custody arguments reveal the cultural conviction that parenthood is good for men as well as women. If parenting is an equal good for both men and women, then equity in certain custody cases seems just, and this sense of justice is embodied in the current legal trend of abandoning maternal preference as the guiding principle for determining custody.[47] If the maternal preference standards in general custody cases are significantly flawed, then it seems as though the biological father, if deemed "fit," should have the right to adoption/custody in early adoption cases based on the universally good nature of parenting. In other words, since parenting is good for men, in cases where the mother does not choose to parent a child, men should not be denied this good based on the choices of the biological mother. Nonetheless, Shanley points out that this standard's potential disregard for the biological mother's wishes in early adoption cases may be construed as an ethical failure.

Shanley claims that a disregard for the mother's wishes in such cases suggests that once a biological mother surrenders the child for custody she lacks any further relevant concern for the child's welfare.[48] This, however, is not necessarily the case. As Shanley points out, choosing to relinquish custody may be due to a variety of factors impacting the biological mother, and need not reflect indifference; in fact this choice is often extremely difficult and painful. When the choice to put a child up for adoption is made, it is not a matter of conflict between the biological father and adoptive parents, but rather an issue between the biological mother and father. Shanley thus argues that the biological mother's unwillingness to give custody to the biological father must at least be considered. She claims:

> At the time of birth the relationship of biological father and mother to the child is neither biologically nor socially symmetrical. She has borne the child for nine months, an activity for which there is no precise male analog. . . . The biological mother's "expectant" state has affected both her own physiological experience and the ways in which others view and interact with her.[49]

This argument suggests an alternative model to understanding custody rights that undermine the simplistic appeals to equity offered by the MRM. Namely, the issue of care creates an ethical and legal demand for an examination of the relationships involved in family and parenting relationships. There is no default position of authority in every case, but issues of women's bodily labor and care must play some role in some custody cases, specifically cases of early adoption, reflecting the ethics discussed in the section on abortion and fathers.

If caring relationships impact these cases of adoption, they become significantly more crucial in determining custody for divorce cases. Courts of law came to rely on the "best interest of the child" standard for determining custody cases after phasing out maternal preference standards. However, the best interest standard is not without its problems, and concepts of "best interest" may be unduly influenced by certain prejudices, such as a preference for two-parent households or upper middle class environments. Martha Fineman argues that the best interest standard should be replaced with a "primary caregiver" standard.[50] In other words, custody should be determined on the basis of who provides (and to what extent) emotional and nurturing care to the child in question. Once this standard is applied, the issue of care and relationships comes to the center, displacing the individual as rights bearer. As Shanley points out, "When someone is considered in the role of parent, he or she cannot be viewed apart from the child that makes him or her a parent; an autonomous (in the sense of unfettered or atomistic) individual is precisely what a parent is *not*."[51] Thus, liberal rhetoric works to obscure the nature of parenting, focusing on what a single individual believes they are owed as opposed to emphasizing communal and relational goods. There are some relational aspects that men cannot biologically access, namely pregnancy. While this gives women certain relational insights and attachments, this does not constitute a harm or deprivation to men. Furthermore, if the MRM is genuinely committed to the creation of fair and just parenting practices, then the care model should replace current rhetoric.

While the liberal values informing MRM custody arguments are clearly problematic, the MRM persistently upholds the equity in access argument by appealing to the damage children suffer as a result of absent fathers. Thus, regardless of the care relationships and investments of mothers, the harm experienced by children is so great in certain custody arrangements that limit or prevent paternal access that it overrides these concerns. Specifically, the MRM claims that parental alienation syndrome combined with the pitfalls of single mother parenting for children create an ethical demand for fathers to have equal access to children and custody on the basis of overall welfare and utility. Notably, such arguments tend to gloss over or ignore completely the variation in care and responsibility that individual fathers exhibit, relying instead upon dichotomous gender constructs positioning all fathers as victims of vengeful or misandrist mothers. Furthermore, there is little to no convincing evidence that parental alienator syndrome is legitimate, nor that single mothers negatively impact children.

Parental alienator syndrome is not currently in the DSM, and thus the label of "diagnosis" is questionable at best. Some critics point out that Richard Gardner, the founder of the theory, did not have adequate empirical evidence to establish his claims. Rather, the theory seems to emerge from Gardner's own clinical experiences with particular clients as opposed to utilizing proper empirical research parameters.[52] This is not to say that instances of parental alienation do not occur. Annelis Haggemeister, associate professor in social work, points out:

> Have there been situations in which either one or the other parent deliberately or otherwise says things that may alienate the child from their relationship with the other parent? Certainly. Yes, there are situations where people may say things or do things that may alienate their children from the other parent. Whether or not that's a full-blown syndrome, I think, is another thing entirely.[53]

However, such incidents do not indicate any sort of established pattern of a harm perpetrated against men. Furthermore, arguing that children's dislike of or aversion to certain adults should be dismissed as mere brainwashing poses a possibly dangerous slippery slope. If children's concerns and reports are not taken seriously, then the possibility arises of dismissing true reports of abuse.

Stating that single mothers pose a danger to children is a traditional and misogynist right wing strategy, and the use of such arguments by the MRM is no different. First, the claim that only fathers can teach boys to be real men relies upon outdated notions of gender rooted in essentialism. Furthermore, many of the problems that the MRM claim children experience as a result of single mother parenting can be attributed to poverty. As Kimmel points out, while criminal behaviors, and so forth, are correlated with fatherlessness, both are a product of poverty.[54] However, the MRM's commitment to focusing only on men as men allows them to ignore issues of class and race, specifically as these identities and contexts impact families. Furthermore, they rarely comment on the fact that divorce or abandonment by biological fathers places many single mothers into poverty, exposing children and mother alike to the negative impacts of severe economic deprivation. Rather, they focus on the alleged exploitation of men as ATM machines in highly privileged contexts.

Thus, while it seems reasonable to request that the judicial system reevaluate its approach to custody, there is no evidence that angry women and feminists in the context of children and custody are victimizing men. Men can and should effectively parent, and the establishment of caring and nurturing bonds with children should give men a right to access and continue such care for children. What MRM arguments do is obscure the most pressing issues facing parents, degrading the model of parenthood from a caring relationship to a matter of individual rights and access.

Conclusion

MRM arguments concerning custody and children demonstrate a characteristic misunderstanding concerning the nature of power. As Foucault argues, power is not something one can simply have or not have, nor is its impact merely limiting or repressive. Rather, power organizes and creates subjects, determining social perceptions and relationships. This understanding of power indicates that the issue for fathers is not a mere inequality in terms of access that gives women power, but rather a gender complex that orders subjects and caring relationships along exploitative lines. While caring for children is rewarding emotional labor, the construct of women as caregivers places an overwhelming amount of responsibility on women, while emotionally stunting men in terms of access to emotional support as well as in emotional development. Since men are socially distanced from families through masculine constructs, the absorption of men into further alienating systems of capitalist exploitation is the next logical step in a power-laden system of domination.

Fathers and Cultural Imperialism

Media images and representations not only reflect cultural standards and norms, but also work to reinforce the norms in question. Thus, popular culture can be understood as a dialectic, both informed by and actively shaping the popular conscious and subconscious. Because media images play this role, the MRM points to cultural representations of fathers as further evidence for the pervasive and oppressive degradation and devaluation of fathers. According to the MRM, fathers in pop culture frequently appear as buffoons, punch lines, or as irresponsible failures, reinforcing an overall negative perception of men and fatherhood. While there are representations fitting such descriptions, I will argue that these images suggest a more complex interpretation that position parents of both genders problematically.

Fathers in Popular Culture

In order to assess the status of fathers in popular culture, I will examine representations that fit two persistent archetypes: father as buffoon/clown and the abusive/absentee fathers. To create this analysis, I will focus on a single example of each that exemplifies many of the criticisms leveled by the MRM. The patterns that emerge will demonstrate that such representations reflect complex family structures and notions of care, indicating that these archetypes do far more cultural work than simply insulting men. Rather, these images create a complex representation of masculinity, creating spaces of both degradation of empowerment that rely upon interactions and relations to women. Overall, the examples I will discuss demonstrate the positioning of men and women both within the family and in the society at large, reflecting the privileges and pains of both gendered positions.

Starting with fathers as buffoons/clowns, the MRM is correct in claiming that such archetypes abound, including such classic examples as: Homer Simpson (*The Simpsons*),[55] Clark Griswold (*National Lampoon's Vacation*),[56] and Daniel Hilliard (*Mrs. Doubtfire*).[57] Because *Mrs. Doubtfire*'s plot centers on issues concerning divorce and custody that relate directly to this discussion, I will focus on Daniel Hilliard as the exemplar of the clownish dad image. In the film, Daniel is a caring but highly irresponsible father. His behavior positions him as a child as opposed to an adult in a mature marital relationship. These qualities result in divorce, and Daniel is denied custody until he can give evidence of steady income and appropriate residence. While attempting to gain such assets, Daniel offers to watch the children while his wife, Miranda, works. When she says no, Daniel hatches a scheme to dress up as a good natured British nanny in order to be hired as the caretaker for his own children, and Miranda ends up hiring Danny under the identity of "Mrs. Doubtfire." Under the care of Danny/Doubtfire, the children's' lives improve greatly, but Danny's ruse is inevitably exposed. Even with income and residence, Danny is denied custody due to his actions. However, upon realizing the positive impact Danny had on the children's lives, Miranda hires him as the full time babysitter, giving him access to the children whenever he likes. Danny then turns Mrs. Doubtfire into a successful television program, and everyone lives happily ever after.

It is possible to read this film as a denigration of fathers, portraying men as incompetent fools and failures. Danny's behavior is childish at best, even though his love for his children is unfailing. He is incapable of relating to his wife due to his immaturity, but his "fun" nature causes her to come off as cold, unreasonable, and vindictive. In other words, this contrast in characters positions Miranda as an unreasonable and disapproving mother who simply cannot let go of her agenda long enough to let her children have a little fun. However, claims to her "unreasonableness" are not obviously true. Danny's behavior is often irresponsible, if not downright disturbing. Danny's inability to contribute in a holistic way to the household is not simply counteracted by his role as the "fun dad." Nonetheless, in the film, Danny is irresistibly charming, and the audience is encouraged to identify and hence root for him throughout. Such identification causes viewers to perceive his loss of custody as some form of injustice. However, requesting that a parent have proper living arrangements and basic income in order to obtain custody is not unfair, much less unjust. Further, such reasonable requests do not legitimate such wildly unreasonable responses that include deception, lying, falsified identity, and a complete invasion of Miranda's personal life without proper consent. Even if Danny does all of this for the children, the intent does not justify the unethical, illegal, and invasive means. In spite of this, while Danny is the clown in some ways, he is truly the heart of the film, making the children happy and melting Miranda's icy walls with his good nature and engaging personality.

Given this analysis, I see very little here to justify any claims that these films insult fathers. Clark Griswold and Homer Simpson follow similar suits, engaging in silly, irresponsible behaviors that, while terribly fun, inevitably lead to some clean up by their respective wives, who often come off as wet blankets. Thus, the goofy dad is not possible without the "adult," overly caring, or possibly authoritarian mother. At the end of the day, Clark, Homer, Danny, and the like, are all good providers economically while keeping children happy with fun and adventures. However, in the background are mothers who perform the housework, family organization, and care work that allow these men to have such fun. Michael Kimmel notes this tendency in wider culture, explaining that, currently, men seem to have changed their approach to fatherhood far more than their approach to marriage. According to Kimmel, in spite of MRM protests to the contrary, men perform less housework than women, but are increasing participation in child care. This creates a disequilibrium that Kimmel characterizes as the dad becoming the "fun parent," taking children out on excursions and playing games while moms complete the housework, cooking, and so on.[58] In any case, the role of the childish father figure is not an overwhelmingly negative portrayal. Rather, these portrayals suggest an imbalance in family and care labor, requiring a woman to do the work that enables the dad to be such a marvelous time. Furthermore, these men are not total buffoons—Clark is a successful businessman, Danny finds success in entertainment, and even Homer is consistently employed. This economic success offsets the carefree attitudes of these characters, making them more admirable than not.

At the other end of the spectrum are fathers as failures: abusive, addicts, or absent. Examples include Royal Tenenbaum, the absentee playboy father in *The Royal Tenenbaums*,[59] Lester Burnham, the emotionally absent father in *American Beauty*,[60] and Ornette Howard, the absentee addict father to Vince Howard in the television series *Friday Night Lights*.[61] Each of these characters is an emotionally impoverished man, unable to connect with their spouses or children in spite of an overwhelming desire to do so. The source of this inability varies by character. Royal is innately selfish, setting up schemes to trick his family into accepting or forgiving him, and ends up dying of a heart attack at the end. Lester is deeply unhappy in his work, and attempts to escape the drudgery of a meaningless job and unfulfilling marriage only to be murdered in the end. Finally, Ornette is an ex-con who returns to his family after serving time in prison, attempting to bond with his son over his football career and get his wife back, only to relapse in to old habits involving violence and substance abuse.

These characters demonstrate significant differences but reflect important themes that persist across genres. Bell hooks analyzes Lester and *American Beauty*, arguing, "Popular culture offers us few or no redemptive images of men who start out emotionally dead. Unlike Sleeping Beauty, they cannot be brought back to life. In actuality, individual men are engaged in the work of emotional recovery everyday, but the work is not easy because they have no support systems within patriarchal culture."[62] In other words, the issue of concern is not an unfair representation of deadbeat dads. Rather, it is the hopelessness that popular culture reflects in terms of men's emotional wellbeing. The male characters outlined here are not punching bags but tragedies, desperate to connect with their families but with no idea how. This is not a simple case of demonizing masculinity or the cultural imperialism Young describes. They should be read as an expression of male pain, and thus as a call to reexamine masculinity and its toxic effects. The inevitable annihilation of such characters is devastating, because each exemplifies some form of hegemonic masculinity. Thus, it is not masculine failure or misandry that destroys them, but rather an overcommitment to masculinity itself. Authentic emotional development becomes impossible.

While popular culture retains men and fathers as punch lines and tragedies in films and television, there is nothing to suggest that the MRM interpretation of such representations is adequate. The problem is not simply stereotypes, but the reinforcement of problematic gender roles across the board through the construction of family images on screen. Comic images do not simply disempower men, but also work to reinforce a lack of responsibility in family contexts, creating a complex message informed by oppressive gender roles. Dramatic roles have much darker suggestions, implying that men cannot succeed in emotional growth, and are often annihilated before any such development can be achieved. Consequently, the MRM argument that men are oppressed as fathers through cultural imperialism must be rejected due to its simplistic and heavy-handed approach to analyzing such images. Men are not simply unfairly bludgeoned in the media; rather, media images serve to subtly reinforce a complex system of gender that creates various privileges and restrictions. The images men receive reinforce hegemonic (and often toxic) masculinity, a gender identity that creates an overall net of privilege in spite of the costs.

CONCLUSION

My analysis concludes that the MRM cannot coherently claim that men are oppressed via fatherhood and marriage, and the harms or restrictions men experience in these contexts cannot be attributed to feminism or women alone. Kimmel suggests that, especially in the context of divorce, that men channel their grief and frustration to MRM-type explanations that exonerate them of responsibility while placing all of the blame on women. Thus, personal tragedy becomes a political strategy.[63] Kimmel points out that it is actually feminist women who cleared the way for men to have greater participation in parenting, and that it is actually work and hegemonic masculinity preventing men from being good, engaged fathers.

Given these issues, fatherhood and parenting need social, legal, and political consideration and intervention, but radically different kinds than what the MRM suggests. First, parental cooperation in marriage and divorce must be emphasized for both parents, and this includes sharing in all levels of responsibility. Second, our legal system should consider different approaches to evaluating custody, taking care relationships and nurturing as central determining factors. Finally, the culture needs to continue to strive to change expectations of masculinity, shifting emphasis to relational models, encouraging emotional expression and development, and teaching children these values consistently. These types of approach suggest a long road but one of high reward. The MRM model promises nothing but more of the same, due to a refusal to build communities, distribute responsibility, and to deconstruct toxic masculinity.

NOTES

1. "96% of Women Are Liars, Honest," last updated October, 2015, http://www.scotsman.com/news/uk/96-of-women-are-liars-honest-1-565123; "Women: 50% Would Lie about Paternity, While 42% Would Lie About Being on Birth Control," last updated July 19, 2014, http://www.avoiceformen.com/allnews/women-50-would-lie-about-paternity-while-42-would-lie-about-being-on-birth-control/.
2. Carnell Smith, "12 Reasons for DNA Paternity Testing," last updated December 17, 2013, http://www.avoiceformen.com/paternity-fraud/12-reasons-for-dna-paternity-testing/.
3. Robert Estephe, "The Lethal Paternity Fraud Racket," last updated February 24, 2014, http://www.avoiceformen.com/series/unknown-history-of-misandry/the-lethal-paternity-fraud-racket/.
4. "Reproductive Health," last accessed November 16, 2016, http://www.who.int/topics/reproductive_health/en/.
5. Janet Bloomfield, "Here's Why Men Should Have the Reproductive Rights That Women Have," last updated May 30, 2014, http://thoughtcatalog.com/janet-bloomfield/2014/05/heres-why-men-should-have-the-reproductive-rights-that-women-have/.
6. Since most of these organizations are pro-life, the rhetoric of baby, child, etc. is common as opposed to neutral terms such as fetus, embryo, etc.
7. Kristi Burton Brown, "Abortion and Men: What's a Father to Do?" last updated June 5, 2013, http://liveactionnews.org/abortion-and-men-whats-a-father-to-do/.
8. Criticisms of marriage generally focus on heterosexual unions in MRM discussions.
9. Warren Farrell, *The Myth of Male Power* (New York: Simon and Schuster, 1993), Kindle edition, 732.
10. Farrell, *Myth of Male Power*, 744.
11. Robert Estephe, "Alimony Slaves Can Do It!" last updated August 7, 2013, http://www.avoiceformen.com/series/unknown-history-of-misandry/alimony-slaves-can-do-it/.
12. Robert Estephe, "Alimony Unlimited (and the Emergence of a Men's Rights Movement)," last accessed November 24, 2013, http://www.avoiceformen.com/series/unknown-history-of-misandry/alimony-unlimited-and-the-emergence-of-a-mens-rights-movement/.
13. Douglas Galbi, "Fathers as Wallets: Legal History of Child Support," last updated January 11, 2016, http://www.avoiceformen.com/men/fathers/fathers-as-wallets-legal-history-of-child-support/.
14. Helen Smith, "8 Reasons Straight Men Don't Want to Get Married," last updated June 23, 2013, http://www.avoiceformen.com/men/mens-issues/8-reasons-straight-men-dont-want-to-get-married/.
15. Farrell, *Myth of Male Power*, 931.
16. Rocking Mr. E, "21st Century Fatherhood," last updated January 18, 2012, http://www.avoiceformen.com/men/fathers/21st-century-fatherhood/.
17. Janet Bloomfield, "6 Truths about Dads Feminists Don't Want You to Know," last updated March 20, 2015, http://thoughtcatalog.com/janet-bloomfield/2015/03/6-truths-about-dads-feminists-dont-want-you-to-know/.
18. Farrell, *Myth of Male Power*, 1188.
19. Patrice Stanton, "Lessons from a Men's Divorce Seminar," last updated October 31, 2012, http://www.avoiceformen.com/mens-rights/family-courts/lessons-from-a-mens-divorce-seminar/.
20. Janet Bloomfield, "Single Women Raising Children Do a Poor Job," last updated July 2, 2015, http://www.avoiceformen.com/mens-rights/single-women-raising-children-do-a-poor-job/.
21. For examples, see: Prentice Reid, "Opposing Shared Parenting: The Feminist Track Record," last updated March 5, 2015, http://www.avoiceformen.com/mens-rights/opposing-

shared-parenting-the-feminist-track-record/ and Illimitableman, 2016, Reddit thread, rant/venting, https://www.reddit.com/r/TheRedPill/comments/3jejin/single_mothers_are_delinquent_subhuman_scum_who/.

22. "Parental Alienation Syndrome," last updated April 22, 2016, http://www.avoiceformen.com/mens-rights/families/parental-alienation-syndrome/.

23. Edward Kruk, "The Impact of Parental Alienation on Children," last updated April 25, 2013, https://www.psychologytoday.com/blog/co-parenting-after-divorce/201304/the-impact-parental-alienation-children.

24. Prentice Reid, "Most Dads Are Deadbeats?" last updated March 20, 2015, http://www.avoiceformen.com/men/most-dads-are-deadbeats/.

25. bell hooks, *The Will to Change: Men, Masculinity, and Love* (New York: Washington Square Press, 2004).

26. Michael Kimmel, *Angry White Men: American Masculinity at the End of an Era* (New York: Nation Books, 2013), 3.

27. Michael Kimmel, *Guyland: The Perilous World Where Boys Become Men—Understanding the Critical Years Between 16–26* (New York, HarperCollins, 2008), 35.

28. hooks, *Will to Change*, 94.

29. hooks, *Will to Change*, 96.

30. Kimmel, *Angry White Men*, 9.

31. Sandra Bartky, *Femininity and Domination: Studies in the Phenomenology of Oppression* (New York: Routledge, 1990), 41.

32. Herbert Marcuse, *One Dimensional Man: Studies in the Ideology of Advanced Industrial Society* (Boston: Beacon Press, 1955), 7.

33. bell hooks, *Feminism: From Margin to Center* (Cambridge: South End Press, 1984), 133.

34. Karl Marx, *Economic and Philosophical Manuscripts of 1844* (Moscow: Progress Publishers, 1959).

35. Marcuse, *One Dimensional Man*, 4.

36. Marcuse, *One Dimensional Man*, 9.

37. Marcuse, *One Dimensional Man*, 7.

38. Kimmel, *Angry White Men*, 43.

39. Bellis, et al., "Measuring Paternal Discrepancy and its Public Health Consequences," *Journal of Epidemiology and Community Health*, 59 (2005): 749–754, http://jech.bmj.com/content/59/9/749.long.

40. Paul Rincon, "Study Debunks Illegitimacy Myth," *BBC News*, February 11, 2005, http://news.bbc.co.uk/2/hi/science/nature/7881652.stm.

41. Bellis, et al., "Measuring Discrepancy."

42. Judith Thomson, "A Defense of Abortion," in *Philosophy and Public Affairs*, 1 (1971).

43. Susan Bordo, *Unbearable Weight: Feminism, Western Culture, and the Body* (Berkeley: California Press, 1995), 89.

44. Bordo, *Unbearable Weight*, 93.

45. Mary Shanley, "Fathers' Rights, Mothers' Wrongs? Reflections on Unwed Fathers' Rights, Patriarchy, and Sex Inequality," in *Reproduction, Ethics, and the Law: Feminist Perspectives*, ed. Joan Callahan (Bloomington: University of Indiana Press, 1995).

46. Kimmel, *Angry White Men*, 155.

47. Shanley, "Fathers' Rights," 228.

48. Shanley, "Fathers' Rights," 230.

49. Shanley, "Fathers' Rights," 231.

50. Martha Fineman, *The Illusion of Equality* (Chicago: University of Chicago Press, 1991).

51. Shanley, "Fathers' Rights," 235.

52. David Surface, "Revisiting Parental Alienation Syndrome," in *Social Work Today*, 9 (2009), http://www.socialworktoday.com/archive/092109p26.shtml.

53. Surface, "Parental Alienation," http://www.socialworktoday.com/archive/092109p26.shtml.

54. Kimmel, *Angry White Men*.

55. *The Simpsons*, created by Matt Groening (Fox Network, 1989–Present).

56. *National Lampoon's Vacation*, directed by Harold Ramis (Warner Brothers, 1983).
57. *Mrs. Doubtfire*, directed by Christopher Columbus (20th Century Fox, 1993).
58. Kimmel, *Angry White Men*, 145.
59. *The Royal Tenenbaums*, directed by Wes Anderson (Buena Vista Pictures, 2001).
60. *American Beauty*, directed by Sam Mendes (DreamWorks Pictures, 1999).
61. *Friday Night Lights*, television series, created by Peter Berg (NBCUniversal, 2006–2011).
62. hooks, *Will to Change*, 101.
63. Kimmel, *Angry White Men*, 139.

Chapter Six

Men, Violence, and Oppression

The problem of masculinity and violence is a well-documented issue that has been examined across many fields and in many contexts. The MRM points to male exposure to violence, harm, and punishment as a significant aspect of male oppression. This chapter will provide an overview of the MRM's conception of masculinity and violence, followed by an analysis of oppression and the gender politics of violence. Violence will be broadly construed, including structural and economic violence as well as direct acts of assault, and so forth. While men do have unique experiences as both forces and victims of violence, these experiences cannot be explained through a simple dichotomous gender framework that claims women have various privileges that men lack. Rather, systemic social violence is the result of complexly overlapping cultural realities and identities that involve, and yet are not limited to, race, class, gender, and education.

THE PROBLEM OF VIOLENCE AND THE MRM

The men's rights movement cites a variety of issues relating to violence as evidence for male oppression. While the examples provided are plentiful, the discussion of violence tends to fall along the lines of four general themes of "male oppression": male sacrifice for women (gynocentrism), male powerlessness, myths concerning gender violence, and discrimination in punishment. Using these themes, the MRM issue of men and violence can easily be related to other issues and concerns argued to revolve around such gendered cultural norms.

Gynocentrism

As discussed in previous chapters, gynocentrism refers to the supposed cultural tendency of men to sacrifice a whole manner of things for the good of women. According to MRAs, gynocentrism is a norm that can be traced back throughout history, and male sacrifice regularly takes the form of economic, sexual, and psychological output creating comfort for women at a great personal cost to men.[1] In terms of violence, many MRAs argue that men's bodily sacrifices in terms of working in dangerous careers as well as through military requirements function as some of the most exploitative manifestations of gynocentric culture.

Warren Farrell points out that men are much more likely to work in dangerous jobs, referring to this phenomenon as the "glass cellar."[2] According to Farrell, the sacrifice many men make in working these jobs reflects the overall demand for men to economically nurture families and women, creating a so-called financial womb.[3] The jobs that Farrell is describing include, but are not limited to: truck drivers, carpenters, lumberjacks, roofers, construction workers, and welders. Other dangerous work includes rescue work such as firefighting. He points out that feminists regularly cite such professions as "boys clubs," and that women are systematically excluded from participation in such work. However, he counters this complaint by arguing that such jobs are actually dangerous and deadly, as opposed to desirable or valued male-only spaces.

In order to establish this point, Farrell then argues that there is a difference between "worst jobs" and merely having low-paying work. He explains, "Because many of the low paid jobs are low paid because they are safer, have higher fulfillment, more flexible hours, and other desirable characteristics that make them more in demand and therefore lower in pay."[4] It is for these reasons that women supposedly choose these types of jobs as opposed to the male-dominated death professions. These reasons follow a specific pattern, Farrell alleges, and this pattern demonstrates seven characteristics of jobs that women prefer: ability to check out at the end of the day, physical safety, indoors, low risk, flexible/desirable hours, no demands to relocate, high fulfillment, and contact with people.[5] Men, however, do not have such luxury, and opt for riskier, less fulfilling work in order to meet the economic demands regularly placed upon them. Knowing that men will take these jobs, Farrell claims that employers put men in danger as a money-saving device, and that there is little business/economic motivation to maintain safety standards for these workers.

In addition to the sacrifices men regularly make in terms of work and exposure, the greatest sacrifice that men are required to make for women involves military service and the draft. Farrell points out that boys are socialized from a very young age to withstand pain, value military actions, and to treat such violence as normal. He calls this the "psychological draft." This then prepares young boys to become men that are forced into dangerous wartime positions and jobs. Unlike men, women in the United States are not required to register for the draft, nor are they required to expose themselves to significantly dangerous combat situations. Consequently, many MRMs point to the military as further evidence that gynocentric norms make it permissible to use men as human shields during wartime in order to minimize and risk to women. This explains why 99 percent of combat deaths are men, not to mention that 94 percent of industrial deaths.[6]

These examples argue that men are economically and sociopolitically exploited through a call to provide for, serve, and protect women and children. At no point do these arguments engage a criticism of capitalism or militarism in the state. Rather, these structures are maintained as preferable or necessary for the good of society, and the criticism is rooted in a rejection of the current applications and manifestations of these concepts. Thus, the MRM argues that gynocentrism has created an unfair, and even oppressive, form of militaristic capitalism that can potentially be corrected through a redistribution of work and draft expectations.

Male Powerlessness

One of the main "truths" told by the MRM is that men are in fact powerless, and that the patriarchy is a myth created and perpetuated by feminists. Such powerlessness is attributed to the economic exploitation of men combined with the devaluation of masculinity. In the context of violence, male powerlessness results in a high suicide rate among men, as well as male experiences of homicide and assault.

The alleged epidemic of male suicide is a centerpiece issue for most MRAs. According to AVFM, 80 percent of suicides are men, making suicide the eighth leading cause of male death, and most victims are divorced men and/or estranged fathers.[7] Farrell argues that people who feel loved and needed rarely commit suicide, and that men who commit suicide often feel like a failure or burden to others. Such men may believe that they are doing everyone a favor, and they do not know how to ask for help.[8] Much of this can be traced back to the dependence men feel on success for personal validation. Any loss of success can create extreme feelings of despair in men. Farrell goes as far as to compare men's experience of unemployment to women's feelings about rape and sexual assault. He claims that both involve a sense of violation, come without consent, and makes individuals feel extremely vulnerable.

In addition to self-inflicted violence, MRAs point out that men are the victims of violent crime from others as well. Farrell argues that men are more likely to be the victims of all violent crimes, and that the more violent the crime, the more likely that the victim is a man.[9] The issue to be explained is then why men are overwhelmingly the perpetrators of such violent crimes as well. Farrell explains, "Murder, rape, spouse abuse, like suicide and alcoholism, are but a minute's worth of superficial power to compensate for years of powerlessness. They are manifestations of hopelessness committed by the powerless, which is why they are committed disproportionately by blacks and men."[10] The solution he proposes is that we, as a society, stop asking men to give more to women than we ask women to give to men. The devaluation of men is causing men to feel and become increasingly disempowered, with violence functioning as a sort of last-ditch attempt to reclaim some form of power.

The argument is then made that this devaluation of men is consistently imposed on individuals in a society starting at a very young age. Farrell points to a variety of examples, including the more frequent use of corporal punishment on boys, and the erasure of male victims of violence, specifically in the context of sexual and domestic abuse. Cultural images and activities further the normalizing of violence against males. Young boys and men are encouraged to play and watch violent contact sports such as football, and movies/television geared toward men is often violent. According to Farrell, male characters in film are killed off without thought, with women only being murdered in horror films or other very specific film contexts.[11] He points to the prevalence of "women-in-jeopardy-films" as paradigmatic of modern day tendencies for women to select the best male protectors, in line with gynocentric tendencies. Furthermore, sometimes the murder of men is framed as female liberation in film, and Farrell cites "Thelma and Louise" as a classic example.

In summary, the MRM claims that violence is not indicative of power, and also that violence regularly impacts men as both perpetrators and victims. This is due to the fact that men are socialized to value violence, expect violence, and to tolerate violence without complaint. There is no social or legal protection set forth to protect men from violence. Thus, men are oppressed both psychologically and distributively by violence, due to constant threat, lack of recognition for male suffering, and a lack of resources to protect men from violence.

Gender and Violence

One of the key issues motivating the MRM is the belief that charges of gender violence, specifically in terms of domestic violence and rape or sexual assault, are widely exaggerated and misrepresented by feminists. In general, the MRM will admit that women do experience rape, sexual assault, and domestic violence; however, they also claim that men experience these issues at comparable rates, but their experiences are diminished or ignored due to feminist rhetoric about rape culture or violence against women. Because feminists control the rhetoric surrounding these issues, men are allegedly damaged by being constantly framed as dangerous perpetrators, and lack the resources to express their unique experiences of such violence. Thus, the MRM argues that feminism contributes to male powerlessness by creating a discourse that erases male experiences, contributes to fear and hatred of men, and diminishes the damage violence inflicts on men as a social group.

Overall, the MRM rejects the feminist notion that culture is structured in such a way as to normalize violence against women, specifically in terms of what is referred to as "rape culture." Many MRMs portray the feminist notion of rape culture as an argument that society trains men to perpetrate rape, thus criminalizing men regardless of actions and contributing to high levels of paranoia concerning the frequency of rape and sexual assault.[12] Paul Elam describes rape culture as a falsely manufactured scare tactic based on an inherent contradiction. According to Elam, feminists claim that women are powerful and equal to men, but, in the context of concepts such as rape culture, simultaneously argue that women are helplessly exposed to the dangers of large, aggressive males.[13] Elam argues that such concepts work to further portray women as victims and men as monsters, further erasing male experiences of violence in terms of sexual assault, domestic violence, and the contexts described earlier in this chapter. Furthermore, this alleged hysteria gives men no protection from false rape or domestic violence allegations from vengeful, angry women.

According to many in the MRM, men experience rape with higher frequency than women, and that the statistics on sexual assault that feminists present are highly inaccurate. Elam points out that men Are raped by women, and in some instances, this sexual assault is framed as a positive experience. For instance, when female teachers engage in sexual relationships with male students, the pain of that experience is often ignored as the young man is congratulated for his "conquest."[14] Furthermore, young boys are sexually abused at alarming rates. Most telling, according to articles posted on AVFM, is the frequency of male rape in prisons, a statistic that allegedly demonstrates that men in the United States experience higher levels of sexual assault than women once these figures are taken into account.[15] However, since feminists monopolize the conversation on sexual assault and abuse, MRAs such as Elam claim that the general social perception is that men cannot be raped, and women cannot be rapists, an unfortunate and dangerous perception that minimizes the very real experiences of men.

The MRM also argues that the instances of false rape claims are significantly higher than feminists admit, pointing to supposedly problematic approaches to reading and analyzing criminal data. AVFM published a list detailing the reasons behind what they allege is the common occurrence of false rape claims.[16] According to this piece, the reasons behind such false accusations vary, but the themes of revenge, political posturing, and regret are prevalent. Combining such motivations with a presumption of guilt in contexts such as college campuses and a lack of consequences for false accusers results in an epidemic experience of persecution for men. Additionally, it can be very difficult to prove the falsity of such a rape allegation, and in some instances women are indoctrinated by feminists to perceive a wide variety of sexual acts that are not rape as rape. Finally, this piece points out that the dark side of women's nature and socialization contribute to this problem, arguing that feminists teach women that all women are good and all men are evil. This represses fair and thoughtful evaluation of specific cases by a presumption of gendered moral natures.

The issue of domestic violence also arises in these discussions, often pointing to a similar gendered division that assumes only men perpetrate violence, and that women do not commit acts of violence against their partners. However, Elam argues that the notion that women are small and weak while men are strong and menacing is a feminist myth, and that men frequently experience domestic violence. Because of the gendered concepts surrounding violence, this violence against men is also often ignored, erased or demeaned. Furthermore, false allegations of domestic violence against men also abound, usually used against men in the context of custody cases and trials.

To conclude, the MRM does acknowledge the existence of gendered violence, but have significantly different understandings of the ways in which such violence manifests itself. According to the MRM, rape and violence impact individuals of both genders, however the experiences of one gender, men, are systematically ignored. Furthering this harm is the fact that, not only are men's experiences demeaned and erased, but men are also labeled as the villains in almost all scenarios of violence. This results in significant legal, personal, and psychological harms with no viable routes for rectification. Overall, the MRM argues that these forms of cultural violence have more serious consequences for men, and that feminism contributes to the oppression of men through the myths of rape culture and violence against women.

Discrimination in Punishment

The final issue concerning violence is the alleged discrimination men experience in terms of punishment. In terms of sentencing, the MRM argues that men consistently receive longer sentences than women, are shown fewer leniencies, and more regularly receive the death penalty. Farrell argues that women's prisons are safer than men's prisons, and more invested in rehabilitation.[17] Overall, the MRM claims that men are discriminated against in terms of punishment, and that this discrimination is sexist and morally wrong/unjust.

Starting with the death penalty, there is a significant disparity in the enforcement of the death penalty along gendered lines at every stage of the process. Two major factors seem to influence this gendered difference, namely the nature of crimes women commit and the way juries view women.[18] While the death penalty is frequently inflicted on individuals who commit crimes such as sexual assault or robbery in addition to homicide, women rarely perpetrate such acts. Rather, women are more likely to commit homicide against someone they know:

> While women commit about 10% of murders, they were responsible for 35% of murders of intimate partners between 1980 and 2008. Most juries consider these crimes of passion arising from disputes—one-time offenses.... Because of the high rate of domestic violence against women, though, juries don't give men the same benefit of the doubt.[19]

However, this article goes on to point out women who kill children or who hire someone to kill for them become more likely to be put on death row.

Furthermore, due to the fact that women are culturally perceived as being more emotional and/or susceptible to fits of passion, juries are often more likely to demonstrate leniency in sentencing. Some MRM sympathizers argue that this is just an extended consequence of gynocentrism manifested in the form of chivalry in the courtroom. Once again, the male/societal impulse to protect women allows women to avoid punishments such as the death penalty.[20] Since women are apparently shielded from the full extent of the law in terms of punishment, women are not likely to support gender equality in terms of the death penalty. Richard Dieter, executive director of the Death Penalty Information Center, argues, "For equality's sake, you would think that women would want the death penalty pursued more often. But of course they don't."[21]

Thus, the alleged sexist disparity that occurs in the death penalty is emblematic of the supposedly unjust gendered distribution of justice on the whole. AVFM lists statistics to support these allegations, arguing that the average incarceration rate for women is 18.51 months as opposed to 51.52 months for men. Additionally, they point out that the U.S. rate of incarceration is the highest in the world, with men making up 93 percent of the prison population.[22] If Farrell is correct, this data then combines with the fact that men are not only in prison more often and for longer periods, but the conditions they suffer in prison are significantly worse than what female prisoners experience. All of this together is argued to demonstrate that society treats men as disposable both physically and economically, while women continue to exist in a protected state, shielding them from the consequences of actions.

A PHILOSOPHICAL ANALYSIS OF VIOLENCE

In order to adequately assess the ways in which men experience violence, a detailed philosophical analysis defining violence and establishing the relevant scope of violence is required. Clearly, violence is both an individual and social phenomenon, and is mediated by social forces such as gender, economics, race, and so forth. Thus, I will propose a definition of violence based on the work of James Gilligan, a clinical psychiatrist, and apply this definition to the broader social phenomenon of aggression and violence in culture. In order to make these points, I will utilize Marcuse's discussion of Eros and Thanatos in order to place Gilligan's definition in the wider context of repression, capitalism, and the reality principles working to shape and inform identity. This discussion will conclude that violence is the result of feelings of shame, and such feelings are distinctly gendered within different contexts, resulting in the central role violence plays in the establishment and maintenance of masculine identity.

Individuals and Violence

Violence is not a unified phenomenon—its applications, usages, and meanings vary across contexts. However, there is a general cultural conception that violence is indicative of power; in other words, the ability to enact violence is to be powerful and the experience of violence indicates a lack of power. The tendency toward violence has been culturally coded as a masculine trait, and explanations of such tendencies abound. Oftentimes, these explanations are rooted in biology, indicating that male violence is an innate and unavoidable aspect of masculinity. Bell hooks argues that such explanations serve to hide the workings of an oppressive patriarchal system, obscuring the fact that violence is socially constructed as a tool for gaining power, evidenced by the fact that patriarchal women also turn to violence as a means for empowerment in such constructs.[23] Violence punishes, silences, and is read as an expression of strength in a patriarchal system deeply invested in dominance and hierarchy.

James Gilligan argues that violence has become an epidemic in U.S. society. While he argues that violence can take many forms, including natural disasters and accidental experiences, the tragedy of violence consists in incidents involving victims and victimizers. He argues that in order to understand violent action, we must approach violent acts as something larger than the individual perpetrator. He states, "Each of us is inextricably bound to others—in relationship. All human action (even the act of an individual) is relational."[24] Thus, we must examine institutional, familial, societal, as well as individual aspects in order to truly gain an appropriate understanding of violent actions.

Gilligan points out that perpetrators of violence often describe their actions as a sort of justice, an undoing of some perceived harm or wrong. If hooks is correct about the perceived connection between violence and power, then the notion of violence as corrective or self-affirming is not surprising. When one is wronged they are disempowered, and violence offers the possibility for a reclaiming of position or dominance. However, the tragedy arises because violence does not provide the desired effect. While individual perpetrators of violence may experience a temporary sense of satisfaction from such actions, this is a short-lived victory. Hooks describes the enactment and maintenance of violence for individuals as emotionally crushing and destructive, and Gilligan describes violent offenders in prison as the "living dead."[25] In his research, Gilligan worked with extremely violent offenders, and his description of them as dead is meant to be literal as opposed to metaphorical. According to Gilligan, many of these men describe an inability to feel anything at all, emotionally or, at times, physically.

Notably, the violent perpetrators that Gilligan works with are overwhelmingly male. However, Gilligan does not believe that this is due to biology or any other innate property of masculinity, mirroring hooks' argument.[26] Rather, since it cannot be explained in biological terms, Gilligan argues that violence is an understandable phenomenon and can be conceptualized as a response to a specific set of cultural conditions. Gilligan describes hearing themes concerning respect and humiliation consistently in his interviews with male inmates, leading him to the conclusion that shame is necessary, but not sufficient, for violence. Shame combines with other factors and emotions that create violent tendencies. Gilligan argues, "The purpose of violence is to diminish the intensity of shame and replace it as far as possible with its opposite, pride, thus preventing the individual from being overwhelmed by the feeling of shame."[27] Thus, Gilligan points out, most violent men are deeply and pathologically insecure and ashamed, feelings they attempt to avoid and bury under violent behavior, bravado, and machismo.

However, if shame is a necessary condition for violence, combining with other factors to produce behavior, this still does not explain why men are often more violent than women, or why certain violent behaviors such as machismo are coded as masculine. Since violence is not an innate, biological trait, then the normalization of violence must be a cultural phenomenon. The following section will examine the ways in which various social structures such as gender and capitalism result in structural violence, and this sort of violence then impacts individuals within a society. The problem of shame is not just an individual phenomenon; rather, it is an emotion that is systematically part of gendered constructs and socialization.

Violence as Social Phenomenon

Violence is not only an individual experience or defect. Rather, violence is a culturally instituted method for distributing individuals, translating power, and controlling various social aspects. Thus, violence can become part of one's identity through socialization, coding certain individuals as naturally violent and rewarding such behavior, as is arguably the case for masculinity. Such manifestations of violence are then complicated and amplified by other forms of structural violence that are directly linked to oppressive forces such as capitalist exploitation. Creating an understanding of these forces clarifies the sources and nature of individual violence, contributing to a clearer theoretical discussion concerning violence as a tool of group oppression and power, as well as experiences of harm and empowerment on an individual level. This section will discuss violence in the context of Marcuse's notions of repression and psychic drives, in order to apply these concepts to the definition of violence established in the previous section.

In *Eros and Civilization*, Marcuse provides a discussion concerning the primary drives present in human consciousness and the repression of those drives in the creation of civilization and society, as Freud describes.[28] Eros is the drive relating to the libido. Freud argues that uncontrolled libido, although it is associated with the gratification of needs required for survival, can be just as fatal as a death drive if uncontrolled. Without a certain amount of repression, Freud claims that an uncontrolled Eros or libido leads a person to seek gratification for its own sake at any moment, and such gratification cannot be granted by civilization. Thus, these instincts must be deflected and inhibited in the creation of a society through delayed gratification. Early forms of gratification in infantile states must be given over to a reality principle governing a civilization in order to create a useful, working member of society. In contrast to Eros, the death instinct is one of aggression. Marcuse explains, "The death instinct is destructiveness not for its own sake but for the relief of tension. The descent toward death is an unconscious flight from pain or want."[29] In the creation of civilization and entrance into society, the aggressive or destructive tendencies of this instinct are deflected away from the self and onto external objects.

The effective repression of these drives requires a certain amount of sublimation. Marcuse points out that contemporary society is one of alienated work and labor. Thus, in order to properly repress these drives and sublimate them effectively, the workings of Eros and the death drive must come to support a civilization in which people become useful members of society through their production. In some sense, the cultural inhibition of aggression for social utilization brings these forces into the service of Eros, as Eros is defined as the builder of culture. However, Marcuse points out that the nature of work itself in a capitalist system offers only a small degree of libidinal satisfaction, because alienated labor is generally painful and unhappy. Free choice in gratification is allowed only within a very restricted confine of choices. Thus, Marcuse claims, "The performance of such work hardly gratifies individual needs and inclinations. It was imposed on man by brute force; if alienated labor has anything to do with Eros, it must be very indirectly, and with a considerably sublimated and weakened Eros."[30] The question then becomes whether or not the inhibition of aggressive impulses works to offset this weakening of Eros.

Externalizing the aggressive tendencies of the ego onto the world is instrumental in establishing civilization. Such domination and destructiveness have led to power over nature, leading to important innovations in technology, and so forth. In this sense, it could be argued that such accomplishment works toward the proper sublimation of the death drive. Marcuse points out, "However, the extroverted destruction remains destructive: its objects are in most cases actually and violently assailed, deprived of their form, and reconstructed only after their component parts are forcibly rearranged. . . . Destructiveness, in extent and intent, seems to be more directly satisfied in civilization than the libido."[31] Thus, in a capitalist society such as ours, the sublimation of aggression is incomplete and leads to an increase in social forms of domination through the matrix of alienated labor relations.

While it is clear that in times of scarcity the repression of Eros is required, Marcuse points out that when there is no longer any such scarcity requirements, the repression of Eros is enacted in other forms. The closer a society comes to being able to liberate itself from toil and labor, the more imperative domination and its maintenance becomes for power groups, turning productivity against people and increasing externalized aggression and domination overall. It is at this point the notion of surplus repression becomes useful. This consists in the restrictions used for specific, historically located domination, and the performance principle relates to the historical form of the reality principle. In a capitalist society focused on making bodies and individuals useful for labor, domination functions as a way to isolate individuals from one another. People's closeness or likelihood of developing spontaneous relationships threatens the order of useful labor. As such capitalist progress increases, the lack of freedom intensifies in order to maintain dominance relations and increase the scope of capitalist motivated efficiency. Such models of domination infuse various aspects of life, including sexuality and gender.

It is clear that the current social structure in western society is not merely capitalist, but is, as bell hooks claims, a white supremacist capitalist patriarchy.[32] Thus, the reality principle as performative principle, the historically prevailing form of the reality principle, is one of masculine dominance and patriarchy. Because the reality/performative principle fails to ever master the repression of feminized Eros, masculinity itself is a tenuously constructed identity. Men must constantly strive to reestablish their masculine power, and this power is always under threat from the cultural mechanisms of shame and potential masculine failure. Michael Kaufman argues that masculinity is terrifyingly fragile. He argues, "But in the end it [masculinity] is just a social institution with a tenuous relationship to that with which it is supposed to be synonymous: our maleness, our biological sex."[33] In other words, the supposed natural sources of masculine identity are merely props to reaffirm a culturally constructed masculine identity that is constantly threatened. To effectively maintain masculinity, a man must never deviate from the norms set out for him, and any behavior perceived as feminine or even slightly less than masculine is met with quick and often devastating forms of cultural punishment. This state of affairs creates a crisis of constant anxiety in many men, because in the creation of a patriarchal power-based identity comes also the ever-present possibility of losing or failing to maintain such power. Timothy Beneke points out, "What makes the need to prove manhood compulsive is that it can never be satisfied; one is momentarily a man and then doubts reassert themselves—you're only as masculine as your last demonstration of masculinity."[34] One way in which men can overcome this anxiety is to enact a denial of powerlessness through aggression, which can be read as a ritualized acting out of power.[35] Consequently, violence becomes a means by which men can concretely demonstrate and confirm their power in the face of any threat to their masculinity. This violence and aggression becomes compulsive and repeated because it effectively asserts masculinity and dominance while effectively, if only momentarily, quelling masculine anxiety.

This reading of masculinity reinforces Gilligan's claim that shame is a necessary condition for violence. Along with Kimmel and Beneke, Gilligan argues that the experience of shame is a common one for men, and Gilligan points to the role of honor and honor codes in the construction of masculine identity to further explain this fact. Such cultures of honor require men to be violent to individuals of both sexes, but much of this violence is directed at other men. He argues, "It is men who are expected to be violent, and who are honored for doing so and dishonored for being unwilling to be violent. . . . Men are honored for activity (ultimately violent activity) and they are dishonored for passivity (or pacifism)."[36] Consequently, not only are men required to compulsively reenact gender norms and masculine performatives in order to maintain masculine identity, but also they are also promised certain cultural accolades and honor if they adhere to these expected codes of conduct. Violence comes to symbolize successful masculinity, and the personal as well as social costs of such success is systematically downplayed and erased.

Clearly, women also have a great capacity for violence, but the system of rewards is very different. Gilligan argues, "Restrictions on their freedom to engage in sexual as well as aggressive behavior is the price women pay for their relative freedom from the risk of lethal and life threatening violence to which men and boys are much more frequently exposed."[37] Thus, in some ways, women are protected from violence in the ways that the MRM claims, however, such protection does not come without a cost. Furthermore, women are also exposed to a complex honor code system as well, however the sense of honor impacting women tends to involve sexuality more than brute physical violence. According to Gilligan, women's role in male systems of honor is the power to destroy the honor of males, because women have the ability to bring dishonor to men through sexual behavior. Thus, women can bring dishonor by being too sexual, sexually aggressive, or by not being faithful. Once again, such restrictive demands limit women's movements and freedom of expression while contributing to the fragility of masculine identity and independent senses of self.

In conclusion, the demands of a repressive society create intolerable amounts of surplus repression for individuals. The inability to adequately repress psychic drives requires significant interventions from the forces of oppression external to the individual in order to maintain the culturally mandated codes of identity imposed on individuals. As a result, the reality principle requires stricter performances, and gender identities become increasingly precarious. Consequently, the frustrations of such repression become directed toward violent and aggressive releases, which are reinforced through assigning honor and diverting shame in response to such expressions. As the reinforcement becomes significantly less rewarding, the more aggression increases toward individual selves and others. Problematically, there is no cultural push toward Eros, thus, men engaging in such escalating cycles of shame, honor, and violence have no recourse to connection or emotion to circumvent this damage, resulting in the walking dead that Gilligan describes. Such cultural conditions also alienate women from men, making women a source of anxiety and frustration, and preventing true connections between the genders. Given such cultural conditions, it is unsurprising that we have a so-called gender war on our hands.

OPPRESSION, VIOLENCE, AND MASCULINITY

As Young points out, violence must be systematic and targeted in order to contribute to oppression. Thus, if men are oppressed by violence, certain conditions must hold. Violent actions must be random and unprovoked, resulting in a diminished sense of overall self-worth and general safety. Generally speaking, oppressive violence acts as a sort of terrorism, restricting the movements and options of the targeted group. Experiences of violence will evoke negative feelings, and will not result in a sense of honor, pride, or accomplishment. Overall, if men are oppressed by violence there should be identifiable psychological and distributive harms, and there should also be a clearly identified source of this oppression. While it seems clear in many respects that men are deeply influenced and harmed by violence in complex ways, it is not a straightforward matter of men being oppressed by women and feminism, nor is violence always strictly oppressive. Relying on the model of violence proposed above, I will investigate the difficulties involved in assessing the social, political, and cultural role that violence has for men, arguing that while the MRM points to important and pressing issues for men, their analysis of the situation and assignments of blame are distressingly inaccurate and misplaced.

Masculine Sacrifice and Economics

The MRM discusses the issue of men working in high-risk jobs as evidence for male oppression and gynocentrism. While the risks men take and the violence they are exposed to in these contexts is unquestionably problematic at times, the argument that such exposure is a result of gynocentrism must be rejected. The restrictions individuals face in terms of work options operate along gendered lines, distributing individuals strategically along the economic spectrum. For example, women are often shuffled into "pink collar" work such as caregiving professions or assistant roles, while men are pushed toward manual labor in the context of "blue collar" roles. In any case, the issue we are confronting in terms of such distribution of labor is a problem of economic exploitation along gendered lines, not the oppression of men by women in the enforcement of such work. In this section, I will argue that the violence men experience as workforce danger is the result of capitalist patriarchy, a system that exploits individuals under the guise of a fair and competitive market.

Gilligan points out that not all violence occurs between individuals; rather, violence can occur within a wider system that distributes and maintains oppression. He defines such structural violence as the higher number of deaths experienced by individuals in the lower tiers of society, and that such disproportionate fatality numbers are caused by class structures.[38] Such structural violence differs from behavioral (individual violence) in three aspects: (1) structural violence operates continuously; (2) structural violence operates independently of individual acts; (3) structural violence is often invisible because it may appear to have other causes.[39] Thus, I would argue that the imposition of high-risk work on lower class males is, in fact, a reflection of structural violence. Men in these positions are often exploited, injured, and underpaid. However, economic strain often causes men to enter these jobs, and the hypermasculinization of such work serves to maintain some level of satisfaction in such work for men.

In the assessment of various blue collar or high-risk work, the rhetoric of honor is often pervasive. This is not difficult to detect in certain careers such as police work and firefighting. While individuals in these careers risk their lives on almost a daily basis, they are simultaneously rewarded with social status and honor, often described as heroes and role models. Thus, the rhetoric of these careers reinforces the masculine code of honor as well as the justification for violence. While women are permitted in such careers, the number of women participating is significantly lower than men, especially for firefighters. For instance, in the United States, less than 5 percent of active firefighters are women, and less than 10 percent are black or Latino.[40] There are higher numbers of women on police forces, with estimates of just over 15 percent as the number of female federal law enforcement officers. Racial minorities compromise approximately 27 percent of police officers overall.[41] Given these statistics, it is clear that men dominate such high risk, honor laden professions, specifically white males. The question is how to read this prevalence in terms of masculinity and violence.

The notion that men are police officers and firefighters far more than women does, in some limited ways, relate to the notion that men are supposed to be protectors of women and children. However, to assess this as a symptom of gynocentrism is to flagrantly ignore the wider cultural forces at work. Police and firefighting work are risky, but as indicated above, not thankless. Honor and respect motivate these individuals to put themselves in such positions, and the prevalence of males is normalized by appeals to allegedly innately masculine traits such as bravery and physical power. While this encourages men to enter such professions, it also works to exclude women from participating. Reports abound concerning the difficulty women have entering such careers, surviving in hypermasculine environments, being taken seriously, and so forth. Furthermore, the fact that white males dominate such careers point to possible evidence of the privilege involved in such positions. The exclusion or low number of racial minorities suggest that white males are dominating these jobs because they are the most honored and culturally valuable work outside of the white collar domain. Consequently, due to the cultural value of such positions, the proliferation of men in such lines of work cannot be explained in terms of male oppression.

The more interesting case is the problem of men in other, less valued, high-risk work. To illuminate the issue, I will examine the career that is described as the most high-risk career in the United States: logging workers, with 110.9 fatal injuries per 100,000 people.[42] There is no explicit cultural sense of honor or admiration attached to this specific career track. According to the U.S. Department of Labor, the median pay for logging is $36,210, with a job outlook on a 4 percent decline. The job is described as physically demanding, at times dangerous, and isolating. The education level required for such work is a high school diploma or the equivalent.[43] Women's share of this industry is 2.8 percent.[44] Other male dominated jobs are also physically demanding and occasionally dangerous, such as mining (13.3 percent women), masonry (0.1 percent women), construction (8.9 percent women), and utilities (22.7 percent women). Noticeably, women-dominated careers in the United States follow along the lines of designated "pink collar" work, such as secretaries (95.3 percent women), child care (94.1 percent women), and nursing (90.6 percent women).[45] In any case, the MRM is certainly correct on one point—there is a distinct and noticeable level of gender segregation in lower and lower middle class careers.

The problem that must be addressed in an assessment of MRM arguments concerning oppression in these contexts is the claim that the oppressive groups involved in such interactions are men and women, with women functioning as the oppressing group. It is undeniable that many of these careers underpay workers, require an unreasonable number of working hours, involve risks not compensated in wages or respect, and draw in individuals with limited economic options due to education level, and so forth. Yet, in the case of male workers, it is difficult to see how women are the oppressing group in these scenarios, once such conditions are analyzed as the consequences of systematic violence. As Gilligan argues, the workings of systematic oppression are often invisible, or deflected onto other naturalized explanations. Thus, in order to maintain this form of class oppression for poor or blue collar men, capitalist systems construct these careers as innately masculine, framing the appeal in terms of traditionally masculine traits like bravery and brute physical force. Fulfilling such masculine ideals and roles is rewarding for men, and capitalist structures promise men personal fulfillment in the context of work and career, obscuring exploitation under the guise of masculine duty, work, and obligation. Consequently, the danger of such work is obscured by promises of masculine fulfillment, resulting in one-dimensional thinking for male workers, in which the rhetoric of capitalism becomes one's own.

Exploitative labor for men in the United States is maintained and encouraged through the complete alienation of the laborer, to the extent that individuals become unable to detect the contradictory nature of capitalist exploitation. The imposition of gender codes onto such labor further entrenches this form of one-dimensional thinking by naturalizing certain careers through an emphasis on essentialist and innate gendered concepts. The systematic violence that men suffer in such dangerous work is not the only way in which capitalism exploits individuals in gendered jobs. Women suffer psychological and emotional stress in so-called pink-collar labor, such as caregiving. Both men and women face various challenges when attempting to cross such gendered lines and enter oppositely gendered careers. The notion that men work in such dangerous careers while women luxuriate at home is simply false and unsupported by any evidence. Low-wage workers of all kinds experience oppression, and this oppression often takes on a gendered nature, but the oppression itself is not simply gender oppression of men by women. Rather, such workers are oppressed by exploitative capitalist structures utilizing gender to keep workers invested in one-dimensional thinking that prevents resistance or revolution.

Masculinity, Honor, and the Military

Perhaps even more than police work and firefighting, military service is often represented as one of the most honorable commitments a U.S. citizen can make. Historically, males in the United States have been required to register for the draft at the age of eighteen, a requirement not asked of women. The draft requirement, combined with the fact that men constitute the majority of armed service members, is used by the MRM as evidence for gynocentrism and male oppression. While military service is certainly male dominated and exposes enlisted men to great risk, the formulation of this situation as a simple case of male exploitation is misguided. Rather, the institution of the military itself as a complex cultural phenomenon must be examined, and the gendered systems occurring within military contexts is significantly more complex than the MRM suggests.

Overall, women are underrepresented in the military, comprising 14.6 percent total, and making up 19.5 percent and 15.5 percent of the Reserves and National Guard, respectively.[46] In 1994, the Department of Justice created a policy effectively banning women from certain combat situations, but the military was ordered in 2015 to open all combat jobs to women.[47] Kristy Kamarck states that individuals resistant to women in combat positions often point to physiological differences between men and women, as well as social issues preventing the full integration of men and women in units.[48] The debate is complicated by counter claims pointing to gender equality, the need for combat experience in order to gain certain promotions, and the leveling of physical differences by modern war weapons and technology. Although the issue of women in the military is complicated, the argument against women in combat is rarely justified by gynocentric calls for men to be protectors of women. In fact, it is quite the opposite, as most arguments point to women's inability or inadequacy in such roles.

Furthermore, the exclusion of women from the draft or selective service is a fact that may change in the very near future. In June of 2016, the Senate passed a defense bill including an amendment requiring women to register for the draft, in line with the recent openings of combat positions for women in the military.[49] Feminists often seem divided on the issue, and feminist resistance to the draft is often read as indicating some legitimacy to MRM complaints. In other words, the MRM argues that if feminists really want equality then they must support equal participation in all arenas, including those that are risky such as registering for selective service. It may be the case that the MRM is correct on this point concerning equality. However, one must also take into account the fact that many feminists oppose selective service issues due to pacifist positions or within a wider critique of militarization and warfare.[50] Thus, it is crucial to assess these arguments within precise contexts. Nonetheless, it seems as though certain potential changes in selective service requirements promise a solution to a long-standing MRM complaint.

What is most curious about the MRM charges of oppression in the context of the military is the fact that women's lack of selective service and combat engagement is not due to women's own actions or demands. The ban on women in combat originated in the Department of Defense, and this ban was used to justify the continued exemption of women from the draft in the Supreme Court decision *Rostker v. Goldberg* in 1981. Various military branches have actively resisted allowing women into the ranks throughout history, and even recently the Marine Corps released statements arguing against women in marine combat situations. In 2015, the Marines sought an exemption from the ban on women in combat situations, citing data and studies demonstrating detrimental aspects of having women in such contexts.[51] The overall point is, that active resistance to women in combat and in the draft is not a case of female refusal or demands for male protection. Rather, complex social, political, and professional issues utilizing essentialist gender concepts interact in military contexts to create resistance to women and assumptions concerning female abilities.

Given such complexities, it is difficult for the MRM to prove that men in the military are victims of a gynocentric culture that demands protection for exploitative women. Rather, the protection of women and children is framed as an inherent aspect of honorable and admirable masculinity, a construct of masculinity that is perpetuated by men as well as women, and used by men not just to demand certain roles from males but to exclude women from certain hypermasculine spaces. Once again, this issue cannot be explained as a simple case of women exploiting men, but rather as a cultural system utilizing masculine gender codes and expectations to elicit complicity and consent to certain sociopolitical demands.

The U.S. military must be analyzed as a complex industrial system that is deeply enmeshed in political and capitalist motivations, goals, and entanglements. As Marcuse notes, the prevalence of war and military entanglements reflect the dominance of unrestrained aggressive instincts. The acceptance of warfare as a natural consequence of social living demonstrates the failure of life instincts, or Eros, to override aggression in the transcending of one-dimensional thinking. Furthermore, the entanglement of capitalist structures with military institutions has resulted in what is referred to as the "military industrial complex," which result in various industries and profit-gaining endeavors influencing military actions, creating an economy dependent on military entanglements, weapon production, and so forth. Feminists and other progressive theorists have thus criticized the draft and the military at large due to pacifist commitments against warfare and violence on the whole, as well as in reaction to concerns about capitalism and the resulting industrial complex.

Consequently, the MRM has little ground to stand on in terms of pointing to the draft and military work as masculine oppression experienced at the hands of women. First, the historic exclusion of women from combat scenarios was not justified in recent times as a means of protecting women, but rather due to women's lack of ability or deficiencies in such contexts. Many women and feminists have opposed such exclusion. Second, the individuals working to keep women out of the draft are often men in the military, not women protesting against exposing women to violence. Third, feminists that oppose the drafting of women tend to be protesting military engagements overall as a result of pacifism or critiques of military structures. Finally, while men in the military experience terrible violence, and so forth. the honor code rewarding men in the military is consistently upheld, creating a sense of psychological reward for supporting and engaging with such activities. While the treatment of veterans is complex and often problematic, the glorification of the military in certain cultural contexts is frequently a masculinist construct. Such recruitment and psychological rewards are not created and sustained by only women, rather, it is a cultural endeavor on the part of many individuals to sustain membership in a risk-laden and dangerous career, promising rewards of honor and other financial incentives. Thus, if men are harmed or exploited by the military the source of this oppression is not women or gynocentrism. Rather, detecting the source of exploitation requires an examination of the prison industrial complex, militarization of the culture at large, and the normalization of all forms of violence within a culture.

Men as Victims of Violence

In order to adequately assess the ways in which men experience violence as individuals, the themes of shame and honor must be revisited. As Gilligan argues, shame is an emotion that not only influences violent actions but also impacts reactions to violence. Consequently, men may engage in violent behavior in order to gain honor and counteract feelings of shame, but the shame of experiencing violence may prevent men from reporting or addressing certain issues that require intervention. This section will argue that men experience violence as a traumatizing and damaging phenomenon in U.S. culture, and that these experiences are the result of patriarchal norms influencing concepts of power and identity as opposed to misandry and gynocentric culture.

Gilligan describes various instances of men inflicting violence on other men as an attempt to gain respect and to establish dominance as evidence of masculine power and honor. Such a system of supposed rewards is instituted and maintained by a patriarchal culture that equates violence with power, and constructs masculinity as an identity reliant upon such power. This patriarchal masculinity is extraordinarily toxic, exposing men to risk and damages for the sake of a tenuously held reward system based on honor. In some respects, the MRM is correct to point out that men are damaged by such demands, and that violence against men is normalized in the context of popular representation such as action films and sports. However, this is only one aspect of the issue, because violence is normalized in many contexts, creating justifications for specific forms of violence against various social groups. For instance, violence against women and minorities is often eroticized in the creation of oppressive sexual identities, and violence is frequently encouraged against Others as a means of controlling social boundaries. Thus, the claim that men experience violence disproportionately is to ignore the complex manifestations of violence and its impact on individuals across contexts. Furthermore, the MRM fails to address the ways that violence works to empower men in patriarchy through the honor system Gilligan describes, while violence often disempowers women and minorities through silencing and creating cultures of fear.

While violence impacts individuals across contexts, the masculine experience of shame is often unique, creating the potential for dire consequences. One particularly pressing issue relating to feelings of shame is suicide; something that the MRM claims is epidemic among men. According to MRAs, men commit suicide at significantly higher rates than women, and this discrepancy is downplayed or ignored in wider cultural conversations. To be clear, the alleged epidemic of suicide for men requires further clarification than what the MRM generally provides. First, while more men die after attempting suicide, the rates of suicide attempts for both genders are generally comparable. However, researchers propose that men are more likely to die as a result of suicide attempts due to factors such as greater lethality of method, a greater willingness to commit disfiguring actions in these attempts, and a higher likelihood of being intoxicated while engaging in suicide behaviors.[52] Furthermore, men face different challenges in dealing with stress and mental illness. Bilsker and White (2011) argue that men are frequently less likely to seek out help and emotional support, and are thus also less likely to visit mental health professionals to deal with various stressors and/or depression. Lack of social support and help-seeking behaviors may also contribute to men's higher rates of substance abuse, which is also correlated with suicide-inducing acts. In general, these factors indicate a problematic inability to ask for help or to admit a problem, reflecting the more general issue of masculinity imposing feelings of shame on men who cannot function completely independently, void of emotional dependence and expression.

In addition to suicide, men who are the victims of violence experience often overwhelming feelings of shame, contributing to cycles of violence enacted in an effort to counteract shame and garner a sense of security and respect. Part of the shame of victimhood is a sense of emasculation, and the issue of emasculation is increased when the experience of violence involves any feminizing or feminine associated aspect. Because of the eroticization of violence against women, sexual assault has been framed as mainly a woman's issue of experience. Thus, the male experience of sexual assault is often perceived as overwhelmingly shameful and anxiety producing, or reframed as a positive encounter for the victim. It must be emphasized that sexual assault is generally a shame-inducing experience for individuals of all identities and genders, leading to significant psychological pain and a lack of official reporting. This underreporting lends some credence to the MRM claim that rape statistics are significantly skewed, however, the issue of false rape accusations remains to be addressed.

According to the MRM, in addition to experiencing rape, men are also violated in terms of false accusations, an issue that MRAs also claim impact domestic violence charges. Thus, the MRM argues, not only do women regularly assault men physically and sexually, but also women additionally disempower men by constructing them as dangerous predators through the maintenance of false notions of rape culture and institutionalized violence against women. Generally speaking, these arguments share the form of claiming that these feminist notions are based on the idea that all men are violent and potential offenders, thus women must actively protect themselves against dangerous men. Furthermore, the MRM argues that women and feminists simultaneously argue that women are not capable of violence, thus ignoring men's experiences and contributing to male oppression.

While there is significant evidence to counteract the MRM claims of false rape accusation rates, the issues that I will be addressing here will focus on the overall concepts of rape culture and victimhood. Beginning with rape culture, the MRM is creating a dichotomous reading of innocents (women) vs. perpetrators (men) as the entirety of this feminist concept. In reality, rape culture is a general term for a complex state of affairs that normalizes violent sexuality for all genders, encourages dehumanization of sexual partners, and clouds issues of consent in sexual interactions. The notions of concern involve many of the dehumanizing aspects of psychological oppression that Bartky describes, including fragmentation and alienation, and such dehumanization can apply to any individual within a problematically gendered context. Consequently, rape culture should not be characterized as a simple "us vs. them" gender war phenomenon. Second, the MRM argues that women have been socialized to adopt a victim role, a role that women use to manipulate and punish men. This is used to explain the so-called prevalence of false rape claims, as well as accusations of punitive false domestic violence charges women use to punish men. Once again, these sorts of complaints may be true concerning individual cases, but there is little evidence demonstrating that this is a full-scale conspiracy of women against men. Rather, it rings more of stereotypes concerning women as manipulating, scheming users, out to punish men who fail to meet certain expectations or standards.

However, it must also be pointed out that women can and are violent to other women, children, and men. Women are certainly capable of sexual assault and domestic violence against intimate partners, and feminists should not minimize or ignore this possibility. Rather, it is imperative to analyze such instances in the context of contemporary gender relations and politics. While the MRM argues that women are capable of violence, this violence is not appropriately contextualized. Historically, women have experienced systemic violence from male offenders in the form of state sanctioned domestic violence and sexual assault.[53] Overwhelmingly, the most violent individuals in a society have been men, as Gilligan points out.[54] If masculinity conditions individuals for violence, then an explanation of female violence must take such norms into account, and explain the ways in which such norms transform and arise for a feminine identified subject. As hooks points out, women in patriarchal society may attempt to access patriarchal power through using its methods, including violence. Such usage should not be considered a moment of equality, but rather as an instance of affirmation for patriarchal society.

Claudia Card argues that individuals experiencing oppression may come to inhabit moral gray zones, in which oppression becomes both an experience and a tool for groups of persons. She explains:

> Gray zones, areas whose inhabitants are both victims and perpetrators of oppression, develop wherever the evils of oppression are severe, widespread, and persistent. The labor of the oppressed in the daily workings of maintaining oppressive power structures frees the energies of those on top for the joyous pursuits of cultural development.[55]

Gray zones allow for an explanation for women's participation in institutionalized racism, classism, violence, and abuse. These instances are not adequate counterexamples for disproving patriarchy, as the MRM argues. Women's access to power and exploitative forces should be understood as a complex reaction to various cultural distributions of power and resources, and such use must be analyzed with reference to standpoint and intersectional identity. Consequently, it is not problematic for feminism to recognize women's tendencies toward violence and oppression within the context of patriarchy. Rather, such instances must be read as further symptoms of the enormous toxicity generated by a society deeply invested in hierarchy, domination, and exploitation.

In conclusion, while men are undeniably harmed by violence and suffer because of it, there is little evidence to suggest that this suffering constitutes oppressive conditions. First, men as a group are not targeted by violence in such a way that it creates an overwhelming sense of fear or restriction of movement, as Young describes in her discussion of oppressive violence. While men can certainly fear assault, they can also simultaneously utilize violence to counteract fear and insecurity, because violence gives men a sense of dominance and control. In terms of the psychological impacts of violence, effective use of violence does not generally imply a decreased sense of self-esteem for men, but rather gives men a sense of power, respect, and honor, as Gilligan argues. Being victimized by violence certainly creates deep and dangerous senses of psychological harm for male subjects, but violence is also offered up as a way to undo such feelings. Finally, men are not being violently oppressed by women. Rather, women participate in and reinforce a patriarchal social structure that offers violence as a solution and mode of power in the maintenance of dominance and hierarchy. Overall, if men are to effectively address the impacts of violence, violence must be analyzed and understood as a dangerous patriarchal methodology that damages others and self, in spite of its promise of power or honor. The issue here is not degradation or oppression by women, but rather a patriarchy that encourages and entrenches violent solutions and actions in a distressingly large number of contexts.

Violence and Incarceration

The fact that men make up the overwhelming majority of the prison population, including individuals facing or undergoing capital punishment, is undeniable. The MRM argues that this is due to the fact that chivalry, a damaging gynocentric norm, causes the justice system to prosecute, incarcerate, and execute men guilty of violent crimes far more often than women. Furthermore, men are more likely to be punished, or more severely punished, for crimes committed against women. In this section, I will analyze these claims, arguing that chivalry plays an important role in punishment and incarceration. However, the function of chivalry is not a straightforward matter of male oppression; rather, chivalry must be understood as a function of problematic and unjust gender norms that position all individuals existing within society's power matrix.

In a 2011 study concerning gender and punishment, Steven Shatz and Naomi Shatz argue for the existence of what they term the "chivalry effect" in death sentencing, pointing out that men are more likely to be sentenced to death than women overall, and also more likely to receive the death penalty for crimes committed against women.[56] Notably, Shatz and Shatz argue that the chivalry effect is a result of norms concerning women, pointing to stereotypes concerning women's roles in society and innate capacity for violence. "[B]ecause women are stereotyped as weak, passive and in need of male protection, prosecutors and juries seem reluctant to impose the death penalty on them." If women are stereotyped as weak, then men are certainly stereotyped as macho, if not brutish. On the other end of this chivalric gender spectrum, Victor Streib argues that the prison and justice system have become a sort of "boys club," where hypermasculine value systems conceptualize male offenders in specific ways.[57] In fact, Streib argues, the entire rhetoric surrounding "crime fighting" and punishment is deeply entrenched in machismo, masculinizing both individuals working in the penal system as well as those convicted of crimes.

If chivalry works to position men and women in specific roles, then punishment is a symptom of larger dichotomous gender norms. Such positioning cannot simply be explained as a devaluation of men in the interest of women. Rather, this manifestation of power places dangerous violent expectations on men while limiting women's autonomy and power. This reflects Gilligan's point that women's exclusion from violent honor codes and consequent protection from certain violent behaviors come at a cost. Furthermore, if Streib is correct, then the entire justice and punishment system is one large boys club, reinforcing "male only" spaces of dominance and control. Thus, even if men are more likely to be incarcerated, they are also more likely to dominate law enforcement, prison work, and legal positions. This being the case, there is no evidence to suggest that women are the oppressors of men in this instance of chivalry. Such a system works to place men in different positions along the functioning lines of power, distributing individuals within the context of masculinity in ways that do not explicitly condemn such gender codes, and in some instances glorify them.

These analyses suggest that chivalry, in line with other gendered norms, create both burdens and benefits for all genders. However, chivalry does not simply make fools of, exploit, or oppress men. Rather, it creates a cost to men for the greater masculine benefit of reinforcing stereotypes concerning men's power, strength, provider role, and overall autonomy. Analogously, it protects women at the cost of autonomy and power. Consequently, one can conclude that there is indeed a gender bias in punishment. However, the source of such injustice is not simply male oppression, but rather a punishment of violent masculinity out of control. Masculinity within appropriate social and legal boundaries is not criticized or devalued. Additionally, the simplistic model of gender bias suggested by the MRM also neglects the ways in which race and class impact masculinity, resulting in the reinforcement of legitimately oppressive racial and other stereotypes. Overall, while there is evidence of disparity and inequality in such examples, masculinity and men do not suffer as a wider group due to such disparities, and suffering within the justice system is significantly complicated by other aspects of identity.

Men, Violence, and Cultural Imperialism

As argued previously, popular culture and images can have a profound impact on individual senses of self, as well as on conceptions of cultural norms and phenomena. MRAs have pointed to violence in popular culture as contributing to both external and internal modes of oppression for men by normalizing women as helpless victims and men as heartless, natural predators. In this section, I will analyze three themes of violence prevalent in popular culture that address these concerns: portrayals of women as victims of violence, men as perpetrators of violence, and male experiences of violence. I argue that while popular culture does perpetrate troubling and problematic norms concerning violence, these representations do not contribute to or reflect male oppression.

Women as Victims

The theme of women as damsels in distress or helpless, sympathetic victims in media is persistently presented as evidence for gynocentrism by the MRM. While women often do fulfill a victim role in such contexts, the status of female victims is far more complex, and female victimhood is often glorified and eroticized in ways that contribute to feminine harm and oppression. To argue this point, I will utilize the role of women in horror films as well as the sexualization of violence against women in various images and ad campaigns.

Horror films are one of the most obvious genres to investigate when considering the nature and representation of victimhood in film. The bodies of both men and women pile up quickly in such films, and the deaths are often gruesome and even pornographic at points. To be fair, men and women both get their turn at victimhood in such films, but authors such as Carol Clover have noted, the deaths of women in such films are often portrayed very differently from the deaths of men. She argues:

> But even in films in which males and females are killed in roughly even numbers, the lingering images are of the latter. The death of a male is nearly always swift; even if the victim grasps what is happening to him, he has no time to react or register terror. He is dispatched and the camera moves on. The death of the male is moreover more likely than the death of the female to be viewed from a distance, or viewed only dimly (because of darkness or fog, for example), or indeed to happen off-screen and not be viewed at all. The murders of women, on the other hand, are filmed at a closer range, in more graphic detail, and at greater length.[58]

The purpose of such attention is not simply because of greater sympathy toward or connection with the female character. While in many ways this presents women in such films as damsels, the intrigue and interest in watching women being brutalized on the screen indicates a far more complex and disturbing tendency. Rather, Clover points out that the death of women as beautiful or engaging is a persistent trope across genres, pointing to Poe's thought that, "The death of a woman is the 'most poetical topic in the world,'" as well as Alfred Hitchcock's claim that you can't torture women enough in film.[59] Such depictions and descriptions hardly seem to reflect a high valuation of women as sacred objects in need of a savior, and rather position the death of women as an almost pornographically gratifying film event.

Examples of aesthetic or "artistic" representations of dead and mutilated women are abundant in contemporary popular culture. Numerous ad campaigns and fashion spreads in recent times have focused on the so-called beauty or edginess involved with the representation of dead and/or mutilated female bodies. One example can be found in a 2008 ad campaign for Wrangler jeans, which used the tagline, "We are animals." In these advertisements, parts of women's bodies are shown in the jeans, but these bodies are lying lifelessly in water, mud, and so on, clearly implying a dead body left at a crime scene. These photographs are stark, gray, and full of dirt and water. It seems curious that such imagery would be used to sell blue jeans, as worn by victims of disturbingly violent actions. However, these images reinforce the notion that there is some sort of beauty to be found in violence, and the reference to our animalistic nature works to naturalize the abuse and degradation of women as some sort of inevitable outcome of male biology.

The Wrangler jeans advertising campaign is by no means an anomaly. There are a variety of other advertising campaigns that use dead women as the theme of pictorials, and most of these dead women have met a violent demise. For instance, Superette, a New Zealand boutique, created an ad campaign based on the novel/film *The Virgin Suicides* with the tagline, "Be caught dead in it." Playing on the clichéd notion of one making a beautiful corpse, these ads show women covered in blood, mangled or stabbed. Their lifeless bodies are supposed to demonstrate that these clothes are so good, that they are good enough to be the last thing a woman ever wears. This campaign suggests several cultural assumptions/norms that are extraordinarily disturbing. First of all, they highlight the fact that women live in constant fear of violence or assault—thus every time a woman dresses, she should be conscious that it may be the last thing she ever puts on. Furthermore, once again, dead women are shown as beautiful, reinforcing the necrophiliac notion that subjectivity or agency only gets in the way of a woman's true worth—her sexualized body. This is objectification at its most virulent, hiding behind the front of artistic expression.

The above examples provide a potent challenge to the MRM conception that female victims in media generally place women in a protected, sympathetic space, with men as the monsters who kill them. Rather, such examples reinforce feminist notions that the MRM regularly reject, such as rape culture, that normalize sexual violence and brutal exploitation. Once again, gendered media representations do not fall along simple, binary, dichotomous lines, but rather reflect complex interactions in terms of violence, power, gender, and identity.

Men as Predators

According to the MRM, men in the media are frequently portrayed as violent, soulless predators of women. While in some respects this claim reflects a certain amount of truth, not all male violent perpetrators in the media are assessed equally. Rather, certain violent males rise to the level of culturally adored anti-heroes or violent archetypes. I argue that the assessment of violent men in the media is often impacted by the level of successful masculinity portrayed by the individual in question, and that violent male characters that reflect successful hegemonic masculinity frequently escape negative cultural reactions.

Contemporary popular culture is rife with male characters and figures that display significantly violent behavior toward both male and female characters. However, many of these individuals have achieved the status of cultural icons as masculine anti-heroes, and most genres have examples of such figures. Films centering on the mafia or mob have resulted in cult followings of Don Corleone, Tony Montana, and Tony Soprano; political shows have given us Frank Underwood and Jack Bauer; serial killers such as Dexter Morgan and Hannibal Lecter have been cultural mainstays; television dramas have given us Walter White. In each case, these characters commit heinous crimes, murders, and acts of violence, but the media encourages the viewer to identify with the character and even root for them in the midst of certain nefarious deeds. All of these men, while obviously morally problematic, are also admirably masculine—successful, powerful, wealthy, or sexually desirable. Clearly, these examples indicate that being a violent male predator is not always considered a terrible thing, as long as the violent male is adequately fulfilling certain aspects of the masculine performative.

Violent males who are demonized in the media are often men who are insufficiently masculine. For instance, in *The Silence of the Lambs*, Buffalo Bill, a serial killer who is effeminate and mistakenly thinks he is transgender, offsets Hannibal Lecter. Carol Clover points out that many of the killers in slasher movies are portrayed as masculine failures, and often display gender confusion, childhood sexual trauma, or sexual disturbances.[60] The focus on sexual dysfunction and gender failure extends to media reactions to real life serial killers as well, such as John Wayne Gacy or Jeffrey Dahmer. Interestingly, even the refusal of such killers and characters in terms of identification or valuation does not result in a complete cultural rejection. Rather, such movie and real life killers, who often target women, often become cultural symbols or icons, resulting in a proliferation of Halloween costumes, posters, references, and so forth. In other words, most people in the United States will recognize a Freddy Krueger or Jason Voorhies mask instantly, marking these individuals minimally as cultural archetypes, even if their failures prevent them from qualifying as anti-heroes.

These characters and their related cultural perceptions and functions undermine MRM arguments that men are simply demonized as violent predators and killers in the media. While men often enact violence in film, reactions to this violence are deeply impacted by the character's masculinity within the performance. Furthermore, not all male killers are definitively denied or rejected. Certain killers, masculine failures though they may be, are sometimes embraced as cultural symbols, archetypes, jokes, or even points of research (like real life serial killers). Consequently, simple charges of men being demonized through violence in the media are woefully inadequate to address such complex spectator reactions.

Men as Victims of Violence in the Media

In spite of the above examples, some MRMs may still object that certain media platforms celebrate the violation of men as victims of violence, especially at the hands of women. To address such arguments, I will analyze the phenomena of women who are violent against men in film as well as the impact of violence on the male body and masculinity in cultural images.

Carol Clover notes that women who kill in films often have significantly different motives than male killers. For instance, in horror films, female killers are often motivated by revenge for experiences in adult life, as opposed to displaying the gender confusion or psychosexual fury often found in male horror film figures.[61] In other films, women's violence against men is often enacted as a mode of self-defense or preservation, such as escape from an abusive home or potential assault.[62] MRAs specifically list *Thelma and Louise* as a problematic source celebrating violence against men at the hands of women. What these analyses do not mention is that Louise, who murders a man who tried to rape Thelma, was a rape survivor and most likely experienced PTSD. Furthermore, the anger and violence coming from Thelma and Louise was almost entirely directed at men who were also violent or harassing. Finally, the film ends tragically—Thelma and Louise choose to die at the end as opposed to being apprehended by law enforcement. Such an ending arguably indicates that women cannot survive after enacting masculine forms of violence, and that the use of violence on the part of female characters results in annihilation and violent death. In this light, the film does not appear to be a simple farce celebrating violence against men by women.

Men's experiences of violence in other contexts is not always devastating, destructive, or even emasculating. Rather, genres such as action films glorify such violence to male characters, using violence against male bodies as reinforcement of masculine power and omnipotence. While violence against women often serves a simple aesthetic purpose, voyeurism, or feminine disempowerment, violence against men can serve to create a masculine spectacle for viewers. Steve Neale argues that masculine norms prevent the male body from being an adequate source of pure eroticism for spectators. Thus, the male body on display in film is often marked by violence, to alleviate the gender tension created by erotic objectification of the male body. He claims that male bodies presented as spectacle are often beaten, bruised, and punished, but such treatment is used to counteract the feminizing impact of objectification and to restore male omnipotence.[63] Thus, violence against men in film can be affirming, exciting, and empowering, and this avoids the feminization of male characters through total victimization or pornographic objectification.

In conclusion, the victimization of men in films in not symmetrical to the victimization of women. First, male victims are not portrayed as sexual spectacle, and there is often little to no aesthetic associated with their deaths. Furthermore, men's experiences of violence in film are not necessarily damaging but often contribute to masculine narcissism, power, and omnipotence. Finally, while male killers in other films might kill due to a hatred of women, the feminine, senses of emasculation, or even a desire for masculine power, female killers are often victims first, with desperate motives and trauma driving their actions. Overall, there is little evidence that popular culture works to actively oppress men externally or psychologically on a consistent basis, and that violent representations often create significantly more perilous representations and consequences for feminine individuals.

CONCLUSION

The MRM arguments concerning male powerlessness fail to establish oppressive conditions for men resulting from violence. Beginning with the overall concept of power, the MRM's explanations of power as a limiting force of domination fails to conceive of power accurately. As Foucault and Young argue, power is productive, aligning individuals across a society in specific ways. Thus, one can argue that violence itself is productive of identity, reinforcing certain stereotypes about masculine dominance, strength, and so forth. While this does entail certain harms, it does not limit men's access to certain goods or expose men to overwhelming psychological harms. Rather, violence can be a source of self-esteem, creating a rewards system in which the benefits outweigh the harms. Furthermore, this system of rewards and cultural esteeming of male violence also counteracts arguments that violence limits male actions or creates a culture of masculine fear. For instance, men of color may have such experiences with violence, but this is due to intersectional identity and racial violence, not simply the fact that they are men. There is no evidence that masculinity on its own creates violently oppressive conditions. Furthermore, the sense of power and identity that men derive from violence or exposure to dangerous conditions counteracts claims of gynocentrism or a total veneration of women and the feminine at the cost of male well-being in material and psychological terms.

Furthermore, the harms men experience resulting from economic conditions, militarization, and a general glorification of violence cannot simply be attributed to abuse and exploitation on the part of women. The inability of the MRM to engage in critiques of wider oppressive structures such as capitalism prevent the creation of radical subjectivity or of genuinely liberatory strategies. Instead, the MRM directs its frustration and pain at women, utilizing misogynistic ideals and stereotypes about women to lash out. This inability to transcend current systems of thoughts leaves the MRM squarely in the grip of one-dimensional thought and democratic unfreedom. While they have the choice to voice their pain and frustration, they fail to see or engage with the possibility for a radically transformed society, instead relying upon traditionalist views of gender and violent rhetoric to justify commitment to oppressive society. Overall, while the MRM does call certain problematic occurrences, norms, and expectations into attention, the analysis of such problems fails to create solutions or radical analysis, quickly slipping into an almost nostalgic masculinity demanding power in the affirmation of identity.

NOTES

1. Adam Kostakis, "The Same Old Gynocentric Story," last updated May 24, 2014, https://gynocentrism.com/2014/05/24/the-same-old-gynocentric-story/.
2. Warren Farrell, *The Myth of Male Power: Why Men Are the Disposable Sex* (New York: Simon and Schuster, 1992), Kindle edition, 2019.
3. Farrell, *Myth of Male Power*, 2099
4. Farrell, *Myth of Male Power*, 2208.
5. Farrell, *Myth of Male Power*, 2218.
6. "The Facts About Men and Boys," last accessed November 17, 2016, http://www.avoiceformen.com/the-facts-about-men-and-boys/.
7. "Facts About Men and Boys," http://www.avoiceformen.com/the-facts-about-men-and-boys/.
8. Farrell, *Myth of Male Power*, 3168.
9. Farrell, *Myth of Male Power*, 3890.
10. Farrell, *Myth of Male Power*, 3921.
11. Farrell, *Myth of Male Power*, 4079.

12. For a full discussion of such examples, refer to: Dave Futrell, "AVFM: Rape Culture Is a Lie but Swolesting Is All Too Real. Also, Women Are Yappy Dogs," last updated May 18, 2016, http://www.wehuntedthemammoth.com/2016/05/18/avfm-rape-culture-is-a-lie-but-swolesting-is-all-too-real-also-women-are-yappy-dogs/comment-page-1/.

13. Paul Elam, "Rape Culture: Female Scam, Male Nightmare," last updated October 19, 2010, http://www.avoiceformen.com/men/mens-issues/rape-culture-female-scam-male-nightmare/.

14. Elam, "Rape Culture," http://www.avoiceformen.com/men/mens-issues/rape-culture-female-scam-male-nightmare/.

15. "More Men Are Raped in the US than Women, Figures on Prison Assaults Reveal," *The Daily Mail*, October 8, 2013, http://www.dailymail.co.uk/news/article-2449454/More-men-raped-US-women-including-prison-sexual-abuse.html; Tara Palmatier, "Our So-Called 'Rape Culture,'" last updated October 29, 2013, http://www.avoiceformen.com/mens-rights/false-rape-culture/our-so-called-rape-culture/.

16. Jonathan Taylor, "Ten Reasons False Rape Accusations Are Common," last updated August 1, 2014, http://www.avoiceformen.com/sexual-politics/ten-reasons-false-rape-accusations-are-common/.

17. Farrell, *Myth of Male Power*, 4399.

18. Christina Sterbenz, "Why the Death Penalty in America is Sexist," *Business Insider*, September 6, 2013, http://www.businessinsider.com/women-and-the-death-penalty-2013-9.

19. Sterbenz, "Death Penalty," http://www.businessinsider.com/women-and-the-death-penalty-2013-9.

20. For a summary of these views, please refer to: Amanda Oliver, "The Death Penalty Has a Gender Bias," *The Huffington Post*, October 1, 2015, http://www.huffingtonpost.com/amanda-oliver/are-women-getting-away-wi_b_8227690.html.

21. Oliver, "Death Penalty Gender Bias," http://www.businessinsider.com/women-and-the-death-penalty-2013-9.

22. "Facts About Men and Boys," http://www.avoiceformen.com/the-facts-about-men-and-boys/.

23. bell hooks, *The Will to Change: Men, Masculinity and Love* (New York: Washington Square Press, 2004), 55.

24. James Gilligan, *Violence: Reflections on a National Epidemic* (New York: Random House, 1996), 7.

25. Gilligan, *Violence*, 33.

26. Gilligan argues that there is a lack of empirical evidence for a biological cause of male violence. He claims that biological explanations, in addition to being unsupported, create dangerous social consequences. The biological approach to violence encourages a general pessimism about violence, framing it as an inevitable aspect of human existence. This can contribute to both individual and social attitudes that treat violence as an inevitable phenomenon, excusing certain tendencies and actions that are, in reality, open to intervention (*Violence*, 209–223).

27. Gilligan, *Violence*, 111.

28. Marcuse is referencing Freud's work, *Civilization and its Discontents* (1929).

29. Herbert Marcuse, *Eros and Civilization* (Boston: Beacon Press, 1955), 29.

30. Marcuse, *Eros and Civilization*, 85.

31. Marcuse, *Eros and Civilization*, 86.

32. hooks uses the term "white supremacist capitalist patriarchy" in many of her works. For the purposes of this paper, please refer to her detailed account of this social structure found in, *The Will to Change: Men, Masculinity and Love* (2004).

33. Michael Kaufman, "The Construction of Masculinity and the Triad of Men's Violence," in *Gender Violence: Interdisciplinary Perspectives* (New York: NYU Press, 2007), 42.

34. Timothy Beneke, *Proving Manhood: Reflections on Men and Sexism* (Berkeley: University of California Press, 1997), 43.

35. Kaufman, "Construction of Masculinity," 42.

36. Gilligan, *Violence*, 231.

37. Gilligan, *Violence*, 229.

38. Gilligan, *Violence*, 192.
39. Gilligan, *Violence*, 192.
40. "Firefighting Occupations by Women and Race," *National Fire Protection Administration*, last accessed November 17, 2016, http://www.nfpa.org/news-and-research/fire-statistics-and-reports/fire-statistics/the-fire-service/administration/firefighting-occupations-by-women-and-race.
41. Victoria Bekiempes, "The New Racial Makeup of U.S. Police Departments," *Newsweek*, March 14, 2015, http://www.newsweek.com/racial-makeup-police-departments-331130.
42. David Johnson, "The Most Dangerous Jobs in America," *Time Magazine*, May 13, 2016, http://time.com/4326676/dangerous-jobs-america/.
43. "Logging Workers," *Bureau of Labor Statistics*, last updated December 17, 2015, http://www.bls.gov/ooh/farming-fishing-and-forestry/logging-workers.htm.
44. "Women in Male-Dominated Industries and Occupations," last updated October 20, 2015, http://www.catalyst.org/knowledge/women-male-dominated-industries-and-occupations.
45. "Women in Male-Dominated Industry," http://www.catalyst.org/knowledge/women-male-dominated-industries-and-occupations.
46. http://www.statisticbrain.com/women-in-the-military-statistics/.
47. "Women in the Military Statistics," last accessed November 17, 2016, https://fas.org/sgp/crs/natsec/R42075.pdf.
48. Kristy Kamarck, "Women in Combat: Issues for Congress," in *Congressional Research Service*, last accessed November 17, 2016, https://fas.org/sgp/crs/natsec/R42075.pdf.
49. "Senate Approves Women Registering for the Draft," *CNN*, last updated June 15, 2016, http://www.cnn.com/2016/06/15/politics/senate-approves-women-draft/.
50. For example, the National Organization of Women opposed the draft in general, but stated that women must be included if a draft exists in a 1980 statement, reflection certain feminists reservations about including the draft in the ERA proposal due to anti-war sentiments: Christina Caterucci, "Should Women Be Required to Register for the Draft?" last updated February 3, 2016, http://www.slate.com/articles/double_x/doublex/2016/02/should_women_be_required_to_register_for_the_draft.html.
51. Gordon Lubold, "Marine Commandant Argues against Women in All Combat Jobs," last updated September 18, 2015, http://www.wsj.com/articles/marines-commandant-argues-against-women-in-all-combat-jobs-1442613875.
52. Dan Bilsker and Jennifer White, "The Silent Epidemic of Male Suicide," *BC Medical Journal*, 53 (2011), http://www.bcmj.org/articles/silent-epidemic-male-suicide.
53. Such examples include rape as a control mechanism or war stratagem. For further discussion, see Claudia Card, "Rape as a Weapon of War," in *Hypatia*, 11: 1996.
54. Jane Caputi further argues for this, pointing out that most serial killers are men. According to Caputi, serial killers are an example of "patriarchal terrorists." See, Jane Caputi, *The Age of Sex Crime* (New York: Popular Press, 1987).
55. Claudia Card, "Groping through Gray Zones," in *On Feminist Ethics and Politics*, ed. Claudia Card (Lawrence: University of Kansas Press, 1999).
56. Steven Shatz and Naomi Shatz, "Chivalry Is Not Dead: Murder, Gender, and the Death Penalty," *Berkeley Journal of Gender, Law, and Justice*, vol. 27 (1): 2012.
57. Victor Streib, "Gendering the Death Penalty: Countering Sex Bias in a Masculine Sanctuary," *Ohio Journal of Law*, vol. 63 (433): 2002.
58. Carol Clover, *Men, Women, and Chainsaws: Gender in Modern Horror Film* (Princeton, NJ: Princeton University Press, 1992) 35.
59. Clover, 42.
60. Clover, 28.
61. Clover, 29.
62. Examples might include: *The Burning Bed* (1984), *Fried Green Tomatoes* (1991), or *Enough* (2002).
63. Steve Neale, "Masculinity as Spectacle," from *The Sexual Subject: A Screen Reader in Sexuality*, ed. Mandy Merck (New York: Routledge, 1992).

Conclusion

In *An Essay on Liberation*,[1] Herbert Marcuse argues that growing opposition to forces of domination and exploitation are often confronted by an escalation of such forces. As the powers of containment are challenged by radical protests, the limits of such containment may be reached, resulting in new forms of control, domination, and even totalitarianism. While the backlash to progressive politics may appear bleak, Marcuse maintains optimism, arguing that beyond these limits exists the space for a freedom not yet existing. The attainment of such freedom must arise from what he terms "the Great Refusal," a refusal that recognizes that freedom cannot be built in the confines of current society. This refusal consists in a rejection of repressive forces, and requires a historical break with both the past and the future, reflecting his notions of negative thinking and transcendence outlined in *One Dimensional Man*.

Achieving these breaks is no simple task. Marcuse points out that it is not sufficient to reject certain aspects of repressive society. Rather, the entire structure of exploitative, dominating, and repressive society must be rejected, in order to create a world based upon freedom and life forces, eliminating human misery and the oppression resulting from current modes of the reality principle. What is required is a rebellion: "To the degree to which the rebellion is directed against a functioning, prosperous, 'democratic' society, it is a moral rebellion, against the hypocritical, aggressive values and goals, against the blasphemous religion of this society, against everything it takes seriously, everything it professes while it violates what it professes."[2] Consequently, the rejection of current oppressive conditions is more than merely political, and the affirmation of life through the enactment of a Great Refusal is ethical in its demands for freedom and liberation.

The MRM characterizes itself as its own form of a "Great Refusal," arguing that there is no place in society for men to thrive, rejecting the mainstream and its various "gynocentric" institutions. This refusal is a ploy, and a co-opting of progressive terms and theories to further the interest of exploitative capitalism, gender norms, and power structures. They hide their role as part of the sustained dominating power structures' reaction to progressive politics through their use of political language and terms originating in feminist circles. Frequent recourse to aggressive tactics and language, outright expressions of rage, and the consistent degradation of feminist women show that the MRM is not committed to Eros or the life forces that Marcuse argues are required for creating a free society. Additionally, their rebellion fails to transcend the realities of contemporary society, as evidenced by their refusal to engage the entire social structure by focusing only on masculine gender.

The MRM holds important lessons for individuals genuinely committed to progressive politics. Currently, oppressive forces are attempting to diminish and erase liberating gains by attempting to frame these gains as oppressive to the powerful. Concepts such as freedom of speech are regularly incited to justify aggressive language and threats, and calls for leveling senses of equality are invoked to reverse gains made by oppressed peoples. Thus, one should read the MRM as emblematic of this, and as a warning of the reenactment of dominating forms to come. However, this also does not mean we should lose hope. Current backlash and reversals indicate a dominating society pushed to its limits, and individuals invested in authentic freedom and liberation must persist in ethical rebellion. This rebellion must be cohesive, and not limited by specific interests. We must persist in the optimism of Marcuse, searching for a free society in which human misery is alleviated and Eros is no longer diminished.

NOTES

1. Herbert Marcuse, *An Essay on Liberation*, 1969, last accessed November 16, 2016, https://www.marxists.org/reference/archive/marcuse/works/1969/essay-liberation.htm.
2. Marcuse, *An Essay on Liberation*.

Bibliography

"96% of Women Are Liars, Honest," *The Scotsman*, December 9, 2004, accessed October 5, 2015, http://www.scotsman.com/news/uk/96-of-women-are-liars-honest-1-565123.

"About Gynocentrism," last modified July 14, 2013, https://gynocentrism.com/2013/07/14/about/.

"Authoring Your Own Life," last modified May 31, 2015, http://www.avoiceformen.com/men/mens-issues/authoring-your-own-life/.

Barry, Ray. "The Facts about Men and Boys," last accessed November 14, 2016, http://www.avoiceformen.com/the-facts-about-men-and-boys/.

Bartky, Sandra. *Femininity and Domination: Studies in the Phenomenology of Oppression.* New York: Routledge, 1990.

Bekiempes, Victoria. "The New Racial Makeup of U.S. Police Departments," *Newsweek*, March 14, 2015, last accessed November 16, 2016, http://www.newsweek.com/racial-makeup-police-departments-331130.

Bellis, Mark, Hughes, Karen, Hughes, Sarah, and Ashton, John. "Measuring Paternal Discrepancy and Its Public Health Consequences," *Journal of Epidemiology and Community Health,* 59 (2005): 749–754, http://jech.bmj.com/content/59/9/749.long.

Beneke, Timothy. *Proving Manhood: Reflections on Men and Sexism.* Berkeley: University of California Press, 1997.

Bilsker, Dan and White, Jennifer. "The Silent Epidemic of Male Suicide," *BC Medical Journal*, 53 (2011), accessed November 16, 2016, http://www.bcmj.org/articles/silent-epidemic-male-suicide.

Bloomfield, Janet. "Here's Why Men Should Have the Reproductive Rights That Women Have," last updated May 30, 2014, http://thoughtcatalog.com/janet-bloomfield/2014/05/heres-why-men-should-have-the-reproductive-rights-that-women-have/.

———. "6 Truths about Dads Feminists Don't Want You to Know," last updated March 20, 2015, http://thoughtcatalog.com/janet-bloomfield/2015/03/6-truths-about-dads-feminists-dont-want-you-to-know/.

———. "Single Women Raising Children Do a Poor Job," last updated July 2, 2015, http://www.avoiceformen.com/mens-rights/single-women-raising-children-do-a-poor-job/.

Bordo, Susan. *Unbearable Weight: Feminism, Western Culture and the Body.* Berkeley: University of California Press, 1995.

Burton Brown, Kristi. "Abortion and Men: What's a Father to Do?" last updated June 5, 2013, http://liveactionnews.org/abortion-and-men-whats-a-father-to-do/.

Butler, Judith. "Imitation and Gender Insubordination," in *The Lesbian and Gay Studies Reader,* edited by Abelove, Barale, and Halperin. New York: Routledge, 1993.

———. *Gender Trouble: Feminism and the Subversion of Identity*. New York: Routledge, 1999.
———. *Precarious Life: The Powers of Mourning and Violence*. New York: Verso, 2004.
———. *Giving an Account of Oneself*. New York: Fordham University Press, 2005.
Card, Claudia. "Groping through Gray Zones," in *On Feminist Ethics and Politics*. Edited by Claudia Card. Lawrence: University of Kansas Press, 1999.
Clover, Carol. *Men Women and Chainsaws: Gender in Modern Horror Film*. Princeton: Princeton University Press, 1992.
Connell, Raewyn. *Masculinities*, 2nd ed. Berkeley: University of California Press, 2005.
Coulombe, Nikita. "Portrayal of Men in the Media: Why There Needs to Be a Reverse Bechdel Test," last updated May 27, 2015, http://www.avoiceformen.com/art-entertainment-culture/portrayal-of-men-in-the-media-why-there-needs-to-be-a-reverse-bechdel-test/.
Cox, Eva. "Boys and Girls and the Costs of Gendered Behavior." Keynote Address (Promoting Gender Equity Conference, Canberra, February 22–24, 1995), 74.
Cudd, Ann. "Analyzing Backlash to Progressive Social Movements," in *Theorizing Backlash: Philosophical Reflections on Resistance to Feminism*. Lanham, MD: Rowman and Littlefield, 2002.
———. *Analyzing Oppression (Studies in Feminist Philosophy)*, 1st ed. New York: Oxford University Press, 2006.
"Defending Freedom with Bricks of Logic," last modified September 28, 2013, http://www.avoiceformen.com/updates/news-updates/defending-freedom-with-bricks-of-logic/.
Devlin, Roger. "Sexual Utopia in Power," last accessed March 2015, https://dontmarry.files.wordpress.com/2009/03/sexualutopia.pdf.
Dewey, Caitlin. "Inside the 'Manosphere' That Inspired Santa Barbara Shooter Elliot Rodger," May 27, 2014, last accessed May 3, 2017 https://www.washingtonpost.com/news/the-intersect/wp/2014/05/27/inside-the-manosphere-that-inspired-santa-barbara-shooter-elliot-rodger/?utm_term=.34b0f4a9079f.
"Don't Be That Girl Sex Assault Posters in Edmonton Spark Anger, Debate," *HuffPost Alberta*, July 10, 2013, accessed November 16, 2016, http://www.huffingtonpost.ca/2013/07/10/dont-be-that-girl-posters-edmonton_n_3575338.html.
Dreyfus, Hubert, and Rabinow, Paul. *Michel Foucault: Beyond Structuralism and Hermeneutics*, 2nd ed. Chicago: University of Chicago Press, 1983.
Elam, Paul. "The Plague of Modern Masculinity," last updated July 1, 2010, http://www.avoiceformen.com/men/the-plague-of-modern-masculinity/.
———. "The Problem with Gay Rights," last modified September 1, 2010, http://www.avoiceformen.com/mens-rights/the-problem-with-gay-rights/.
———. "Rape Culture: Female Scam, Male Nightmare," last updated October 19, 2010, http://www.avoiceformen.com/men/mens-issues/rape-culture-female-scam-male-nightmare/.
———. "Counterculture," last modified October 22, 2013, http://www.avoiceformen.com/mens-rights/counterculture/.
———. "The X%: What Feminism Is Really About and Why Anyone Who Values Freedom Should Fight against It," last updated November 19, 2013, http://www.avoiceformen.com/feminism/the-x-what-feminism-is-really-about-and-why-anyone-who-values-freedom-should-fight-against-it/.
———. "Welcome to AVFM," last modified June 5, 2014, http://www.avoiceformen.com/a-voice-for-men/welcome-to-avfm/.
———. "A Little Blood in the Mix Never Hurt a Revolution," last updated March 26, 2015, http://www.avoiceformen.com/mens-rights/a-little-blood-in-the-mix-never-hurt-a-revolution/.
———. "Preparing for the Next Conquest," last modified July 30, 2015, http://www.avoiceformen.com/a-voice-for-men/preparing-for-the-next-conquest/.
Esmay, Dean. "Alimony Unlimited (and the Emergence of a Men's Rights Movement)," last accessed November 24, 2013, http://www.avoiceformen.com/series/unknown-history-of-misandry/alimony-unlimited-and-the-emergence-of-a-mens-rights-movement/.
———. "The Lethal Paternity Fraud Racket," last updated February 24, 2014, http://www.avoiceformen.com/series/unknown-history-of-misandry/the-lethal-paternity-fraud-racket/.

———. "Breaking the Pendulum: Tradcons vs. Feminists," last modified March 26, 2014, http://www.avoiceformen.com/gynocentrism/breaking-the-pendulum-tradcons-vs-feminists/.

———. "Gays against Feminism: Because Gay People Are Not Your Property, Feminists," last modified June 26, 2015, http://www.avoiceformen.com/feminism/gays-against-feminism-because-gay-people-are-not-your-property-feminists/.

"The Facts About Men and Boys," last accessed November 17, 2016, http://www.avoiceformen.com/the-facts-about-men-and-boys/.

Faludi, Susan. *Backlash: The Undeclared War Against American Women*. New York: Three Rivers Press, 1991.

———. *Stiffed: The Betrayal of the American Man*. Harper Collins, 2011. Kindle edition.

Farrell, Warren. *Why Men are the Way They Are*. New York: Berkeley Books, 1986.

———. *The Liberated Man*. New York: Berkeley Books, 1993.

———. *The Myth of Male Power: Why Men Are the Disposable Sex*. New York: Simon and Schuster, 1993. Kindle edition.

Fineman, Martha. *The Illusion of Equality*. Chicago: University of Chicago Press, 1991.

"Firefighting Occupations by Women and Race," *National Fire Protection Administration*, last accessed November 17, 2016, http://www.nfpa.org/news-and-research/fire-statistics-and-reports/fire-statistics/the-fire-service/administration/firefighting-occupations-by-women-and-race.

Foucault, Michel. "Disciplines and Sciences of the Individual," in *The Foucault Reader*. Edited by Paul Rabinow. New York: Pantheon Books, 1984.

———. *The History of Sexuality, Vol. 1: An Introduction*. New York: Routledge, 1990.

———. *Discipline and Punish: The Birth of the Prison*. New York: Random House, 1995.

Friedan, Betty. *The Feminine Mystique*. New York: W. W. Norton, 1963.

Frye, Marilyn. "The Possibility of Feminist Theory," in *Women, Knowledge, and Reality*. Edited by Ann Garry and Marilyn Pearsall. New York: Routledge, 1996.

———. "Oppression," in *Gender Basics: Analyzing Women and Men*. Edited by Anne Minas. Belmont: Wadsworth Publishing, 2000.

Futrell, Dave. "Register Her Was a Fake 'Offenders Registry' Run by Misogynists, Designed to Vilify and Intimidate Women," last modified December 17, 2016, https://manboobz.com/2012/12/17/register-her-is-a-fake-offenders-registry-run-by-misogynists-designed-to-vilify-and-intimidate-women/.

Galbi, Douglas. "Fathers as Wallets: Legal History of Child Support," last updated January 11, 2016, http://www.avoiceformen.com/men/fathers/fathers-as-wallets-legal-history-of-child-support/.

Gallagher, B. J. "The Problem of Political Correctness," last modified February 25, 2015, http://www.huffingtonpost.com/bj-gallagher/the-problem-political-correctness_b_2746663.html.

Gallagher, Ken. "Feminism for Beginners," last updated April 19, 2015, http://www.avoiceformen.com/feminism/feminism-for-beginners/.

Gerard, Sage. "Dissecting the New American Racist," last modified December, 28, 2015, http://www.avoiceformen.com/featured/dissecting-the-new-american-racist/.

Gilligan, James. *Violence: Reflections on a National Epidemic*. New York: Random House, 1996.

Goldberg, Herb. *The Hazards of Being Male: Surviving the Myth of Masculine Privilege*. Berkshire: Nash Publishing, 1976.

Herring, Susan. "Posting in a Different Voice: Gender and Ethics in CMC," in *Philosophical Perspectives on Computer-Mediated Communication*. Edited by Charles Ess. Albany: State University of New York Press, 1996.

———. "Men's Language on the Internet," in *Norlyd* (28), 1996.

———. "The Rhetorical Dynamics of Gender Harassment Online," in *The Information Society* (15), 1999.

———. "Gender and (A)nonymity in Computer Mediated Communication," in *Handbook of Language and Gender*, 2nd ed. Edited by J. Holmes, M. Meyerhoff, and S. Ehrlich. Hoboken, NJ: Wiley-Blackwell Publishing, 2013.

hooks, bell. *Feminist Theory: From Margin to Center*. Cambridge: South End Press, 1984.

———. *The Will to Change: Men, Masculinity, and Love.* New York: Washington Square Press, 2004.

———. *Writing Beyond Race: Living Theory and Practice.* New York: Routledge, 2013.

Jackson, Keith Burgess. "The Backlash against Feminist Philosophy," in *Theorizing Backlash: Philosophical Reflections on the Resistance to Feminism.* Edited by Anita Superson and Ann Cudd. Lanham, MD: Rowman and Littlefield Publishers, 2002.

Johnson, David. "The Most Dangerous Jobs in America," *Time Magazine,* May 13, 2016, last accessed November 16, 2016, http://time.com/4326676/dangerous-jobs-america/.

J T, "On Masculinity," last updated May 16, 2016, http://www.avoiceformen.com/men/on-masculinity/.

Kamarck, Kristy. "Women in Combat: Issues for Congress," in *Congressional Research Service,* last accessed November 17, 2016, https://fas.org/sgp/crs/natsec/R42075.pdf.

Kaufman, Michael. "The Construction of Masculinity and the Triad of Men's Violence, in *Gender Violence: Interdisciplinary Perspectives.* New York: NYU Press, 2007.

Kimmel, Michael. *Guyland: The Perilous World Where Boys Become Men—Understanding the Critical Years between 16 and 26.* New York: HarperCollins, 2008.

———. *Angry White Men: American Masculinity at the End of an Era.* New York: Nation Books, 2013.

Kinkade, Tyler. "'Men's Rights' Trolls Spam Occidental College Online Rape Report Form." *The Huffington Post,* December 18, 2013, http://www.huffingtonpost.com/2013/12/18/mens-rights-occidental-rape-reports_n_4468236.html.

Kostakis, Adam. "Gynocentrism, Humanism and the Patriarchy," last updated May 24, 2014, http://gynocentrism.com/2013/08/15/gynocentrism-humanism-and-the-patriarchy/.

———. "Gynocentrism Theory Lecture Series: Chasing Rainbows," last modified May 24, 2014, https://gynocentrism.com/2014/05/24/chasing-rainbows/.

———. "Gynocentrism Theory Lecture Series: The Eventual Outcome of Feminism, Part I," last modified May 24, 2014, https://gynocentrism.com/2014/05/25/the-eventual-outcome-of-feminism-part-i/.

———. "Gynocentrism Theory Lecture Series: The Eventual Outcome of Feminism, Part II," last modified May 24, 2014, https://gynocentrism.com/2014/05/25/the-eventual-outcome-of-feminism-part-ii/.

———. "Gynocentrism Theory Lecture Series: False Consciousness & Kafka Trapping," last modified May 24, 2014, https://gynocentrism.com/2014/05/25/false-consciousness-kafka-trapping/.

———. "Gynocentrism Theory Lecture Series: Old Wine, New Bottles," last modified May 24, 2014, https://gynocentrism.com/2014/05/24/old-wine-new-bottles/.

———. "Gynocentrism Theory Lecture Series: Pig Latin," last modified May 24, 2014, https://gynocentrism.com/2014/05/24/pig-latin/.

———. "The Same Old Gynocentric Story," last updated May 24, 2014, https://gynocentrism.com/2014/05/24/the-same-old-gynocentric-story/.

Kruk, Edward. "The Impact of Parental Alienation on Children," last updated April 25, 2013, https://www.psychologytoday.com/blog/co-parenting-after-divorce/201304/the-impact-parental-alienation-children.

"Logging Workers," *Bureau of Labor Statistics,* last updated December 17, 2015, http://www.bls.gov/ooh/farming-fishing-and-forestry/logging-workers.htm.

Love, Dylan. "Inside the Red Pill, the Weird New Cult for Men Who Don't Understand Women," *Business Insider,* September 15, 2013, last accessed May 4, 2017, http://www.businessinsider.com/the-red-pill-reddit-2013-8.

Lubold, Gordon. "Marine Commandant Argues against Women in All Combat Jobs," last updated September 18, 2015, http://www.wsj.com/articles/marines-commandant-argues-against-women-in-all-combat-jobs-1442613875.

Marcuse, Herbert. *Eros and Civilization.* Boston: Beacon Press, 1955.

———. *One Dimensional Man: Studies in the Ideology of Advanced Industrial Society.* Boston: Beacon Press, 1964.

———. *An Essay on Liberation,* 1969, last accessed November 16, 2016, https://www.marxists.org/reference/archive/marcuse/works/1969/essay-liberation.htm.

———. "Repressive Tolerance," in *A Critique of Pure Tolerance*. Boston: Beacon Press, 1969.
Marx, Karl. *Economic and Philosophical Manuscripts of 1844*. Moscow: Progress Publishers, 1959.
Matchar, Emily."'Men's Rights' Activists are Trying to Redefine the Meaning of Rape." *New Republic*, February 26, 2014, http://www.newrepublic.com/article/116768/latest-target-mens-rights-movement-definition-rape.
Matthews, Steve. "Identity and Information Technology," in *Information Technology and Moral Philosophy*. Edited by Jeroen Van Den Hoven and John Weckert. New York: Cambridge University Press, 2008.
Messner, Michael. "The Limits of 'The Male Sex Role': An Analysis of the Men's Liberation and Men's Rights Movements' Discourse." *Gender and Society*, vol. 12 (1998): 255–276.
"moralfag," last modified July 28, 2016, https://en.wiktionary.org/wiki/moralfag.
"More Men Are Raped in the US than Women, Figures on Prison Assaults Reveal." *The Daily Mail*, October 8, 2013, http://www.dailymail.co.uk/news/article-2449454/More-men-raped-US-women-including-prison-sexual-abuse.html.
Morrell, Dre. "Black Men and Men's Rights: Where Do We Fit?" last updated June 16, 2015, http://www.avoiceformen.com/art-entertainment-culture/black-men-and-mens-rights-where-do-we-fit/.
Mulvey, Laura. "Visual Pleasure and Narrative Cinema," in *Film Theory and Criticism*. Edited by Leo Braudy and Marshall Cohen. New York: Oxford University Press, 1999.
Neale, Steve. "Masculinity as Spectacle," in *The Sexual Subject: A Screen Reader in Sexuality*. Edited by Mandy Merck. New York: Routledge, 1992.
Oliver, Amanda. "The Death Penalty Has a Gender Bias." *The Huffington Post*, October 1, 2015, http://www.huffingtonpost.com/amanda-oliver/are-women-getting-away-wi_b_8227690.html.
Palmatier, Tara. "Our So-Called 'Rape Culture,'" last updated October 29, 2013, http://www.avoiceformen.com/mens-rights/false-rape-culture/our-so-called-rape-culture/.
Parsell, Mitch. "Pernicious Virtual Communities: Polarization and the Web," in *Ethics and Information Technology* (10).
Preysler, Walter. "Why Black Men Need the MRHM and Not Feminism," last modified February 19, 2016, http://www.avoiceformen.com/mens-rights/why-black-men-need-the-mhrm-and-not-feminism/.
"The Reality of Feminism," video, last updated December 19, 2015, http://www.avoiceformen.com/feminism/the-reality-of-feminism/.
"Reproductive Health," last accessed November 16, 2016, http://www.who.int/topics/reproductive_health/en/.
Rincon, Paul. "Study Debunks Illegitimacy Myth." *BBC News*, February 11, 2005, http://news.bbc.co.uk/2/hi/science/nature/7881652.stm.
Rocking Mr. E. "21st Century Fatherhood," last updated January 18, 2012, http://www.avoiceformen.com/men/fathers/21st-century-fatherhood/.
Schechtman, Marya. *The Constitution of Selves*. Ithaca, NY: Cornell University Press, 1996.
Scott, Travis. "The Role of Masculinity," last updated August 15, 2016, http://www.avoiceformen.com/feminism/the-role-of-masculinity.
"Senate Approves Women Registering for the Draft." *CNN*, last updated June 15, 2016, http://www.cnn.com/2016/06/15/politics/senate-approves-women-draft/.
Shanley, Mary. "Fathers' Rights, Mothers' Wrongs? Reflections on Unwed Fathers' Rights, Patriarchy, and Sex Inequality," in *Reproduction, Ethics, and the Law: Feminist Perspectives*. Edited by Joan Callahan. Bloomington: University of Indiana Press, 1995.
Shatz, Steven and Shatz, Naomi. "Chivalry Is Not Dead: Murder, Gender, and the Death Penalty." *Berkeley Journal of Gender, Law, and Justice*, vol. 27 (1): 2012.
Smith, Carnell. "12 Reasons for DNA Paternity Testing," last updated December 17, 2013, http://www.avoiceformen.com/paternity-fraud/12-reasons-for-dna-paternity-testing/.
Smith, Helen. "8 Reasons Straight Men Don't Want to Get Married," last updated June 23, 2013, http://www.avoiceformen.com/men/mens-issues/8-reasons-straight-men-dont-want-to-get-married/.

Spelman, Elizabeth. *Inessential Woman: Problems of Exclusion in Feminist Thought*. Boston: Beacon Press, 1988.
Stanton, Patrice. "Lessons from a Men's Divorce Seminar," last updated October 31, 2012, http://www.avoiceformen.com/mens-rights/family-courts/lessons-from-a-mens-divorce-seminar/.
Sterbenz, Christina. "Why the Death Penalty in America Is Sexist." *Business Insider*, September 6, 2013, last accessed November 16, 2016, http://www.businessinsider.com/women-and-the-death-penalty-2013-9.
Streib, Victor. "Gendering the Death Penalty: Countering Sex Bias in a Masculine Sanctuary." *Ohio Journal of Law*, vol. 63 (433): 2002.
Sunstein, Cass. "Democracy and the Internet," in *Information Technology and Moral Philosophy*. Edited by Jeroen Van Den Hoven, John Weckert. New York: Cambridge University Press, 2008.
Superson, Anita. "Sexism in the Classroom: The Role of Gender Stereotypes in the Evaluation of Female Faculty," in *Theorizing Backlash: Philosophical Reflections on the Resistance to Feminism*. Edited by Anita Superson and Ann Cudd. Lanham, MD: Rowman and Littlefield, 2002.
Superson, Anita, and Cudd, Ann. *Theorizing Backlash: Philosophical Reflections on the Resistance to Feminism*. Lanham, MD: Rowman and Littlefield, 2002.
Surface, David. "Revisiting Parental Alienation Syndrome," in *Social Work Today*, 9 (2009). http://www.socialworktoday.com/archive/092109p26.shtml.
Taylor, Jonathan. "Ten Reasons False Rape Accusations Are Common," last updated August 1, 2014, http://www.avoiceformen.com/sexual-politics/ten-reasons-false-rape-accusations-are-common/.
Thomson, Judith. "A Defense of Abortion," in *Philosophy and Public Affairs*, 1 (1971).
"Women: 50% Would Lie about Paternity, While 42% Would Lie About Being on Birth Control," last updated July 19, 2014, http://www.avoiceformen.com/allnews/women-50-would-lie-about-paternity-while-42-would-lie-about-being-on-birth-control/.
"Women in Male-Dominated Industries and Occupations," last updated October 20, 2015, http://www.catalyst.org/knowledge/women-male-dominated-industries-and-occupations.
"Women in the Military Statistics," last accessed November 17, 2016, https://fas.org/sgp/crs/natsec/R42075.pdf.
Wright, Peter. "Damseling, Chivalry, and Courtly Love," last modified July 17, 2016, http://www.avoiceformen.com/feminism/damseling-chivalry-and-courtly-love-part-two/.
Young, Iris Marion. *Justice and the Politics of Difference*. Princeton, NJ: Princeton University Press, 1990.

Index

abortion and paternity rights, 108, 123
accountability, necessity of, 73
action films, 42
advertising campaigns, 162
age and Guyland, 19
Agent Orange, 12, 21
alienation/alienated individual: in capitalism, 119–120, 146–147; completion of, 55; exploitative labor and, 152
alimony, 110
alpha males, xvii
American Beauty, 131
American Dream, as myth, 18
"An Essay on Liberation" (Marcuse), 78
anger, role of, 15
angry white men. *See* men's rights movement adherents (MRAs)
arrogance, 66, 73
AVFM. *See* A Voice for Men (AVFM)

backlash to feminism: ignoring, 23; intensification of, online, 47, 48; justifiability of loss and, 39; as result of threat to hegemonic masculinity, 39; using for self-reflection and reassessment of men as comrades, 23
Bartky, Sandra: feminine narcissism, 118; gender roles as morally and psychologically reprehensible, 96; psychological oppression, 92, 96, 97

basic repression, 54
Bellis, Mark, 122
Beneke, Timothy, 148
Bilsker, Dan, 156
"Black Men and Men's Rights: Where Do We Fit?" (Morrell), 70
black racists, 70
Blake, Mariah, xviii
blame culture, 73
Bloomfield, Janet, 107–108, 112
bodies: discipline and, 32; docile, 32, 33; importance of, in establishing identity, 34–35; as limiting factor in expressing gender, 33; online communication and, 37; public aspect of, 35; in social frameworks, 36; as symbols of culture, 31, 33
Bordo, Susan, 31, 64, 123, 124
Butler, Judith: body as cultural symbol, 31, 33; creation of self-narratives, 36; gender as disciplinary production, 33; gender as performative, 68; gender demands, 89; heterosexuality as contributing to dichotomous division of gender roles, 68; homosexual identities as inversions of heterosexual identities, 69; public aspect of bodies, 35

capitalism, 53–55, 56, 59; exploitation of workers, 119; military and, 154; work in, 115, 116, 117–121

Card, Claudia, 158
catfishing, 29, 49n6
character identity, 28, 34–35
chivalry: cost of, to men and women, 160; as historical basis of gynocentrism, 57, 62, 68; incarceration and, 143, 159–160; as marginalizing men, 97
Civilization and its Discontents (Freud), 54
Clover, Carol, 161–162, 164
Coalition of Free Men, xiii
Collins (no given name), 45
compensation, as feature of identity, 28
competing victim syndrome, 7; liberal feminism and, 21; MRAs and, 21
Connell, Raewyn W., 13, 16, 17
Cox, Eva, 7, 21
Cudd, Ann, 39, 85; impacts of constraint of oppression, 96; psychological oppression, 92; recognition of one's oppression, 102n20
cultural domination, 97
cultural imperialism, 100, 129–132. *See also* media representations
culture: bodies as symbols of, 31, 33; construction of gender identity and, 60; emasculation and, 38; gender as construct of, 86; as gynocentric, 54; justifiability of loss and societal changes, 39; men as embedded in, 18; necessity of changing, for men to self-heal, 76; normalization of violence and, 145, 146; parenting as good, 125; western, as based on repression, 54–56; wimpification of men and societal changes, 15
culture of ornament, 18
custody: biological basis for fathers' rights, 125; courts' deference to mothers, 124; denying, to fathers harms children, 112, 127; examination of relationships, 126; feminism and men's liberation movement and, xii–xiii; parents without relationships, 125; portrayal of fathers in popular culture and, 129–130; rights of fathers trump relationships, 125; rights of mother, 125–126; women as controlling, 106
cyberlibertarianism, 48

damsel in distress, 63, 157
Dartmouth, 12
death, representations in media, 161–162
death penalty, 143, 159
democratic unfreedom, 55, 60, 74, 77–78
Devlin, Roger, 3
Dewey, Caitlin, xv
Dieter, Richard, 143
discipline, bodies and, 32
Discipline and Punish (Foucault), 14, 88
disruption, as MRM strategy, viii, 10, 11, 12–13, 49, 117
"Dissecting the New American Racist" (Gerard), 70
distributive model of justice, 91
distributive model of power, 88, 94
diversity, 10, 74
diversity and white supremacist thinking, 73
divorce, xii, 110, 111
domestic violence, 142, 157
domination, violence as method of, 13
dominator thinking, 73
doxxing, 13, 25n25, 25n27
Dreyfus, Hubert, 90

Elam, Paul: counterculture nature of MRM, 10; emotional nature of women, 6; essentialist masculinity and, 68; feminism as tool to control women, 6; feminists as dupes, 6; gay men and MRM, 67; myth of weakness of women, 142; necessity of changing cultural narrative for men to self-heal, 76; protection of women, 4; rape culture as myth, 141; rape of men, 141; use of doxxing, 13, 25n25, 25n27. *See also* A Voice for Men (AVFM)
equality: feminism as striving for, with certain types of men, 20–21; as goal of MHRM, 9; as ideal of MRM, 74; indiscriminate, 78; reproductive rights after birth and, 107–108; as seen by MRAs, 7
Eros, 55, 146, 147, 149, 154
Eros and Civilization (Marcuse), 146
Esmay, Dean: feminism as wanting privileges without responsibility, 5–6; gay men, 67; stereotypical masculine

identity and, 68; traditional family structure, 62–63
An Essay on Liberation (Marcuse), 169
essentialist masculinity: AVFM and, 66; dangerous jobs and, 150–151, 152; described, 65; of Elam, 68; elimination of narratives on nonprivileged men, 60, 66; military service and, 154; in MRM rhetoric, 66; power and, 94–95; race and, 71; stereotypes, 96, 160; as true enemy, 116
Estephe, Robert, 107, 110
exploitation: as aspect of oppression, 99, 118, 150, 151–152; of married men and fathers, 109, 110, 115; of masculine labor, 56, 100

failure, fear of, 29–30
Faludi, Susan, 16; creation of culture of ornament, 18; effect of limits on male power, 17; Farrell's views, xiv; inability of men to establish new identity, 18
family, MRM recognition and definition of, 114
Farrell, Warren, x; AVFM and, xviii; commonalities between slave and male experiences, 71, 72; definition of power, 93; divorce, 111; economic exploitation of married men, 109, 110; economic objectification, 98; as father of men's liberation movement, xi; feminism as not taking men's complaints seriously, xiv; as feminist, xii; joint custody and, xii; male labor, 56, 138; men as sacrificing for women, 2; men as victims of violent crimes, 139; slavery and gender, 71; spending gap, 57, 118; suicide due to despair, 139; violence as part of socialization of boys, 138, 140; women-in-jeopardy-films, 140; women's prisons versus men's, 142
fathers' rights: abortion and, 108; after birth, 107; as central to MRM, xiii; child support and, 110; economic exploitation of men and, 110, 115; loss of personal connection with children, 110; parental alienator syndrome and, 112–113; paternity fraud and, 106–107, 121–122; portrayal in popular culture and, 129–132; tension between feminism and men's liberation movement, xii–xiii. *See also* custody
feminine narcissism, 3, 57, 113, 118
femininity, mutually dependent identification with masculinity, 16
feminism: ampersand problem, 65–66; as attracting misandric women, 57–58, 62; as cause of "wimpification" of men, 15; as control tool, 6; as corrupting modern culture, xv; damaging representations of masculinity, 62; as driving force behind oppression of males, 5–8; as duping women, 6, 58; endorsement by men as part of protector role, 2; as entrenching women's power, 2; gay men as aligned with, 67; increased participation of men in child-care and, 132; as increasing oppression of men, 2; men's rights versus, xi; military service and, 153, 155, 168n50; as movement out of control, 5; MRAs infiltration of social media sites and blogs, 12; MRM and, xii–xiii, 11; myth of weakness of women and, 142; as not taking men's complaints seriously, xiii, xiv; organizations as hate groups, 14; patriarchy as myth of, 2, 3; race as aligned with, 71; as scapegoat, 18, 22; second wave, 10; sexuality and, 17; as theft, 93; third wave, 20; as tool of government, 93; as usurped by bourgeoisie white women, 66; as wanting privileges without responsibility, 5–6
Fineman, Martha, 126
flaming, as male, 43
Foucault, Michel, 32, 33, 88–89; body as cultural symbol, 31; dominance, 90; nature of power, 128; power as disciplinary, 14; power as productive, 165; power as type of relationship, 88, 94; self-policing nature of individuals, 89; sex as artificial concept, 89
fragmentation mechanism, 96, 97
freedom of speech, 46, 75
Freud, Sigmund, 54, 146

Friday Night Lights, 131
Frye, Marilyn, 86–87, 98, 101
"fuck their shit up" (FTSU) method, 76

Gallagher, Ken, 94
Gamer Gate, 48
Gardner, Richard, 127
"Gays against Feminism: Because Gay People Are Not Your Property, Feminists" (Esmay), 67
gender: body as limiting factor in expressing, 33; as construct of culture, 86; as disciplinary production, 33; distribution of justice and, 142–143; as fabrication, 33; identity, 60, 61, 68; as inherent determining factor of self within bodily limits, 32; as performative, 68; position as slave and, 71; sex versus, 32; as social group, 85; violence and, 140–142
gender harassment, defining, 44–45
gender roles system and expectations: as harmful to men and women, xi, xii, xiv; as highly dichotomous and stereotypical, 31, 32, 64, 68; military service and, 154; as morally and psychologically reprehensible, 96; online identity and, 30, 31–34; parental, 112; reinforced by media, 129–132; shame as part of, 145; violence and, 148
Gerard, Sage, 70
Germany, 71, 72
Gilligan, James: honor codes, 148, 160; shame, 13, 40, 155; violence, 13, 144–145, 150, 156, 158, 167n26
Giving an Account of Oneself (Butler), 32
glass cellar, 138
Goldberg, Herb, xiii
Gotell, Lisa, 12
gray zones, 158
"the Great Refusal," 169–170
group polarization, 47–48
Guyland, 18–19, 41, 42
gynocentrism: arguments for, 2–3; as culturally dominant, 97; described, 2, 57, 138; historical basis, 62, 68, 97; maintains patriarchy myth, 58; as source of oppression, 93; as source of repression, 56; as true source of men's problems, 54; violence as manifestation of, 138

Haggemeister, Annelis, 127
harassment: defining gender, 45; as justified, 14–15; online vulnerability of women, 44; stages of online, 45. *See* doxxing
hegemonic masculinity: backlash to feminism as response ti threat to, 39; described, 16; emasculation for failure to uphold, 40; group polarization online and, 48; media representations, 41; as more available online, 42; MRM refusal to engage politically and, 11; narcissistic world view and, 11; truth and, 14; used by MRM to explain male experience, viii
Herring, Susan, 30, 43–46, 48
heterosexuality and gender roles, 68
The History of Sexuality (Foucault), 89
homophobia: accusations against MRM of, 67; AVFM and, 67–68; essentialist masculinity and, 60, 66; homosexual identities as inversions of heterosexual identities, 69
honor codes, 148, 160
hooks, bell: blame culture, 73; employment and male identity, 115; feminism as striving for equality with certain types of men, 20; feminism's potential to end war between sexes, 65; male identity as economic provider, 16; men as suffering from sexism, 23; popular cultural images of fathers, 131; satisfaction from violence, 145; usurping of feminism by bourgeoisie white women, 66; victim competition, 21; violence and power, 144; white supremacist capitalist patriarchy, 147; white supremacist thinking, 72–73; working black women, 118; work's effect on family, 116
humanism. *See* men's human rights movement (MHRM)
human rights, use of term, by MHRM, 9–10
hypermasculinity, 19, 31

identity: characterization of, 28, 34–35; creation of self-narratives, 36; establishment of, 28; features of, 28; gap between real and ideal, 38; homosexual, as inversion of heterosexual, 69; importance of bodies in establishing, 34–35; relationships and creation of, 36; social group membership and, 84; violence as part of, 146. *See also* male identity; online identity
identity politics, 86–87
incarceration, 143, 159–160
indentured servitude, 71
industry, 72
information filtering, 47
Internet, xv–xviii, 14. *See also* manosphere; A Voice for Men (AVFM)

Jackson, Keith Burgess, 23
jargon and rhetoric: AVFM, xviii; of crime fighting and punishment, 160; discussion and, 7; of emasculation, 93; essentialist masculinity in MRM, 66; about gendered violence as controlled by women, 141; importance of, to MRM, 11; MRM use of feminist, 4; MRM working within system by use of, 60; of Red Pill subreddit, xvi–xvii; use of insults without arguments, 12; use of term "human rights" to deny misogyny, 9; of women versus of men, 43–46
Jarvis (no given name), 45
Joblin, Mark, 122
justice as distributive, 91

Kamarck, Kristy, 153
Kaufman, Michael, 148
Kimmel, Michael: celebration of traditional masculinity, xv; creation of male homosocial bonding spaces, 41; custody rights, 125; definition of misandry, 4; essentialist masculinity as true enemy, 116; fathers' participation in child-care, 130; Guyland, 18; male anger and women's refusal of sex, 17; masculinity crisis, 38; meaningful work myth, 116; men's changed approach to fatherhood, 130, 132; projection of anger against women serves system, 120; rise of MRM, 15; role of anger, 15; romanticized past of male identity, 17; scapegoating by MRAs, 22; single motherhood, 128
King, Turi, 122
Kostakis, Adam: definition of gynocentrism, 57; dehumanization campaign of feminists, 58; emotional nature of women, 6; feminism as attracting misandric women, 57; feminist fear of logic, 63; feminists as responsible for damaging representations of masculinity, 62; gynocentrism, 2; impressionable nature of women, 6; patriarchy myth, 3, 58; women's hatred for men, 5
Kruk, Edward, 113

liberal/egalitarian feminism, 20–21
The Liberated Man (Farrell), xii
Love, Dylan, xvi

male homosocial bonding spaces, as escapism, 40–41
male identity: commodification of, 119–120; in culture of ornament, 18; dangerous jobs, 152; decreasing commodification of women and, 120; as economic provider, 16, 98, 109, 115, 116, 138; inability of men to establish new identity, 18; military service, 154; online, 48; perceived degradation of, 13; romanticized past, 17; tenuous nature of, 147; women's refusal of sex, 17. *See also* online identity
male power: constant need to reestablish, 148; effect of limits on, 17; feelings of loss concerning, and shame, 13; men as lacking claim, 93; myth of, xiii, 16, 56, 100; nature of disciplinary, 14; reinforcement of, by Guyland culture, 19; violence as demonstration and confirmation of, 148. *See also* patriarchy
manosphere, xv–xviii, 8, 12. *See also* Red Pill subreddit; A Voice for Men (AVFM)

Marcuse, Herbert: alienation and capitalism, 119; backlash to progressive movements, 169; primary drives, 146; progressive criticism of MRM and, 59–60; requirement of social change, 76; student protests of 1960s, 78; sublimation of aggression, 146–147; tolerance and illusion of freedom, 77; war, 154; western society as based on repression, 54–56

marriage: divorce and, 110, 111; domestic violence, 142, 157; economic/distributive harms in, 109; psychological and personal harms, 110

Marx, Karl, 119

masculinity: anxiety levels due to continuous maintenance of, 40; as conditioning for violence, 158; crisis, 15, 38; dismissal of intersectionality and, 69; as fragile, 148; innate characteristics, 40; mutually dependent identification with femininity, 16; traditional, xv, xvi–xvii; violence as tendency and, 144

matriarchal gynocentric culture, as real, xiii, xiv

Matthews, Steve, 34, 35, 37–38

meaningful work myth, 115–116

media representations: fathers in, 129–132; gender roles system and expectations reinforced by, 129–132; hegemonic masculinity in, 41; men as predators, 163–164; men as victims, 140, 164–165; violence as glorified, 165; women as killers, 164; women as victims, 161–163

Men Going Their Own Way (MGTOW), xvii, 48, 75, 78

men's human rights movement (MHRM), xix, 9–10

Men's Rights Inc., xiii

men's rights movement (MRM): absentee father as portrayed by, 114; accusations of homophobia against, 67; alienation of men, 54; as appealing to specific group of men, xi; capitalism and, 59; causes of, vii, xi, 5–8, 15, 59; central claims, viii; core principles. *See* gynocentrism; misandry; as creating bonds based on anger, resentment and perceived oppression/persecution, 15; dismissal of intellect of women, 64; dominator thinking in, 73; equality as ideal of, 74; Farrell as father of, xi; as feminist doppelganger, 8; feminists and, xii–xiii; first wave, x, xiii–xiv; fissure within, xi; focus on radfems, 20, 22; gendered violence and, 140–142; as "Great Refusal," 170; Guyland and, 19; hegemonic masculinity used to explain male experience, viii; humanism of, 8; libertarian values and, 74; media presents men as predators, 163–164; media presents women as damsels in distress, 161–163; men's lack of power, 93; methods of intervention, 11–14; misidentification of source of servitude, 120; as more backlash than progressive movement, 76; as movement of disruption and resistance, viii, 10, 11, 12–13, 49, 79, 117; as nostalgic and conservative movement, 114; as online movement, 46–48; overview of characteristics, 56; political strategy, viii; rage and, 11; refusal to recognition of complexities of oppression, 77–78; as working within system, 60. *See also* A Voice for Men (AVFM)

men's rights movement adherents (MRAs): dichotomous nature of gender identity and, 61; equality as seen by, 7; hypermasculine online identities, 31; infiltration of feminist social media sites and blogs, 12; levels, xviii; MGTOW, xvii, 48, 75, 78; Red Pill, xv–xvii, 67; Return of Kings, xvii; scapegoating of radfems by, 22; as tellers of truth, ix, 14, 58; traits, ix; trolling by, 11–12; typical described, 8; victim competition and, 21

Messner, Michael: early MRM, xiii–xiv; false symmetry of oppressiveness of gender roles, xi; over-reliance on sex-role theory, xi–xii

military service, 138, 153–155

misandry: as characteristic of gynocentrism, 57; feminism and, 5, 57–58, 62; as inversion of misogyny, 4;

men as scapegoats, 4; cf radfems, 21; as source of repression, 56; violence by women and, 107
misogyny, misandry as inversion of, 4
moralfags, 67
moral responsibility, as feature of identity, 28
Morrell, Dre, 70
Mrs. Doubtfire, 129–130
Mulvey, Laura, 42
mystification mechanism, 96, 97
The Myth of Male Power (Farrell), x, xiv, 71

narrative identity, 27–30, 34, 36
National Lampoon's Vacation, 130
National Organization of Women, 168n50
Neale, Steve, 165
negative thinking, 55, 59, 60
"neomasculinity," central beliefs, xvii

objective oppression, 91
Occidental College, 12
one-dimensional thinking, 55–56, 117, 120
online communication: bodies and, 37; group polarization and, 47–48; harassment of women, 44–46; heightens MRM as movement of disruption and resistance, 12–13, 49; as ideal platform for MRM, 46–48; information filtering and, 47; masculine space, 43–46; posting by women versus by men, 43–46
online identity: catfishing and, 29, 49n6; as challenge to understanding self, 37; establishment of, 28–29; gender performance, 31–34; as generally honest, 30; idealized gender identity and, 30; text-based anonymity, 37
oppression: ampersand problem and, 65–66; capitalist nature of, 55, 56, 152; defining, 91; as distributive, 91; essentialist gender theories and, 65, 66; exploitation as aspect, 99, 118, 150, 151–152; gray zones, 158; impacts of constraints, 96, 98; marginalization as aspect, 99; models, 90–92; MRM on source of, 56, 59; objectification and, 97–98; patterns of, 87; of pink-collar labor, 152; powerlessness as aspect, 100; psychological, 92, 96–98; recognition of complexities of, 77; recognition of one's, 102n20; as shared by all men, 61, 83; between social groups, 87, 89–90; social groups as necessary for, 83; violence as aspect, 100–101, 149, 159

parental alienator syndrome, 112–113, 127
Parfit, Derek, 28
Parsell, Mitch, 47
paternity fraud, 106–107, 121–122
patriarchy: fragile nature of male identity and, 148; legitimacy of, 16; violence and, 144, 156, 159; white supremacist capitalist, 147; women's refusal of sex and, 17
patriarchy myth: maintains gynocentrism, 58; maintenance of all-encompassing, 59; as source of repression, 56; as ultimate feminist, 2, 3, 54; violence and, 139–140
performance principle, 54–56
"pick-up artist" (PUA) sites, xvii
pleasure principle, 54–56
political correctness, 75
political party/ideology, AVFM's refusal to align with, 75
power: as disciplinary, 88–89; as distributive, 88, 94; domination in, 90; as lack of control, 93; nature of, 128; as productive, 165; social groups and, 89–90; as type of relationship, 88; violence and, 144
Preysler, Walter, 71
protector role of men: economic, 3, 109, 151; endorsement of feminism and, 2; error of, 4
prudential concern, 28, 29
psychological draft, 139
punishment. *See* incarceration

Rabinow, Paul, 90
race: as aligned with feminism, 71; AVFM and, 70–71, 74; ROK and, 70
radical feminism (contemporary), 12, 20, 21–22
rage, 6, 11

rape: doxxing of "false accusers," 13, 25n25; false claims of, 141, 158; of men, 141; as normal aspect of heterosexual experiences, xvii; spamming of false reports, 12
rape culture, 141, 157
reality principle, 54–56
rebellion, 169–170
Reddit and redditors, xv–xvi, 12
Red Pill subreddit, xv–xvii, 67
regimes of truth, 32
RegisterHer.com, 13
register-her site, 76
reidentification, 28
relationships, identity creation and, 36
repression: as basis of western society, 54–56; capitalism and, 53–55; sources of, 56; surplus, 54–56, 149
"Repressive Tolerance" (Marcuse), 77
reproduction: WHO definition of, freedom of, 107; women as controlling, 108, 122–124
resources, competition for, 7
Return of Kings (ROK) site, promotion of neomasculinity, xvii
ROK, 67, 70
Roosh V, xvii. See also Return of Kings (ROK) site
Rostker v. Goldberg (1981), 154
The Royal Tenenbaums, 131

Sabath, Joseph, 110
Schechtman, Marya, 28, 29, 34, 49n4
second order desires, 29, 49n4
sex-role theory, xi–xii
sexual assaults: false accusations of, against men, 157; against men, 157; spamming of false reports, 12
sexuality: used by women to dishonor men, 149; women's refusal and shame, 17
sexual objectification, 97–98
shame: feelings of loss concerning male power and, 13; less likely online, 42; as part of gender roles system and expectations, 145; suicide and, 156; violence and, 13, 145, 155, 157; women refusing sex, 17
Shanley, Mary, 125–126
Shatz, Naomi, 159

Shatz, Steven, 159
The Silence of the Lambs, 163
The Simpsons, 130
slavery, 71
Smith, Helen, 110
social groups: defining, 84; identity and, 84; as necessary for oppression, 83; nonvoluntary, 85; patterns within, 86–87; power and, 89–90
social media, 11, 12. See also specific sites
spamming, fake rape reports, 12
Spelman, Elizabeth, 65–66
spending gap, 57, 109, 118
standpoint theory, 70, 74
Streib, Victor, 160
subjective oppression, 91
suicide, 139, 156
Sunstein, Cass, 47
Superson, Anita, 39
surplus repression, 54–56, 149
survival, as feature of identity, 28

Thelma and Louise, 164
Theorizing Backlash: Philosophical Reflections on the Resistance to Feminism (Superson and Cudd), 39
throwness issue, 85
tolerance and freedom, 77
"trad-con" women, 62
trolling: described, 11; goal, 12; as male, 43
truth: hegemonic masculinity and, 14; MRAs as tellers of, ix, 14, 58; norms within regimes of, 32; power through controlling, of narrative, 14; tolerance and, 77
"21st Century Fatherhood" (AVFM blog), 110
two-dimensional thought. See negative thinking

uber masculinity, xv
University of Alberta, 12

victim feminism, 63, 64, 157
victimhood, competition for, 7, 21
violence: alienated individual and, 146–147; biological explanations for, 144, 145, 167n26; corporal punishment

and, 140; as cultural phenomenon, 145, 146; dangerous jobs of men, 138, 150–151; as demonstration and confirmation of male power, 148; domestic, 142, 157; domination as goal, 13; doxxing as form of, 13; as epidemic in U.S., 144; forms of, 144; gendered, 140–142; individuals and, 144–145; lack of online embodiment and, 48; as manifestation of gynocentric culture, 138; masculinity as conditioning for, 158; men as victims of, 107, 139, 140, 142–143, 149, 155–159; military and, 138; MRM working within system and, 60; oppression and systemic, 100–101, 149; as oppressive, 149, 159; patriarchy and, 139–140, 144, 156, 159; power and, 144; as productive, 165; satisfaction from, 145; shame and, 13, 145, 155, 157; structural, 150; suicide and, 139, 156; by women, 107, 149, 158; women's refusal of sex and, 17

A Voice for Men (AVFM): central focus, xix; diversity of opinions, xix; equality in mission statement of, 75; essentialist masculinity and, 66; false rape claims and, 141; feminist fear of logic, 63; feminists' use of victim identity, 64; focus on radfems, 21–22; gay men as aligned with feminism, 67; gender models used by, 63; heteronormative framework of, 68; homophobic rhetoric, 67–68; importance of, xviii; launched, xviii; loss of personal connection with children, 110; male suicide, 139; nature of power, 93; oppressive experiences shared by men, 61; as organizing point for MRM, xix–xx; parental alienator syndrome, 112–113; paternity fraud claims, 106–107; as platform for MHRM, 9; race, 70–71, 74; recognition of diversity in experience on, 68; refusal to align with political party/ideology, 75; tactics and language, xviii–xix; waves of MRM, x; women as consuming, demanding, and overbearing, 64; women writing for, 62

White, Jennifer, 156
white supremacist thinking, 72–73
"Why Black Men Need the MHRM and Not Feminism" (Preysler), 71
Why Men Are the Way They Are (Farrell), xiv
Winfrey, Oprah, xiv
women: avoidance of all interactions with, 75; brainwashing of, by feminists, 58; as consuming, demanding, and overbearing, 64, 118; as controlling reproductive decision-making, parenting and custody, 106; decreasing commodification of, 120; dismissal of intellect of, 64; domestic violence and, 142, 157; exclusion from honor codes, 148, 160; as having more desirable jobs, 138; male homosocial bonding spaces and, 41; as manipulators and liars, 64; in military, 153; online behavior, 43; online harassment of, 44–46; refusal of sex, violence and, 17; as single mothers, 114, 127, 128; society as revolving around, 2; victimhood myth, 3; as victims in media, 161–163; violence by, 107, 149, 158; weakness of, as myth, 142
World Health Organization (WHO), 107

Young, Iris Marion: defining social groups, 84; faces of oppression, 98–101; impacts of oppression, 96; issue of throwness, 85; oppressive violence, 149, 159; power as distributive, 88; power as productive, 165

About the Author

Christa Hodapp is a senior lecturer in philosophy at the University of Massachusetts Lowell. She received a bachelor's degree in women's studies from Denison University, a master's degree in women's studies from Florida Atlantic University, and a PhD in philosophy from the University of Kentucky. Her research interests include masculinity and the media, as well as gender, violence, and popular culture.

Lightning Source UK Ltd.
Milton Keynes UK
UKHW041712221118
332646UK00028B/354/P